Global Catholicism, Tolerance and the Open Society

Arno Tausch • Stanislaw Obirek

Global Catholicism, Tolerance and the Open Society

An Empirical Study of the Value Systems of Roman Catholics

 Springer

Arno Tausch
University of Innsbruck
Innsbruck, Tyrol, Austria

Stanislaw Obirek
American Studies Center
University of Warsaw
Warsaw, Poland

Additional material to this book can be downloaded from http://extras.springer.com.

ISBN 978-3-030-23238-2   ISBN 978-3-030-23239-9   (eBook)
https://doi.org/10.1007/978-3-030-23239-9

This Springer imprint is published by the registered company Springer Nature Switzerland AG.
The registered company address is: Gewerbestrasse 11, 6330 Cham, Switzerland

Show proper respect to everyone
1 Peter 2:17
(The Holy Bible, New International Version
(NIV))
Only the person who cries out for the Jews
may sing Gregorian chants
Dietrich Bonhoeffer, after the German
November Pogrom of 1938

Contents

About the Authors

Arno Tausch is Honorary Associate Professor of Economics, Corvinus University, Budapest, Hungary (since Fall Semester 2010), and Adjunct Professor (Universitaetsdozent) of Political Science at Innsbruck University, Department of Political Science, Innsbruck University, Austria (since 1988). He authored or coauthored books and articles for major international publishers and journals, among them 21 books in English, 2 books in French, 8 books in German, and over 100 articles in peer-reviewed journals, and also numerous articles in the media of several countries. He wrote several analyses for leading strategy think tanks in several countries, most recently for the Jerusalem Center for Public Affairs in Israel. For the Springer publishing group, he published three books (with coauthors): *Towards a Socio-Liberal Theory of World Development, 1993; Economic Cycles, Crises, and the Global Periphery, 2016;* and *Islamism, Arab Spring, and the Future of Democracy, 2018*, and an essay for the collective Palgrave volume *European Studies in Development, 1980* (Chaps. 2–8).

Stanislaw Obirek a culture anthropologist, is Professor at the American Studies Center at Warsaw University, Poland. He was a visiting professor at Holy Cross College in Worcester, MA (2000), and a fellow at St. Louis University (2004). His books include *Catholicism as a Cultural Phenomenon in the time of Globalization: A Polish Perspective* (2009); *Winged Mind. Walter Ong's Anthropology of Word* (2010); *Liberated Mind. In Search of a Mature Catholicism* (2011); *Pole Catholic?* (2015); with Zygmunt Bauman, *Of God and Man* (2015); and *On the World and Ourselves* (2015) (both published with *Polity Press*). He is interested in the place of religion in modern cultures, interreligious dialogue, and strategies for overcoming conflicts between different civilizations and cultures. He also published articles with journals such as *Shofar. An Interdisciplinary Journal of Jewish Studies*. For the Springer book publishing company group, he contributed the essay "The Many Faces of John Paul II" in *Religion, Politics and Values in Poland* (Ed. Ramet S. Borowik), pp. 41–59 (Palgrave Series "*Studies in Religion, Politics and Policy*") (Chap. 1).

List of Figure

List of Tables

List of Maps

List of Graphs

Chapter 1
The Failure of the Catholic Church in Postsecular Context?

Bringing the Church into the Twentieth Century

The purpose of the present chapter is to encourage readers to reflect on some of this book's topics which are relevant for modern life in the global world. In my deliberations I would like to concentrate here on Antisemitism and on the possible collaboration of believers and nonbelievers.

At the end of the 1950s of the twentieth century, the Catholic Church entered into a new epoch of its history, thanks to the charismatic Pope John XXIII. After more than fifteen centuries (from 413 to 1965) of confrontation with other cultures and religions, the Catholic Church started at last a new chapter of dialogue and openness. Particularly two documents, accepted by the participants of the Second Vatican Council (1962–1965), *Nostra Aetate* (Our Age) and *Dignitatis humanae* (On Human Dignity), were decisive in this process. In fact, both commenced a very vivid theological debate of Catholic theologians with representatives of other religions and with secular culture.

Unfortunately, after a few years of spiritual and theological enthusiasm of some theologians, particularly in the Western Hemisphere and in Latin America, the so-called postconciliar Popes—Paul VI, John Paul II, and Benedict XVI—were more preoccupied with the restoration of traditional (that means post-Constantine) Catholicism than with the continuation of the *Aggiornamento* of Catholicism to the modern world.[1] This ambivalent message to the global Church (on the one hand, declaration of openness and dialogical attitude and on the other hand, the closing of

---

[1] The original first use of this term, meaning "bringing up to date" occurred in a speech by Pope John XXIII on "The Ecumenical Council will reach out and embrace under the widespread wings of the Catholic Church the entire heredity of Our Lord Jesus Christ. Its principal task will be concerned with the condition and modernization (in Italian: aggiornamento) of the Church after 20 centuries of life. May it be that side by side with this, God will add also, through whatever edification we may offer, but above all by merit of the omnipotence of the Most High who can draw new chosen sons from the very stones, one other result: a movement toward recomposition of the whole Mystical

© Springer Nature Switzerland AG 2020
A. Tausch, S. Obirek, *Global Catholicism, Tolerance and the Open Society*,
https://doi.org/10.1007/978-3-030-23239-9_1

the theological debate on the most relevant issues for reform of the Church) brought as a result a confrontation of Catholics with modernity and postmodernity. Liberal theologians were marginalized and deprived of academic positions in Catholic institutions, and conservatives were promoted. In addition, the nomination of bishops was used as an instrument to eliminate dissenters from the hierarchy. This process was particularly visible during the long papacy of John Paul II (1978–2005). The literature on this topic is vast and the number of critical publications is growing.

This critical evaluation of the changes in the Catholic Church is not generally accepted by the majority of Catholic scholars who share the official interpretation of the Second Vatican Council. According to this interpretation, the most important achievement of the Second Vatican Council was the introduction of vernacular languages in the liturgy that changed radically the role of lay people. Liberal Catholic theologians, who were excluded from the debate, underlined that not the language but the content of the debate was relevant, for example, the role of the bishops and of the local churches, sexual ethics (contraception et cetera), the possible ordination of women, and celibacy. But debates concerning these important issues were not possible. The same should be said about the ecumenical movement and interreligious dialogue, which were strictly controlled by the Roman Curia.

It is not the aim of these introductory remarks to preview the results of the present study. I would limit myself to underline its importance for the present debate on the place of religion in the public sphere. Some philosophers, anthropologists, and sociologists of religion proposed the concept of postsecularism (Rosati 2015) as the most adequate description of the relationship between sacred and secular (Norris and Inglehart 2011) in the twenty-first century. I will return to this proposal later. Now I would like to discuss the present study.

In the present book, we are informed how complex, globally speaking, is the situation of the Catholic Church and how different attitudes toward various values could be observed among followers of this institution. Almost all analyses are based on the *World Values Survey*, available online. The data are accessible to all interested in the confrontation of the Catholic doctrine with the daily praxis of its adherents. One of the most surprising phenomena in the twenty-first century is a growing Antisemitism also in countries where Catholics constitute the majority of the society. It is not easy to explain this tendency in the light of the declaration *Nostra Aetate*, accepted by the Catholic Church in year 1965 during the Second Vatican Council, in which it was more than clearly underlined that Antisemitism is incompatible with Catholicism.

Flock of Our Lord." *The Criterion*. Archdiocese of Indianapolis (United States of America), July 7, 1961.

Between Jerusalem and Rome

How is it possible to understand this disturbing trend? The majority of theological studies of Jewish and Catholic theologians are focused on the analysis of the common biblical sources and on the process of separation of the two respective religious traditions in the first centuries after the death of Jesus of Nazareth and the destruction of the Jerusalem temple. There is no doubt that the Second World War and the destruction of European Jews had a great impact on these studies. Besides, the importance of the Second Vatican Council and, particularly, the declaration *Nostra Aetate* (1965) should be taken into account. A new perspective was gained thanks to two Jewish responses to the Catholic declaration: first *Dabru Emet* (2000) and second *Between Jerusalem and Rome* (2017). In both documents, one can observe the awareness of the profound changes in the Catholic Church, which are welcomed by Jewish authors.

In the light of the positive development of the doctrinal debate between representatives of the Catholic Church and Jewish religious communities, it is hard to understand why—as the present study documents at length—

about one in five practicing Roman Catholics still rejects to have a Jewish neighbor.

For the possible explanation of this sociological and religious phenomenon, we have to look into the history of Jewish-Christian relations.

From Enemy to Brother

The French historian Jules Isaac is enormously important in this context. He made an important contribution to the study of Antisemitism in the years after the Holocaust. He was the first who drew attention to the complex issue of the teaching of contempt toward Judaism and Jews in Christian theology since its beginning, namely, since the New Testament. Moreover, thanks to Isaac's personal involvement in the Jewish-Christian dialogue and his meetings with two Popes (with Pius XII in 1949 and John XXIII in 1960), he influenced Catholic doctrine.

Of course, it is impossible to reduce the changes in Catholic doctrine to the influence of one person. A highly significant role had a growing group of Catholics (most of them were converts from Judaism), who realized that the traditional language of Catholic theology had to be transformed. Thus, Catholicism abandoned its Antisemitism and elaborated a more positive approach toward Judaism and Jews. It was a long and painful process as we know from John Connelly's reconstruction of its history. It was exactly the aim of Connelly's book *From Enemy to Brother. The Revolution in Catholic Teaching on the Jews 1933–1965* to demonstrate that the revolutionary change which happened at the Second Vatican Council

resulted from the struggle among theologians extending from the 1930s to the 1960s (Connelly 2012, p. 10).

Nevertheless, it is important to underline that for many Catholic scholars, Isaac's book *Jesus and Israel* written during the Second World War and published in French in 1948 was a very sobering experience. Just to quote Gregory Baum, who took part in the final formulation of the declaration *Nostra Aetate*. He once wrote:

> Isaac's book *Jesus et Israel* opened my eyes. More than that, the book deeply troubled me; it shook the foundations upon which I had built my file. (Tobias 2017, p. VIII)

In this statement, Baum drew attention to the fact that in order to discover the antisemitic dimension of Christianity, it is necessary to go through the process of deep conversion. It is not enough to gain knowledge but to be ready to change one's own worldview, in this case to reject the apologetic and defensive attitude toward one's own tradition. Baum is one of the many converts from Judaism who were the pioneers in the critical debate on the role of Christianity in the Holocaust. For him, there is no doubt that without Isaac's inspiration, the radical change of Catholic doctrine concerning Jews and Judaism would not have been possible. As Baum wrote:

> *Nostra Aetate* (. . .) echoed the ideas Jules Isaac had passionately promoted and that Catholic theologians had made their own. (Tobias 2017, p. X)

It was so because:

> *Jesus et Israel* was the first sustained, wide-ranging, well-grounded, and passionately argued intellectual assault upon Antijudaism in history. (Tobias 2017, p. 123)

The Foundations of Anti-Judaic Thought Were Laid in the New Testament

But not only the converts from Judaism saw the necessity to re-evaluate the Christian tradition regarding Jews and Judaism. Similar awareness could be found in many books written by Catholic theologians such as Rose Thering who wrote, in 1958, her doctoral dissertation which portrayed the attitudes toward Jews in Catholic text-books. John Pawlikowski published in 1973 the book *Catechetics and Prejudice* based on Catholic teaching materials on Jews, protestant, and ethnic minorities (Pawlikowski 1973). Rosemary Radford-Ruether's study describes the theological roots of Antisemitism (Radford-Ruether 1974). It seems that the monograph by Radford-Ruether was the first, which drew attention to the antisemitic character of the New Testament. Isaac didn't go that far; he was much more cautious, as we will see later. For Radford-Ruether, there is no doubt that:

> The foundations of anti-Judaic thought were laid in the New Testament. They were developed in the classical age of Christian theology in a way that laid the basis for attitudes and practices that continually produced terrible results. (Radford-Ruether 1974, p. 226)

Nevertheless, most of Christians were unaware of this antisemitic dimension of the New Testament:

Christians have generally suppressed a knowledge of their own history on this matter and preserve an obliviousness to the results of their anti-Judaic language. (Radford-Ruether 1974, p. 229)

One of the reasons why it happened was that the new identity of the followers of Jesus Christ was based not only on faith in Him but also on a radical rejection of Judaism. In other words:

For Christians to incorporate the Jewish tradition after Jesus into their theological and historical education would involve ultimately the dismantling of the Christian concept of history and the demythologizing of the myth of the Christian Era. (Radford-Ruether 1974, p. 257)

In fact, the author of these words did demythologize Christianity in its subsequent theological development. Nevertheless, already in the book *Faith and Fratricide*, she drew radical conclusions combined with a radical call to take seriously the existing Judaism in defining Christian identity. For her, it is a condition sine qua non if one wishes to avoid the destructive tension between the two religions:

The fratricidal side of Christian faith can be overcome only through genuine encounter with Jewish identity. (Radford-Ruether 1974, p. 261)

Perhaps the most radical position was taken by John Dominic Crossan (1996) who convincingly demonstrated that the narrative of the passion and death of Jesus had an anti-Jewish character. Although at the same time Crossan underlines the difference between racial Antisemitism and theological anti-Judaism in his book *Who Killed Jesus: Exposing the Roots of Anti-Semitism in the Gospel Story of the Death of Jesus*, the distinction is important because only the first has an eliminatory character. However, the relation between these two categories of Antisemitism could not be denied, and the history of Christian anti-Judaism made possible the almost general acceptance of Antisemitism in Christian Europe. Another important distinction introduced by Crossan is between

history remembered and prophecy historicized

which he applied to the way how the authors of the New Testament used the Hebrew Bible in portraying the passion of Jesus. In a similar way, using rigorous philological methods, Bart Ehrman in his bestseller book *Misquoting Jesus: The Story Behind Who Changed the Bible and Why* underlined the antisemitic character of many changes in the final edition of the New Testament, as we know it today. Ehrman also pointed out the paradoxical attitude of the first Christian communities toward the Jews and their mother religion, Judaism. On the one hand, they were born inside Judaism and used extensively the Jewish Scripture, and even their religion's founder was a Jew, but on the other hand, they rejected the Jewish tradition with contempt:

One of the ironies of early Christianity is that Jesus himself was a Jew who worshiped the Jewish God, kept Jewish customs, interpreted Jewish law, and acquired Jewish disciples, who accepted him as the Jewish messiah. Yet, within just a few decades of his death, Jesus's followers had formed a religion that stood over-against Judaism. (Ehrman 2005, p. 187)

According to Ehrman, it is disturbing to find that the very text, which for centuries was considered by Christians inspiring and infallible, was in fact a human construction. As he wrote in the concluding chapter to the above quoted book:

> This conviction that scribes had changed the Scripture become an increasing certitude for me as I studied the text more and more. (Ehrman 2005, p. 210)

Jules Isaac: A New Era

The problem is not that we have to reject the New Testament as a human construction, but that we have to adopt the correct way to interpret it and to discover its hidden message. An interesting proposal was elaborated by Norman A. Beck, a Lutheran American pastor and an expert in New Testament study (Beck 1994). He offered practical advice on how to implement the new reading of the New Testament as an antisemitic text in the daily life of modern Christian communities. What is important in our context is the fact that also members of other Christian denominations and Jewish authors as well wrote extensively on the topic, just to mention John Gager (1985) and one of his books *The Origins of Anti-Semitism: Attitudes Toward Judaism in Pagan and Christian Antiquity* in which he analyzed the sources of Christian Antisemitism. Also, for Gager, Isaac's monograph (1971) is seen as crucial for the new way of approaching the topic of the relationship between Christianity and Judaism:

> With the publication in 1948 of Jesus and Israel, the French historian Jules Isaac inaugurated a new era in the study of pagan and Christian views of Judaism. (Gager 1985, p. 15)

Let us now return to Jules Isaac's main ideas expressed in his pathbreaking books which really determined the new awareness in the perception of Christian Antisemitism.

It is worthwhile to have a closer look not only at the aforementioned book by Jules Isaac but also on his life achievement, i.e., making Christian communities aware that they have to change their attitude toward Jews and Judaism. Jules Isaac was born in 1887 in France and till 1939 was not only a widely respected scholar, a professor of history, and the author of classical textbooks for schools, but in 1936, he became the Inspector General of Education in France in the Popular Front Government headed by Prime Minister Leon Blum. In the Second World War, the Germans occupied France, and the Vichy government introduced discriminatory measures against Jews, and Isaac lost almost his entire family in Auschwitz. His wife was able to convey him a message:

> Save yourself for your work; the world is waiting for it. (Isaac 1965, p. 9)

Isaac took it not only as the last will of his wife but also as a life program. So, he began to reflect on the sources of Christian Antisemitism and collected materials for his book *Jesus and Israel*. Norman Tobias, the author of a monograph dedicated to Jules Isaac's contribution to the Second Vatican Council, convincingly demonstrated that without Isaac's passionate defense of his historical findings during his meetings with Pope Pius XII and John XXIII, the Vatican hardly would have been able to change its traditional view of Jews and Judaism (Tobias 2017, pp. 166, 187–188).

As was mentioned, Isaac was a recognized author of textbooks for schools and probably for this reason also his book *Jesus and Israel* has a structure of four parts constructed from 21 propositions, instead of chapter titles, that make the content of the book easy to remember. From all these propositions, I would like to underline only some of them, which entered later in the official documents elaborated by the Catholic Church and by Jewish scholars and religious authorities. The first proposition states that:

the Christian religion is the daughter of the Jewish religion

and that the New Testament is founded on the Hebrew Bible. The second reminds us that:

Jesus, the Jesus of the Gospels, only Son and Incarnation of God for the Christians, in his human lifetime was a Jew, a humble Jewish artisan.

And this basic fact should be part of the Christian historical memory and religious identity. The third is focused on Jesus's family:

Insofar as we can know of them through the Gospels, Jesus's family was Jewish: Mary, his mother, was Jewish, and so were all their friends and relatives.

The second part of the book (propositions 7–10) deals with religious life during the life of Jesus and his teaching, which

took place in the traditional Jewish setting (proposition eight).

Jules Isaac also underlined that:

nothing will be more futile than to try to separate from Judaism the Gospel that Jesus preached in the synagogues and in the Temple (proposition 10).

From part three (propositions 11–15) dedicated to the relationship between Jesus and his people, I would like to mention two, which are closely connected. In proposition 11, Isaac said that:

Christian writers deliberately omit the fact that at the time of Christ the Dispersion of Jews had been a fait accompli for several centuries.

So, as a consequence:

no one has any right to say that the Jewish people "as a whole" rejected Jesus.

From the fourth and last part (proposition 16–20), it is important to quote one proposition dedicated to the long Christian tradition to impute Jewish people with the responsibility for the death of Jesus:

For eighteen hundred years it has been generally taught throughout the Christian world that the Jewish people, in full responsibility for the Crucifixion, committed the inexpiable crime of deicide.

And Isaac rightly added:

> No accusation could be more pernicious—and in fact none has caused more innocent blood to be shed.

And the final proposition underlines once again that the people of Israel are:

> totally innocent of the crimes of which Christian tradition accuses them: they did not reject Jesus, they did not crucify him.

Jules Isaac ended his book with an ardent appeal to both religious groups, Christian and Jews:

> I urge true Christians, and also true Israelites, to undertake this effort of renewal, of purification, this strenuous examination of conscience. Such is the aim I have envisaged. Such is the major lesson that emerges from meditation on Auschwitz, which I cannot release myself from, which no man of heart could abstain from. (Isaac 1971, p. 400)

Seelisberg

This appeal was heard by few; nevertheless, these few people initiated the movement which was unstoppable. After the war, in the year 1947, Jules Isaac met with a group of Jewish and Christian intellectuals to whom he submitted the main theses of his book which were to form the basis for the so-called Ten Points of Seelisberg. As Christian Rutishauser wrote:

> The final statement, including the now famous Ten Points of Seelisberg, which focused on Christian's roots in Judaism, became one of the most important cornerstones of the Jewish-Christian dialogue. (Rutishauser 2007, p. 35)

They were elaborated by a group of 65 conference participants—members of the Roman Catholic and the Reformed Churches and of the European and American Jewish communities in Seelisberg, Switzerland, in 1948 under the shock of the destruction of European Jewry. This catastrophe was the result of the crimes of Nazi Germany but also of the Antisemitism not only of French society, which was the personal experience of Isaac's family and of all French Jews, but also of other European countries. Many European Christians were not only witnessing the Holocaust but also actively collaborated with the Nazi perpetrators. For the participants of the meeting in Seelisberg, it was clear that the Antisemitism of European Christian nations was also responsible for what had happened during the Second World War. They decided to work together, as Christians and Jews, to elaborate a program which could be helpful in fighting and overcoming Antisemitism and its consequence. Christian Rutishauser, recalling the significance of the Seelisberg Conference from today's perspective, wrote:

> Looking back at the Seelisberg Conference from the vantage point of the present day, it is remarkable to note with what farsightedness and socio-political realism the participants were able to lay a foundation for a Jewish-Christian dialogue and for the fight against Antisemitism. (Rutishauser 2007, p. 47)

Rutishauser added also that:

Jules Isaac, the French historian of Jewish descent, was a significant protagonist at the Conference. (Rutishauser 2007, p. 37)

Unfortunately, this new understanding of the Christian role in the destruction of the European Jews did not enter into the conscience of all the adherents of the Catholic Church. At the end of his long struggle with Christian Antisemitism, Jules Isaac wrote his last book entitled *Teaching of Contempt: Christian Roots of Anti-Semitism*. It could be considered as his spiritual legacy and was published by Isaac in 1962 at the age of 85, just 1 year before the author's death. The departure point of the analysis of Christian Antisemitism is the thought that the situation is really paradoxical. In the long history of Christian theology, Isaac stated, on the one hand:

All authorities are agreed that Antisemitism is by definition unchristian, even anti-Christian. (Isaac 1965, p. 21)

but on the other hand:

There is a Christian Antisemitism. Whether conscious or subconscious, it is perennial and virulent, of great scope and intensity. (Isaac 1965, p. 24)

In his book, he tried to cope with this paradox. Presenting the main three themes of the teaching of contempt toward Jews and Judaism, Jules Isaac repeated some prepositions from his book *Jesus and Israel* and observed that they are deprived of any historical or factual basis. The first of these themes deals with the false accusation that the dispersion of the Jews is a providential punishment for the crucifixion of Jesus. But the historical reality indicates that the dispersion of Jews from their homeland began more than five centuries before the Christian era.

The second topic is connected with the negative evaluation of Judaism at the time of Jesus, which is not justified and also not necessary:

For the Christian religion does not require for her own glorification a corresponding disparagement of ancient Israel, of the people of the Old Testament, the people of Jesus and the Apostles, and of the first Christians. God gives her the power to break at last with these evil habits of mind and heart and tongue, contracted over a period of nearly two thousand years as a result of what I have called the teaching of contempt. (Isaac 1965, p. 146)

And the third theme is the absurd accusation of deicide with the most murderous consequences. Unfortunately, it is not only the problem of knowledge of historical facts but also the question of changing wrong attitudes:

Evil habits persist; they are too old to be uprooted overnight. (Isaac 1965, p. 147)

It seems that the most difficult obstacle which Catholics have to overcome is the fact that the very basis of their identity, namely, the New Testament, is not only very problematic but is a source of Antisemitism. It is not easy to admit that the New Testament, which for centuries was considered by Christians as inspired by Holy Spirit and the word of God, should be rejected in many parts. The basic fear relates to the possible loss of Christian religious identity. As we will see, this fear is not only unjustified, but, thanks to the process of purification of the anti-Jewish elements, the New Testament will gain its original legacy.

Beyond the Anti-Jewish Legacy

One of the most important theological contributions dealing with the New Testament's anti-Jewish legacy was published in the collection of essays dedicated to Jewish-Christian relations in the year 1994 (*Jewish-Christian Encounters over the Centuries. Symbiosis, Prejudices, Holocaust, Dialogue*) by Perry and Schweitzer (1994). One of the contributors to that volume, Norman A. Beck, in a footnote to his essay entitled "New Testament and the Teaching of Contempt: Reconsideration" wrote:

> This article is offered in appreciation for James Parkes and Jules Isaac, who first identified in detail the Christian teaching of contempt for Jews. (Beck 1994, p. 83)

In the same year, Beck published also a book dedicated to the same topic under the title *Mature Christianity in the 21st Century: The Recognition and Repudiation of Anti-Jewish Polemic in the New Testament*, which could be perceived as a kind of manifesto for all future New Testament studies. Perhaps it can be said that it is a utopian hope that most of New Testament scholars will change their mind and admit its anti-Jewish character. Nevertheless, the first step to solving a problem is defining the very nature of the problem—we have to underline: the New Testament is by its nature an anti-Jewish text. Only by recognizing this obvious fact will Christians be able to start new hermeneutics of their basic source of identity. One of the reasons why Antisemitism is still an important factor in the Catholic perception of Jews and of Judaism is the fact that the abovementioned impressive achievement of historical and biblical scholarship is almost entirely ignored by the masses belonging to the Catholic Church. This fact also explains the paradox which was mentioned at the beginning—the positive doctrine of this institution toward Judaism and Jews elaborated during and after the Second Vatican Council is almost unknown to the masses of Catholics around the globe.

The Framework of the Present Study

Now it will be possible to confront the theoretical declaration of this institution with the factual state of mind of its adherents. The first part of the present study, quite following the logic which we have presented, focuses its attention on Catholic Antisemitism, particularly in regard to the declaration *Nostra Aetate* and the emphasis given in this document on a positive view of Jews and Judaism. Unfortunately, the careful presentation of the available data shows that Catholics, globally speaking, are still presenting strongly antisemitic positions although theological reflection should encourage more open and positive attitudes toward Jews and Judaism.

The second chapter of the present study deals with attitudes of Catholics toward migration and exhibits that in most Catholic countries the followers of this institution demonstrate xenophobic and hostile positions toward all immigrants, including

Jewish immigrants. The result of these opinion surveys is also in strong contrast with the theological reflection on migration generally or on the essence of Abrahamic religions in relation to the migration issue (Padilla 2014; Padilla and Phan 2013).

It seems that Catholics are tolerant when they constitute minorities in societies, but when they are presenting the dominant religion or culture, their tolerance is fading. Particularly disquieting is Chap. 6 of this study, which analyzes the attitude of Catholics toward homosexuality, because in this case not only the attitude of the average Catholic is negative but also the official doctrine of the Church is discriminatory and stigmatizing of homosexual persons. Also, in this case, the historical research done by John Boswell in his book *Christianity, Social Tolerance, and Homosexuality: Gay People in Western Europe from the Beginning of the Christian Era to the Fourteenth Century* demonstrates how deeply this discriminatory attitude is rooted in Catholic theology from the very beginning of Christianity onward (Boswell 1980). In the context of how the Catholic Church treats the problem of homosexuality and of homosexual priests, it is particularly disturbing if one takes into account the fact that a high percentage of gay people can be found among the clergy. The influence of this group on the current policy of the Vatican is a well-documented fact, which illustrated the degree of hypocrisy of this institution (Martel 2019).

Chapter 7 is dedicated to the problem of the Open Society or democracy. In many aspects this chapter is similar to the fifth in which the problem of tolerance was discussed. But it is important that the present study confronts the topic once again and from a different angle—how, and if at all, the Catholic Church is compatible with modern and liberal democracies? The answer to this question is very important and even vital for the future of this institution. On the one hand, the theology of John Courtney Murray was decisive in the elaboration of the declaration *Dignitatis humanae*, which encouraged Catholics to accept liberal democracies and religious pluralism, but on the other hand, in many countries, the Catholic Church is unwilling to accept democratic rules (e.g., in Poland after the political changes in 1989).

Faith Lies Beyond Theology

In order to better understand the cultural and theological background of the attitudes of so many Catholics and perhaps to help them to overcome them, it is appropriate to introduce the concept of postsecularism as a kind of hermeneutical key for the present pluralistic character of contemporary societies. It is important to situate the reality of postsecularism in the context of the vivid debate which is taking place in Europe and in the United States and in other Western democracies since the beginning of the twenty-first century. In this debate, the representatives of different humanistic disciplines are involved: for example, philosophers of religion (Leszek Kołakowski, Jurgen Habermas, Charles Taylor), political scientists (Massimiliano Rosati, Kristina Stoeckl), sociologists (Zygmunt Bauman, Ulrich Beck), sociologists of religion (Peter L. Berger, Michele Dillon), and theologians (Joseph Ratzinger,

Pope Francis). It seems to me that with the introduction of the concept of postsecularism, we gain a new analytical tool to interpret the present human condition. As we will see, traditional categories as secularization and de-secularization, privatization and de-privatization, and the return of religion or politicization of religion are not adequate any more to describe the new position of religion in the public sphere and its relation to the secular reality. In a certain sense, with the acceptance of the concept of postsecularism, it is possible to speak about a change of paradigm in religious studies in the sense given to this term by Thomas Kuhn in his classical study *The Structure of Scientific Revolutions*:

> To be accepted as a paradigm, a theory must seem better than its competitors. (Kuhn 1970, p. 17)

Today, it is more evident that each religion has an historical and evolutionary character and also that religious pluralism seems self-evident and is more and more accepted as a matter of fact also by adherents of different religions (in previous epochs religious pluralism was rejected). In this new context, the necessity is to elaborate a new paradigm of the coexistence of different religions and worldviews in a pluralistic society.

It seems to me that the criticism of the way in which the concept of religion (and probably also the concept of God) was used and abused in Western theology is not only justified but also finds confirmation in books dealing with religion without God. In addition, the recent analysis of the secularization process has drawn attention to the phenomenon of essentialization of Christianity which, in effect, provoked Ivan Illich to introduce the concept of the "corruption of Christianity," namely, the betrayal of its original legacy (Taylor 2007, p. 737). In this context, it is good to remember the proposal by Wilfred Cantwell Smith to reject the traditional concept of religion. Thanks to his radical position, Smith helps to overcome the negative heritage of the concept of religion because it is a theoretical construction, which does not correspond to the fullness and richness of religious experience. Theology, in fact, as an intellectual reflection on religious reality is a part of this construction and has to be abandoned as well:

> Theology is part of the traditions, is part of this world. Faith lies beyond theology, in the hearts of men. Truth lies beyond faith, in the heart of God. (Smith 1964, p. 167)

The conclusion at which Smith arrived is his appeal to reformulate also the traditional names of world religions:

> On the verbal plane, I seriously suggest that terms such as Christianity, Buddhism, and the like must be dropped, as clearly untenable once challenged. (Smith 1964, p. 175)

In this context, it is possible not only to discuss concrete religious traditions but also to negotiate their quality. And it is exactly what postsecularism is suggesting. As an example of this negotiation, I see an interesting proposal elaborated by the German sociologist Ulrich Beck in his book *A God of One's Own* which is directed both at secular and religious audiences, including Christians. According to Beck's vision, the crucial criteria for a believer is not an external doctrine elaborated in the history of Christianity, but a personal and individual decision to choose one's God. Therefore, in his view:

> Christianity may have undergone a conversion from an intolerance prosecuted with fire and sword to the limited form of tolerance. (Beck 2010, p. 99)

It seems to me that exactly this "limited form of tolerance" is now at stake when we discuss the concept of religion and its impact on human history. The awareness of a mutual correlation between religion and culture, on the one hand, and the dependence of both on life experience, on the other hand, could be a good departure point for a process of "conversion" of all the participants in the public debate in this regard. I believe that a stronger awareness of the limitations of respective worldviews as an essential element in what heretofore has been known as "religion" would be helpful not only in the accurate understanding of that concept but also it will create the possibility to enter into a creative dialogue between representatives of secular and religious worldviews.

A good example of the practical consequences of the acceptance of a postsecular worldview is the meeting between Jürgen Habermas and Joseph Ratzinger in 2004 in Munich, Germany. It was an academic exchange of two German intellectuals who have never met before and whose' widely recognized academic achievements are related to completely different fields. Habermas is a well-known philosopher not interested in religion, and Ratzinger is a very influential Catholic theologian known for his critical attitude toward modern culture. In this debate, the term postsecularism was introduced by Habermas (who followed the German sociologist Klaus Eder and his article from 2002) as a way to create a dialogical space for secular and religious positions. In his response, Ratzinger not only accepted the proposed term but saw in postsecularism a chance to overcome the existing impasse between religious and secular worldviews and underlined the positive contribution of critical thinking for the purification of religious fanaticism. To illustrate this process of mutual learning, I would like to quote just two statements in which they both recognized the necessity to hear one another. Habermas said that:

> In the postsecular society, there is an increasing consensus that certain phases of the "modernization of the public consciousness" involve the assimilation and the reflexive transformation of both religious and secular mentalities. If both sides agree to understand the secularization of the society as a complementary process, then they will also have cognitive reasons to take seriously each other's contributions to controversial subjects in the public debate. (Habermas and Ratzinger 2006, pp. 46–47)

Ratzinger, in his lecture, accepted Habermas' suggestion by saying:

> With regard to the practical consequences, I am in broad agreement with Jurgen Habermas's remarks about a postsecular society, about the willingness to learn from each other, and about self-limitation on both sides. (Habermas and Ratzinger 2006, p. 77)

A very similar approach to the mutual relation between the religious and the secular dimension of our reality and with a practical application of postsecular thinking is present in Ulrich Beck's book (2010) with the interesting subtitle *Religion's Capacity for Peace and Potential for Violence*, which was already mentioned earlier. It is worth mentioning that Beck, as Habermas, was not particularly interested in religious questions. Only in this book, Beck decided to cope with religion as an important element of the public sphere, and he wrote:

> The secular society must become postsecular, i.e. skeptical and open-minded towards the voices of religion. Permitting religious language to enter the public sphere should be regarded as enrichment, not as an intrusion. Such a change is no less ambitious than the general toleration of secular nihilism by the religions. (Beck 2010, p. 156)

My final example is the last book by Zygmunt Bauman *Retrotopia* which could be seen as his intellectual legacy. In the final chapter entitled "Epilogue: Looking Forward, for a Change," he made an enthusiastic reference to Pope Francis' texts and gestures. Specifying a number of problems, which humanity has to cope with in the present moment of history, Bauman finds one person who is able to supply an adequate answer:

> I found in Pope Francis, currently the person among public figures of considerable great planet-wide authority who is bold and determined enough to raise and tackle these sorts of questions. (Bauman 2017, p. 138)

Bauman quotes extensively the speech given by Pope Francis on May 6, 2016, when he received the European Charlemagne Prize. For Bauman, the Pope's speech is inspiring because he sees in it a concrete suggestion to resolve some problems of our world. For Bauman:

> The intention behind Pope Francis' message is to bring the fate of peaceful cohabitation, solidarity and collaborations of humans from the fuzzy and obscure realm of high politics. (Bauman 2017, p. 139)

And for this reason, Bauman concluded his book with a positive note:

> The chances of fruitful dialogue, as Pope Francis remind us, depend on our reciprocal respect and assumed, granted and mutually recognized status equality. (Bauman 2017, p. 140)

The postsecular understanding of religious and secular mutuality is exactly about this. Bauman's appreciation for Pope Francis could be confirmed by Michele Dillon, an American sociologist of religion:

> The Catholic Church has many resources that well match the postsecular turn. (Dillon 2018, p 165)

Dillon made reference to Habermas' concept of "contrite modernity" which she applied also to the Catholic Church. And in the light of the recent statements made by Pope Francis in the context of the clergy sex abuse in Pennsylvania, we can see that "contrite Catholicism" might be real:

> With shame and repentance, we acknowledge as an ecclesial community that we were not where we should have been . . . realizing the magnitude and the gravity of the damage done to so many lives.

At the end of the letter, Francis says:

it is essential that we, as a Church, be able to acknowledge and condemn, with sorrow and shame, the atrocities perpetrated by consecrated persons, clerics, and all those entrusted with the mission of watching over and caring for those most vulnerable.

In other words, if we combine contrite modernity with contrite Catholicism, a real and mutually fruitful dialogue will be possible. As writes Dillon:

A contrite modernity, just as contrite heart, does not give into despair over past failings. Rather, it has the values and cultural resources to amend its shortcoming, and to steer society back on track so that it can better realize its potential. (Dillon 2018, pp. 2–3)

It is an open question if postsecularism could constitute a change of paradigm (Charles Taylor expressed his skepticism when I asked him what he thinks about this). We are still at the beginning of the debate. But I hope that I suggested some examples of constructive application of a postsecular way of thinking in which religious and secular values are perceived not as opposed to each other but as complementary perspectives. A similar approach (although without mentioning postsecularism) was offered by the late Peter Berger in his last book *The Many Altars of Modernity: Toward a Paradigm for Religion in a Pluralist Age*, published in 2014. In this book, Berger used the religious pluralism of the modern world as a hermeneutical key for interpreting religious changes in the twenty-first century.

Bauman's *Retrotopia*

Let me conclude these reflections about the importance of a postsecular attitude in the modern world with a passage from Bauman's *Retrotopia*:

We need to brace ourselves for a long period marked by more questions than answers and more problems than solutions, as well as for acting in the shadow of finely balanced chances of success and defeat. But in this one case, in opposition to the cases to which Margaret Thatcher used to impute it, the verdict "there is no alternative" will hold fast with no likelihood of appeal. More than at any other time we—human inhabitants of the Earth—are in the either/or situation: joining either hands, or common graves. (Bauman 2017, p. 140)

In my Preface I concentrated myself only on two aspects: Antisemitism and pluralism. First, it is clear that the Catholic Church has a problem with popularization of its own doctrine, and second, it seems obvious that many global Catholics have a problem with the acceptance of religious, cultural, and political pluralism. I'm sure that familiarity with the results of the present study will be helpful not only for Catholics but also for all interested in the understanding of the paradoxical presence of religion in public sphere today. But even more, the awareness of the existing gap between the official doctrine of the Church (open toward immigrants, dialogical, friendly attitudes toward Jews and other religions) and the practical attitudes of Catholics (hostile toward immigrants, antisemitic, unwilling to accept democratic rules of an Open Society) will provoke new and creative solutions to overcome the present *malaise*.

Literature

Bauman, Z. (2017). *Retrotopia*. Cambridge, CA: Polity Press.

Beck, N. A. (1994). New testament and the teaching of contempt: Reconsideration. In M. Perry & F. M. Schweitzer (Eds.), *Jewish-Christian encounters over the centuries: Symbiosis, prejudices, holocaust, dialogue* (pp. 83–100). New York: Peter Lang.

Beck, U. (2010). *A God of one's own: Religion's capacity for peace and potential for violence*. Cambridge, MA: Polity Press.

Beck, N. A., & Mazal Holocaust Collection. (1994). *Mature Christianity in the 21st century: The recognition and repudiation of the anti-Jewish polemic of the new testament* (Expanded and rev. ed., Shared ground among Jews and Christians, Vol. 5). New York: American Interfaith Institute/World Alliance.

Between Jerusalem and Rome. (2017). Download April 10, 2019, from http://www.rabbis.org/pdfs/BetweenJerusalemRome.pdf

Boswell, J. (1980). *Christianity, social tolerance, and homosexuality. Gay people in Western Europe from the beginning of the Christian Era to the fourteen century*. Chicago, IL: The University of Chicago Press.

Connelly, J. (2012). *From enemy to brother. The revolution in catholic teaching on the Jews 1933–1965*. Cambridge, MA: Harvard University Press.

Crossan, D. (1996). *Who killed Jesus. Exploring the roots of antisemitism in the gospel story of the death of Jesus*. San Francisco, CA: Harper Collins.

Dabru Emet. (2000). Download April 10, 2019, from http://www.jcrelations.net/Dabru_Emet_-_A_Jewish_Statement_on_Christians_and_Christianity.2395.0.html

Dillon, M. (2018). *Postsecular Catholicism: Relevance and renewal*. New York: Oxford University Press.

Eder, K. (2002). Europäische Säkularisierung—ein Sonderweg in die postsäkulare Gesellschaft? *Berliner Journal für Soziologie, 12*(3), 331–343.

Ehrman, B. (2005). *Misquoting Jesus. The story behind who changed the Bible and why*. San Francisco, CA: Harper Collins.

Gager, J. G. (1985). *The origins of antisemitism. Attitudes toward Judaism in Pagan and Christian antiquity*. New York: Oxford University Press.

Habermas, J., & Ratzinger, J. (2006). *The dialectics of secularization: On reason and religion*. San Francisco, CA: Ignatius Press.

Isaac, J. (1965). *Teaching of contempt. Christian roots of antisemitism*. New York: McGraw-Hill.

Isaac, J. (1971). *Jesus and Israel*. New York: Holt, Rinehart, Winston.

Kołakowski, L. (2002). *Co nas łączy?: Dialog z niewierzącymi. Kraków: WAM* [What connects us? Conversations with non-believers].

Kuhn, T. (1970). *The structure of scientific revolution*. Chicago, IL: The University of Chicago Press.

Martel, F. (2019). *In the closet of the Vatican. Power, homosexuality, hypocrisy*. London: Bloomsbury Continuum.

Norris, P., & Inglehart, R. F. (2011). *Religion and politics worldwide*. Cambridge, CA: Cambridge University Press.

Nostra Aetate. (1965). Download April 10, 2019, from http://www.vatican.va/archive/hist_councils/ii_vatican_council/documents/vat-ii_decl_19651028_nostra-aetate_en.html

Padilla, E. (Ed.). (2014). *Theology of migration in the Abrahamic religions* (1st ed., Palgrave Macmillan's Christianities of the world). New York: Palgrave Macmillan

Padilla, E., & Phan, P. (2013). *Contemporary issues of migration and theology (Christianities of the world)*. New York: Palgrave Macmillan.

Pawlikowski, J. (1973). *Catechetics and Prejudice. How catholic teaching materials view Jews, protestants and radical minorities*. New York: Paulist Press.

Perry, M., & Schweitzer, F. (1994). *Jewish-Christian encounters over the centuries: Symbiosis, prejudice, holocaust, dialogue*. New York: Peter Lang.

Pope Francis [Bergoglio Jorge Mario]. *Letter of His Holiness Pope Francis to the People of God.* Download April 10, 2019., from http://w2.vatican.va/content/francesco/en/letters/2018/documents/papa-francesco_20180820_lettera-popolo-didio.html

Radford-Ruether, R. (1974). *Faith and Fratricide. The theological roots of antisemitism.* New York: The Seabury Press.

Rosati, M. (2015). *The making of a postsecular society. A Durkheimian approach to memory, pluralism and religion in Turkey.* Farnham: Ashgate.

Rutishauser, C. (2007). The 1947 Seelisberg conference. *Studies in Christian-Jewish Relations, 2* (2), 34–53.

Smith, W. C. (1964). *The meaning and end of religion.* New York: Mentor Book.

Stoeckl, K. (2011) Working paper "*Defining the Postsecular*". In Document Collection of the Italian-Russian Workshop "Politics, religion and culture in postsecular society (Faenza, 13–14 May 2011)", PECOB – Portal of East Central and Balkan Europe. Download April 10, 2019, from http://www.pecob.eu/flex/cm/pages/ServeAttachment.php/L/EN/D/7%252Fd%252F1%252FD.1f1f8fddc2dd41df40ac/P/BLOB%3AID%3D3100

Taylor, C. (2007). *A secular age.* Cambridge, CA: The Belcamp Press of Harvard University Press.

Tobias, N. C. (2017). *Jewish conscience of the church. Jules Isaac and the Second Vatican Council.* Cham: Palgrave Macmillan.

Chapter 2
Developing the Research Strategy

Why did we write this book? And what are we aiming at? At a time of rising global Antisemitism, we thought that a systematic study on the active adherents of the West's largest religious denomination, Roman Catholicism, especially focusing on their overcoming of Antisemitism, on their commitment to democracy and the Open Society, and on their religious and social tolerance is highly necessary. While there is a growing research literature on traditional and growing right-wing Antisemitism (Rubinstein 2015), Muslim Antisemitism (Curtis 2017; Israeli 2017; Jikeli 2015; Kressel 2012; Pollack 2017; Rosenfeld 2013; Tausch 2016; Wistrich 2002), and left-wing Antisemitism (Hirsh 2017; Rubinstein 2015), Goldhagen (2003) was right in emphasizing that with 450 Antisemitic statements in the 4 Christian Gospels and the Acts of the Apostles from the New Testament alone, it is time to reflect anew as well on the Antisemitism in the Christian tradition. Two New Testament quotations might suffice here in this context to underline the real problem, correctly identified by Goldhagen (2003), of this existing Antisemitism in the New Testament at the very root of Christianity, other contradicting passages of the New Testament, which clearly show the Jewish roots of Christianity notwithstanding. Such quotations worked over the centuries as a real fire accelerator of hatred and persecution:

> For you, brothers and sisters, became imitators of God's churches in Judea, which are in Christ Jesus: You suffered from your own people the same things those churches suffered from **the Jews who killed the Lord Jesus** and the prophets and also drove us out. **They displease God and are hostile to everyone** in their effort to keep us from speaking to the Gentiles so that they may be saved. In this way **they always heap up their sins to the limit. The wrath of God has come upon them at last**. (1 Thessalonians 2: 14–16, New International Version (NIV))

> **If you were Abraham's children," said Jesus, "then you would do what Abraham did. [...] You belong to your father, the devil, and you want to carry out your father's desires. [...] The reason you do not hear is that you do not belong to God**. (John, 8: 39–47, New International Version, NIV)

Our empirical study on the opinions of regular Church service attenders among the global Catholics should be a tool for the scientific community in the field of the

A. Tausch, S. Obirek, *Global Catholicism, Tolerance and the Open Society*,
https://doi.org/10.1007/978-3-030-23239-9_2

social sciences, the humanities, and divinity studies, but it should also serve as a tool for international decision makers at the levels of governments, NGOs, and, above all, it should serve the global publics, interested in issues of religion.

Fukuyama: Beyond the Western Consensus of the 1990s

Why should we study the attitudes of active global Catholics at all, and why should we focus on the hard-core issues of Antisemitism, on attitudes toward the Open Society, on religious tolerance, and on attitudes on homosexuals and homosexuality?

Francis Fukuyama, in an essay published in *Foreign Affairs* in summer 2016 (Fukuyama 2016), correctly highlighted that the Western ideological consensus, which characterized much of the 1990s and the first decade of the New Millennium, rested on the acceptancy of globalization, migration, and the integration of religious, ethnic, or sexual minorities. Fukuyama's hypothesis in the context of the election victory of Mr. Donald Trump in the November 2016 Presidential Election in the United States and the electoral swings toward the populist right in many other democracies ever since is that this consensus is now breaking up under the pressures of globalization.

We argue that apart from the now decimated ranks and files of global social democracy, now losing election after election around the world, Roman Catholicism ever since the days of the Second Vatican Council became a global voice of the democratic center, positioned against Antisemitism, supporting democracy and free and fair elections and supporting religious tolerance and integrating immigrants. If global support for liberal Catholicism among the active rank and file of global Catholicism erodes, it is yet another sign of how the democratic center of the Free World itself erodes progressively.

Now, the current Pope of the Roman Catholic Church is not only the first Pope to have published a book together with a Jew prior to his election now also available in English (Pope Francis and Skorka 2014). The current leadership of the Roman Catholic Church, headed by Pope Francis, also takes an especially liberal and conciliatory view of migration and refugee issues, which is in stark difference to the restrictive attitudes taken by populist politicians like Mr. Donald Trump in America or the current Hungarian Prime Minister Viktor Orban in Europe. For many, Roman Catholicism with its already 1.3 billion global adherents[1] would appear as the new, natural partner of those who contest the rise of populism in the West. More than half a century after the Second Vatican Council, did its conciliatory messages and humanistic values finally take hold of the hearts and minds of the Catholic global faithful? This question is especially relevant, as only the Second Vatican Council put an end to Catholic Antisemitism, which lasted for 2000 years.

---

[1]https://international.la-croix.com/news/worldwide-catholic-population-grows-to-just-under-13-bil lion/6172 (Download April 10, 2019).

Table 2.1 Fukuyama's categories of the waning Western consensus and our investigation

Fukuyama's elements of the waning Western ideological consensus (Fukuyama 2016)	Our analysis of key global Catholic opinion structures
Globalization and democracy	Catholic acceptancy of democracy and the market economy
Open migration regime	Catholic opinions on migration: supporting Chancellor Angela Merkel's culture of "welcome" or supporting policies of walls and fences; Catholic opinions on global religious tolerance
Integration of religious, ethnic, or sexual minorities	Catholic opinion on Antisemitism and Catholic opinion on homosexuality

Independent from one's religious affiliation, it is certain that current global developments, characterized by mass migration and the rise of populism in the industrialized West, but also increasingly in the global South (Brazil, Philippines et cetera), suggest to take a closer look again at the values held by global adherents of the Roman Catholic Church, which is the religious organization, which still commands the largest following of any religion among the citizens of Western democracies, and which, by its self-definition, should be a religious congregation committed to the ideals of neighborly love to the needy, openness for the weakest, and human understanding. Do Roman Catholics, practicing their faith, the so-called *Dominicantes*, who attend each week—as strictly prescribed in Catholicism—the Catholic Sunday Church Service, today follow the advice of their Church leaders on issues of migration and xenophobia, and is the Roman Catholic Church really now a remaining bastion of the democratic center in the West? And, furthermore, are Roman Catholics *Dominicantes* today a global best practice community of religious tolerance, the overcoming of Antisemitism, and the inclusion of minorities like homosexuals?

So, we have decided to test in the framework of Fukuyama's proposed ideological categories of the waning liberal Western consensus (see above) the opinions of global Catholics on Antisemitism, on the Open Society and democracy and the market economy, on religious tolerance, and on homosexuality (Table 2.1).

We are not interested here in the question, which asylum and migration policies are correct, or which path should be followed in this respect by the developed, rich, Western democracies. We are only interested in what the active Roman Catholics—in comparison with overall society—think about some of the most pressing issues of our time. Global secularization trends notwithstanding, the Roman Church still not only commands the fellowship of more than 1.3 billion global citizens, but it also continues to be a highly significant actor in international relations, with 183 nations now having diplomatic relations with the Vatican, disposing of a highly respected, powerful, and efficient foreign policy machinery.[2]

---

[2]https://press.vatican.va/content/salastampa/en/bollettino/pubblico/2018/01/08/180108a.html (Download April 10, 2019).

Needless to say, that in view of the current global migration and political processes, which suggest a sharp polarization in the Western countries on the issues of migration, such solid social scientific information is ever more necessary. The path-breaking studies by Hadler (2012) and Hadler and Symons (2018) on the values of global Catholics suggest indeed that there are good sociological reasons to combine the study of the acceptancy of democracy and the market economy with a study on the opinions on migration, global religious tolerance, and Antisemitism and opinions on homosexuality. Hadler's evidence, based on 32 countries, strongly suggested that the interconnections between these dimensions are very strong and—as also suggested by Fukuyama (2016)—that they should be studied in conjunction.

The Role of the *World Values Survey* in Mapping the Global Value Landscapes of Today

But while empirical studies, using global opinion surveys from the *World Values Survey* data base on Islam, now abound, far-reaching comparisons of the values of global Catholics, based on global opinion surveys, like the *World Values Survey*, are still not too frequent in the literature. Here, we highlight only some international high-profile studies, which indicate the directions, where current research is heading for, and also how the dimensions, focused on by Hadler (2012) and Hadler and Symons (2018), could further be used in empirical studies on global Catholicism. Our survey is thus not intended to be exhaustive, but rather it should show to our readers where such research is heading for and what kind of conclusions the social sciences might draw on the basis of the multivariate analysis of these data.

The systematic social scientific study of global values and opinions, used in this essay, has of course a long and fruitful history in the social sciences. Such studies are made possible by the availability of systematic and comparative opinion surveys over time under the auspices of leading representatives of the social science research community, featuring the global and/or the European populations with a fairly constant questionnaire for several decades now. The original data are made freely available to the global scientific publics and render themselves for systematic, multivariate analysis of opinion structures on the basis of the original anonymous interview data. Our data are mainly from two sets of such reliable and regularly repeated global opinion surveys: the *World Values Survey* (*WVS*) and the *European Social Survey* (ESS). Add to this the data from the *PEW Institute* in Washington, DC.

Some Leading *World Values Survey* Studies on Global Catholicism

In the following, we will attempt to provide our readers with a "map" of what has been already achieved in our field, i.e., the study of global Catholicism with the methods of quantitative sociology, based on global opinion surveys. Gu and Bomhoff (2012), for example, found that public support for democracy is stronger among the better educated in both 11 Catholic and 9 compared Muslim countries. The study attempted to answer two fundamental questions: (1) Does a strong Islamic or Catholic commitment encourage more authoritarian political views? Are pious Muslims and Catholics less open to democracy? (2) What do Muslims and Catholics associate with democracy: a tolerant society or an efficient and responsive government? The study took particular care to measure the following factors:

1. Tolerance of diversity. This included tolerance of racial diversity and tolerance of divergent social behavior such as homosexuality, prostitution, abortion, divorce, euthanasia, and suicide.
2. Support for gender equality in work, politics, and education. This measures the level of agreement with the following: "when jobs are scarce, men should have more right to a job than women"; "On the whole, men make better business executive than women do"; "On the whole, men make better political leaders than women do"; "A university education is more important for a boy than for a girl."

Contrary to the conventional belief that pious believers are less receptive to democracy; individual religiosity, measured by the belief in God, was found to have a significant positive impact on the desire for democracy in both types of societies. Overt support for democracy is consistently and positively correlated to the attachment of a set of more implicit tolerant civil values in Catholic-majority countries. According to the study, the pious believers in the Catholic countries are people who attach greater importance to democracy. They associate democracy with better economic performance and are also more likely to endorse liberal self-expression values, described in all details in the sociological studies by Ronald F. Inglehart and his associates. Both global Muslim and global Catholic publics are equally likely to treat free and fair elections as a defining element of democracy. Catholic publics are much more likely to identify democracy with greater gender equality than Muslim publics do, with an average of 61% of respondents in the 11 countries under survey versus 46% in the 9 Muslim-majority countries.

In their insightful study, Feess et al. (2014), also using the *World Values Survey* from 57 countries as a data source, were demonstrating a large and robust positive impact of the degree of religiosity on the work ethic. The study started from the assumption that there is no good reason to assume that specific religions are per se superior for fostering economic growth and economic productivity. The interesting hypotheses tested in this study were the following:

Hypothesis 1 The higher the degree of religiosity of individuals, the higher is their work ethic.

Hypothesis 2 Given the degree of religiosity, the religion of the individuals has no significant impact on their work ethic. The average work ethic is the same among different religions, but does not exclude that the variable impact of religiosity on work ethic differs.

The third hypothesis directly tested the sociological theory of Max Weber (1904) who famously argued that the Protestant worldview is anchored in the value system of an entire society, rather than being restricted to those who are particularly religious. He argued that religiosity might only be the primary trigger for a *Protestant work ethic* but that the impact of religiosity erases when the value system is stable even without religious foundation. This suggests that religiosity may have played a major role for the initial development of a Protestant work ethic but that the link between religiosity and work ethic shrinks particularly fast for Protestants.

Hypothesis 3 The impact of religiosity on the work ethic is smaller for Protestants compared to Catholics.

While the impact of religiosity is robust and pronounced for all religions, the study found more differentiated results for the effect of different religions themselves. Muslims report a remarkably higher work ethic than Christians do. Disaggregation shows that this effect is mainly driven by the high work ethic of Muslims in Europe and America and, correlated with that, in wealthier countries where Protestantism or Catholicism dominates. The work ethic of Protestants and Catholics is relatively low in these countries, while Muslims are characterized by a high work ethic even in highly developed economies. Furthermore, the average work ethic in each single country where Islam is the prevalent religion is above the average work ethic of Catholics and Protestants.

Amidst all the debate which is now raging in Europe, whether "Islam" "belongs" to "Europe" or not, the next study under scrutiny here attempts to answer the absolutely untrivial question whether or not Catholic culture is conducive to religious tolerance of minorities. May and Smilde (2016) examined in their *World Values Survey*-based study on the "real existing" conditions of tolerance of non-Catholics in mainly Catholic countries the effect of religious majority size on religious minority well-being. Religious minorities face a number of challenges, ranging from deliberate discrimination to inadequate worship space and accommodations. Yet, for many of the members of religious minority groups, religion remains an important part of community organizing and individual well-being. Using data on non-Catholics in majority Catholic nations, the study demonstrated that the personal benefits of participation in a minority religion are dependent on the size of the Catholic majority. Although religious minorities generally experience health and wellness gains via their engagement with religious communities, the non-Catholic residents of some Catholic nations score higher on self-reports of mental and physical health, when they are not actively engaged with their religious tradition.

Conway and Spruyt (2018) finally investigated variations in Catholic religious commitment in different macro world regions. The study tested the drivers of the self-rated importance of God, private prayer, and church attendance across 52 countries in 5 world macro-regional contexts—Africa, Asia, Europe, Latin America, and Oceania. Among a group of traditionally Catholic countries, what explains why some countries have fewer or more Catholics today than they did before? The study found that rather than Catholicism being more competitive at fulfilling spiritual needs and tastes or being more culturally defensive (and thus keeping commitment for longer through developing institutions such as trade unions, youth clubs, and other social organizations), Catholic identity and practice are being eroded by modern society (albeit at different paces in different world regions), where existential security, that is to say, social safety nets, functioning pension systems, employment, and the overall fulfillment of basic human needs, has made significant inroads among the general populace within the all-Catholic group, i.e., when governments enacted legislation, inspired by the Roman Catholic Social Doctrine to provide societies with adequate safety nets against poverty (see Müller et al. 2000). Indeed, when evaluated in a single quantitative model, the *existential security perspective* (a term coined originally by Ronald F. Inglehart and his associates) outperforms in respect of all three indicators of religiosity the classical secularization perspective. In addition, the effect of existential security on religiosity is stronger for the self-rated importance of God than for the other two religion indicators. It may be that for devotees facing strong day-to-day survival challenges, the "costs" in terms of time and effort are lower for religious orientations than for engaging in more time-intensive behaviors such as prayer and church attendance. Thus, the findings stress the significance of differentiating between different kinds of religious involvement in comparative research and theory. The study also tested the effects of the occurrence of Catholic Church clergy-related pedophilia and sex scandals but found that the effects of these scandals on religious commitment are a gradual process and thus may best be observed over time in each country, rather than between countries.

Current World Affairs Reasons for an Analysis on the Opinions of Active Global Catholics

From the above, we can already draw the fairly robust conclusion that quantitative comparative sociology, based on global opinion surveys, is already well-equipped to face the task of studying the real landscape of active Catholicism concerning the hard-core and cutting-edge issues chosen for our analysis (Antisemitism, attitudes toward the Open Society, religious tolerance, and attitudes on homosexuals and homosexuality). But there were not only scientific reasons to write the present study. There were also very immediate and very pressing current world affairs reasons suggesting that it is time to write an analysis on where the active global Catholic rank and file is currently positioned:

- The current Pope of the Roman Catholic Church, Pope Francis already celebrated his 82nd birthday on December 17, 2018, 6 years older than the threshold age when Catholic bishops usually have to offer their resignation.[3] "The ministry of a bishop in a diocese or in the Roman Curia requires a total commitment of energy, and anything—including age—that decreases the ability to dedicate oneself fully to serving the church and the faithful is a valid reason for offering to retire." What basic trends characterize the convictions of the global Catholic rank and file in this context?
- Like Pope Francis, the current Secretary General of the United Nations, Antonio Guterres, is generally being referred to as a "progressive Catholic" who shares with the current Pope the values of social inclusion and openness for refugees. With a representative of moderate liberation theology at the helm in the Vatican and a like-minded Portuguese Roman Catholic Social Democrat in charge at the UN headquarters in New York, even a new axis of "progressive Catholicism" in international relations could develop as a counterweight to the tendencies toward populism and xenophobia in the Western world.
- In the United States, the values of Roman Catholic immigrants have become the subject of heated and divisive controversies. During the election campaign of Mr. Donald Trump, he repeatedly used very strong insults against the majority Roman Catholic 12 million Mexican immigrants describing them as "rapists" and "thieves," indicating that he firmly thinks that they fundamentally differ in their basic societal values from mainstream American society. But really how different the values of the Catholic US population are from the general population in the United States?

Where do global and where do European Roman Catholics really stand in this context regardless of what the Church officially pronounces in its official teaching, called *magisterium?*

Bergson, Maritain, Postwar Christian Democracy, and the Open Society

As we will explain in greater detail in Chap. 4 of this work, one must consider that centuries of Roman Catholic opposition against Human Rights, the Enlightenment and "Modernism" to the contrary, there is now a solid tradition of Roman Catholic thinking in favor of democracy ever since the writings of the influential French theologian Jacques Maritain (1882–1973) and the Jewish philosopher Henri Louis Bergson (1859–1941). Of course, Bergson formally was not a Roman Catholic, but was a Jew who felt very close to Roman Catholicism during his later years and who

---

[3]http://www.catholicnews.com/services/englishnews/2014/pope-confirms-retirement-age-of-75-for-bishops-including-in-curia.cfm (Download April 10, 2019).

strongly influenced the intellectual climate of global liberal Catholicism. And yet Bergson died as a Jew during the Vichy Government's persecution of Jews in France in 1941. His *Two Sources of Morality and Religion* even proved to be an important inspiration for Poppers *Open Society and Its Enemies*. He provided Catholicism with the most consistent philosophical reasoning in favor of a democratic Open Society ever to have been authored. The pre-Second World War liberal democratic Catholicism came to bear its full fruits in the trajectory of the Christian democratic parties in Europe and in Latin America after the Second World War, which were so instrumental in the postwar period in countries like Germany and Italy and which also played a major role in the democratization of the countries of Latin America in the 1980s and 1990s and in Eastern Europe after the transformation starting in 1989.

The interesting research question already voiced by Lipset (1959) about the affinity of the Judeo-Christian heritage to democracy is now of course open to further empirical investigations. Without question, towering figures of Western democratic political leadership after 1945, like the German Konrad Adenauer, the Chilean Eduardo Frei Montalva, and the Italian Alcide de Gasperi, were deeply motivated by the idea of a combination of Christian values and democracy.

As we also will explain in greater detail in Chap. 4 of the present work, Catholic authoritarian and Antisemitic traditions, positioned against democracy, are too well known in history and still plagued many countries, especially in Europe, for much of the nineteenth century and the first half of the twentieth century. Then, just how thin is the ice that now separates global contemporary Catholic publics from the temptations of a re-emergence of Catholic authoritarianism? After all, regimes, where Catholics played a prominent role, such as Croatia or Slovakia in the Second World War, were not only "clerical fascist" dictatorships, but they were also allied with Hitler's Germany and played a terrible and active role in the *Shoah*.

Or is Roman Catholicism today a real stable upholder of democracy and the market economy? And is democratic Roman Catholicism symbolized by such personalities as the Frenchman Jean Monnet and the German Konrad Adenauer, not only at the cradle of the process of European integration, but has the *Open Society* now finally triumphed over its enemies in the minds and hearts of the global Catholics, including a permanent resistance to the temptations of a return to Roman Catholic authoritarianism?

Outlining the Research Direction of the Empirics of the Present Study

As already highlighted above, the issue of immigration, on which we focus in Chap. 4 of this work, now polarizes more and more opinions in the developed Western democracies. This sharp polarization in Germany and other European countries about the future of immigration policy gathered pace especially since Chancellor Angela Merkel's policy of invitation and welcoming refugees in late summer, 2015. Also, in other Western countries, there seems to be a strong backlash against liberal immigration policy. Prominent examples would be the case of the United States and Australia. For the first time since 1945, the chance is real that far-right-wing parties and candidates will further gain power at the ballot boxes in many Western countries. Asylum and migration greatly polarize the political landscape everywhere. This book, finalized in the days shortly before the European parliamentary elections of spring 2019, risks a strong and yet fairly safe prognosis: the European right will gain in strength, and the European left—especially the Social Democrats—will be decimated at the ballot boxes. What can we already say about the positioning of active Catholics in these macro-ideological "equations"?

In this study, we also aim to find out in Chap. 5 something about the religious tolerance among global Catholic *Dominicantes*. Today, the measurement of religious tolerance across nations has become possible. The *World Values Survey* offers fairly encompassing and comparable data on tolerance items. Our newly developed index of religious tolerance combines the performance of five tolerance components.

With the publication of Reverend Charamsa's book (Charamsa 2016), written by a Polish former official at the Congregation for the Doctrine of the Faith in the Vatican, accusing the Roman Catholic Church of making the lives of gay and transgender people "a hell," the entire issue of homosexuality and Roman Catholicism has moved again into the focus of international media attention. While Pope Francis went on the record to say "Who am I to condemn the homosexuals," the influential Cardinal Robert Sarah of Guinea, certainly to be considered as a future contender for Saint Peter's throne in Rome, said: "What Nazi-Fascism and Communism were in the 20th century, Western homosexual and abortion ideologies and Islamic fanaticism are today." But global value change in favor of accepting homosexuality increasingly also affects the faithful Roman Catholics.

We also present a brief synoptical promax factor analysis of our data, in which the following dimensions from the *World Values Survey* data base were studied in conjunction with Catholic Antisemitism in Chap. 7:

- Acceptancy of homosexuality versus homophobia
- Age
- Attitudes on family and work
- Attitudes on labor and labor rights
- Attitudes on the sociopolitical and economic
- Position in the economic and social hierarchy
- Strength of the adherence to the church in fundamental religious questions
- Value in education
- Xenophobia versus a culture of welcome

Is it still true that there is close connection between tolerance for homosexuals and overall tolerance in a society (Hadler 2012; Hadler and Symons 2018; Inglehart 2008; Inglehart and Baker 2000; Inglehart and Welzel 2010)?

And finally, which are the best and worst practice models of global Catholicism in the light of our data?

Christianity Is the Most Persecuted Religion, Worldwide

Last but not least, our interest to study active global Roman Catholicism also has another and final background, lamentably often overlooked in Western countries: today, Christianity is the most persecuted religion, worldwide. One does not necessarily have to share the values and convictions of the Religious Right in America to arrive at the conclusion that in view of the massive persecution of Christians around the world, there is a conspicuous silence about this in the West.[4]

While empirical studies on global Islam abound, especially after 9/11, there is a real dearth of sociological, value-oriented surveys on global Catholicism or Christianity in general.[5] As the Organization "Open Doors," documenting human rights violations against Christians, worldwide, every month around our globe:

- 255 Christians are killed
- 104 are abducted
- 180 Christian women are raped, sexually harassed, or forced into marriage
- 66 churches are attacked
- 160 Christians are detained without trial and imprisoned

215 million Christians experience high levels of persecution. This represents 1 in 12 Christians worldwide. Apart from the notorious case of the dictatorship in North Korea, Islamist repression fuels Christian persecution in 8 of the top 10 countries. It is expanding in Asia (the Philippines, Bangladesh, Indonesia) and Africa (Egypt, Nigeria, Somalia). Also, insecure governments are using the country's majority religion to marginalize Christians and other religious minorities. This phenomenon has been observed in some parts of Asia with Hindu nationalism (India, Nepal) and Buddhist nationalism (Myanmar, Sri Lanka) both gaining ground.

Literature

Anti-Defamation League (ADL). (2014). *ADL 100 Index*. Download April 10, 2019, from http://global100.ADL.org/

Bergson, H. L. (1935). *The two sources of religion and morality* (R. Ashley Andrà & C. Brereton with the assistance of W. Horsefall Carter, Trans.). New York: Henry Holt.

Bible Gateway. (2019). Download April 10, 2019, from https://www.biblegateway.com/

Charamsa, K. (2016). *La Prima Pietra. Io, prete gay a la mia ribellione all'ipocrisia della Chiesa*. Milano: Rizzoli.

Conway, B., & Spruyt, B. (2018). Catholic commitment around the globe: A 52-country analysis. *Journal for the Scientific Study of Religion, 57*(2), 276–299.

Curtis, M. (2017). *Jews, Antisemitism, and the Middle East*. Milton: Taylor and Francis.

---

[4]http://www.abc.net.au/news/2014-08-01/moore-why-dont-we-hear-about-persecuted-christians/5641390 (Download April 10, 2019).

[5]https://www.opendoorsusa.org/christian-persecution/ (Download April 10, 2019).

Feess, E., Mueller, H., & Ruhnau, S. G. (2014). The impact of religion and the degree of religiosity on work ethic: A multilevel analysis. *Kyklos, 67*(4), 506–534.

Fukuyama, F. (1995). *Trust*. New York: Free Press.

Fukuyama, F. (2006). *The end of history and the last man*. New York: Simon and Schuster.

Fukuyama, F. (2016, Summer). American political decay or renewal? The meaning of the 2016 election. *Foreign Affairs*. Available at: https://www.foreignaffairs.com/articles/united-states/2016-06-13/american-political-decay-or-renewal

Goldhagen D. (2003). *A moral reckoning: The role of the catholic church in the holocaust and its unfulfilled duty of repair* (First Vintage Books ed.). New York: Vintage Books, a division of Random House.

Gu, M. L., & Bomhoff, E. J. (2012). Religion and support for democracy: A comparative study for Catholic and Muslim countries. *Politics and Religion, 5*(2), 280–316.

Hadler, M. (2012). The influence of world societal forces on social tolerance. A time comparative study of prejudices in 32 countries. *The Sociological Quarterly, 53*(2), 211–237.

Hadler, M., & Symons, J. (2018). World society divided: Divergent trends in state responses to sexual minorities and their reflection in public attitudes. *Social Forces, 96*(4), 1721–1756.

Hirsh, D. (2017). *Contemporary left Antisemitism*. London: Routledge.

Inglehart, R. F. (1988). The renaissance of political culture. *American Political Science Review, 82* (04), 1203–1230.

Inglehart, R. F. (1990). *Culture shift in advanced industrial countries*. Princeton, NJ: Princeton University Press.

Inglehart, R. F. (2000). Globalization and postmodern values. *Washington Quarterly, 23*(1), 215–228.

Inglehart, R. F. (2006). Mapping global values. *Comparative Sociology, 5*(2), 115–136.

Inglehart, R. F. (2008). Changing values among western publics from 1970 to 2006. *West European Politics, 31*(1–2), 130–146.

Inglehart, R. F. (2015). *The silent revolution: Changing values and political styles among Western publics* Princeton, NJ: Princeton University Press.

Inglehart, R. F., & Baker, W. E. (2000). Modernization, cultural change, and the persistence of traditional values. *American Sociological Review, 65*(1), 19–51. Download April 10, 2019, from http://my.fit.edu/~gabrenya/cultural/readings/Inglehart-Baker-2000.pdf

Inglehart, R. F., & Norris, P. (2003). *Rising tide: Gender equality and cultural change around the world*. New York: Cambridge University Press.

Inglehart, R. F., & Norris, P. (2009, November 4). The true clash of civilizations. *Foreign Policy*. Download April 10, 2019, from http://foreignpolicy.com/2009/11/04/the-true-clash-of-civilizations/

Inglehart, R. F., & Norris, P. (2012). The four horsemen of the apocalypse: Understanding human security. *Scandinavian Political Studies, 35*(1), 71–95.

Inglehart, R. F., & Norris, P. (2016). *Trump, Brexit, and the rise of populism: Economic have-nots and cultural backlash*. Download April 10, 2019, from SSRN: http://ssrn.com/abstract=2818659 HKS Working Paper No. RWP16-026.

Inglehart, R. F., & Welzel, C. (2003). Political culture and democracy: Analyzing cross-level linkages. *Comparative Politics, 36*(1), 61–79.

Inglehart, R. F., & Welzel C. (2009, March, April). How development leads to democracy. What we know about modernization. *Foreign Affairs*. Download April 10, 2019, from http://www.foreignaffairs.com/articles/64821/ronald-Inglehart-and-christian-welzel/how-development-leads-to-democracy

Inglehart, R. F., & Welzel, C. (2010). Changing mass priorities: The link between modernization and democracy. *Perspectives on Politics, 8*(02), 551–567.

Inglehart, R. F., Ponarin, E., & Inglehart, R. C. (2017). Cultural change, slow and fast: The distinctive trajectory of norms governing gender equality and sexual orientation. *Social Forces, 95*(4), 1313–1340.

Israeli, R. (2017). *Muslim anti-Semitism in Christian Europe: Elemental and residual anti-Semitism*. Milton: Taylor and Francis.

Jikeli, G. (2015). *European Muslim antisemitism: Why young urban males say they don't like Jews (Studies in Antisemitism)*. Bloomington: Indiana University Press.

Kressel, N. (2012). *"The sons of pigs and apes": Muslim Antisemitism and the conspiracy of silence* (1st ed.). Washington, DC: Potomac Books.

Lipset, S. M. (1959). Some social requisites of democracy: Economic development and political legitimacy. *American Political Science Review, 53*(01), 69–105.

Lipset, S. M. (1969, December). The socialism of fools—The left, the Jews and Israel. *Encounter,* 24.

Maritain, J. (1936). *Humanisme integral. Problemes temporels et spirituels d'une nouvelle chretiente*. Paris: Aubier (1936). 334 S. 8°. Aubier.

Maritain, J. (2012). *Christianity and democracy, the rights of man and natural law*. San Francisco, CA: Ignatius Press.

May, M., & Smilde, D. (2016). Minority participation and well-being in majority Catholic Nations: What does it mean to be a religious minority? *Journal of Religion and Health, 55*(3), 874–894.

Müller, A., Tausch, A., Zulehner, P. M., & Wickens, H. (Eds.). (2000). *Global capitalism, liberation theology, and the social sciences: An analysis of the contradictions of modernity at the turn of the millennium*. Hauppauge, NY: Nova Science.

Pollack, E. (Ed.). (2017). *From Antisemitism to anti-Zionism: The past & present of a lethal ideology (Antisemitism in America)*. Boston, MA: Academic Studies.

Pope Francis, I., & Skorka, A. (2014). *On heaven and earth: Pope Francis on faith, family, and the church in the twenty-first century* (A. Bermúdez & H. Goodman, Trans.; D. Rosemberg, Ed.). London: Bloomsbury Continuum.

Rosenfeld, A. (Ed.). (2013). *Resurgent antisemitism: Global perspectives (Studies in Antisemitism)*. Bloomington, IN: Indiana University Press.

Rubinstein, W. D. (2015). *The left, the right and the Jews*. London: Routledge.

Rudin, J. (1987). *Dietrich Bonhoeffer: A Jewish perspective*. By Rabbi A. James Rudin. National Interreligious Affairs Director, The American Jewish Committee, New York. Presented at the Evangelische Akademie Nordelbien, Hamburg, June 17, 1987. Available at: https://www.jamesrudin.com/uploads/5/8/6/3/58633797/dietrich_bonhoeffer.pdf

Tausch, A. (2016). Islamism and Antisemitism. Preliminary evidence on their relationship from cross-national opinion data. *Social Evolution and History, 15*(2), 50–99. Available at: https://cyberleninka.ru/article/n/islamism-and-antisemitism-preliminary-evidence-on-their-relationship-from-cross-national-opinion-data

Weber, M. (1930 [1904/05]). *The protestant ethic and the spirit of capitalism*. London: Allen and Unwin

Wistrich, R. (2002). *Muslim anti-Semitism: A clear and present danger*. New York: American Jewish Committee.

Chapter 3
The Second Vatican Council in the Hearts and Minds of Global Catholics: The Open Society, Catholic Antisemitism, and the Effects of *Nostra Aetate*

Introduction

One popular and very common hypothesis nowadays is that the Roman Catholic Second Vatican Council (October 11, 1962–December 8, 1965) with its commitment to interreligious tolerance, especially toward Judaism and Islam (see Bea 1966; Connelly 2012; Cunningham 2015; D'Costa 2014; Heschel 1966; Kimelman 2004; Valkenberg and Cirelli 2016), paved the way for the high contemporary degree of societal religious tolerance in predominantly Catholic Western countries, irrespective of the fact whether Catholics in those countries today live a secular or a more religious life. With its declaration *Nostra Aetate* (promulgated on October 28, 1965), the argument runs, the Church buried the demons of Catholic Antisemitism for good.[1] But just how thick is the ice that now separates global contemporary Catholic publics from the temptations of a re-emergence of Catholic authoritarianism and Antisemitism (Pollard 2007)? After all, regimes, where Roman Catholics played a prominent role, such as Croatia or Slovakia in the Second World War, were not only *clerical fascist* dictatorships, but they were also allied to Hitler's Germany, and they played a more than active role in the *Shoah* (Goldhagen 2007; Hoppenbrouwers 2004; Phayer 2000). Given the fact that today global Antisemitism is again on the increase in many regions and countries (ADL 2014), the analysis of the opinions of the active segment of the 1.3 billion global Roman Catholics is of strategic importance and relevance for the entire West and not just an exercise in retrospective political culture research and what in Christian theology is being called *pastoral theology* (Rahner 1963).

While the study of global Antisemitism received important new and global empirical insights from the ADL (Anti-Defamation League) so-called 100 study

---

[1] http://www.usccb.org/beliefs-and-teachings/ecumenical-and-interreligious/ (Download April 10, 2019). For all matters of Jewish-Christian Dialogue, see also https://sites.sju.edu/ijcr/ (Download April 10, 2019).

© Springer Nature Switzerland AG 2020
A. Tausch, S. Obirek, *Global Catholicism, Tolerance and the Open Society*,
https://doi.org/10.1007/978-3-030-23239-9_3

(ADL 2014) covering more than 100 countries, comparative studies on Antisemitism among *practicing* global Roman Catholics are rather lacking.

At least 26% of the citizens of our globe—more than one billion people—today are Antisemitic. But the ADL maintains in its 2014 study that while fewer than 20% of Christians in the Americas and Oceania are Antisemitic, the share of Christians with Antisemitic attitudes in Western Europe is already 25%; in Eastern Europe, it is a high 35%; and in the MENA region, it has reached a staggering 64%.

Our study is thus intended to focus on indicators of global Antisemitism of entire countries in comparison with the Antisemitism of their practicing Roman Catholic communities, i.e., those Catholics who attend Sunday Mass regularly, the so-called Dominicantes, which still make up according to our (country population-weighted) data some 45% of the global 1.3 billion Roman Catholics.

The lack of global empirical studies on contemporary Catholic Antisemitism is all the more intriguing since among all global religious denominations, the Roman Catholic Church is the religious organization, which still commands the largest single following held by any Christian Church among the citizens of the Western democracies in the Americas, Europe, Africa, and the Asia-Pacific region.[2] One could even say that Roman Catholicism per se is the leading religion of the West. By its self-definition (John Paul II 1994), the Church should be a religious congregation committed to the ideals of neighborly love to the needy, openness for the weakest and by universal human understanding, and brotherly/sisterly affection to Judaism, the "older brothers in faith."[3] This term used for the first time ever by the late Pope John Paul II during his historic visit to the synagogue in Rome on April 13, 1986,[4] is a far step away from all the declarations of the Heads of the Roman Catholic Church on Judaism and the Jews during the past 2000 years (Kertzer 2007).

From its early days, Antisemitism was the *original sin* of Roman Catholicism (Bauer 1993; Brustein 2003; Grümme 1997; Wistrich 2004, 2007, 2010). Catholic authoritarian and Antisemitic traditions are too well known in history, and they plagued many countries, especially in Europe, well into much of the nineteenth century and the first half of the twentieth century (Conway 2008; Laqueur 1997; Phayer 2000; Pollard 2007; Ward 2013).

In this chapter, we will thus first look into the cross-national evidence as to whether the share of Roman Catholics per total population or for that matter also the share of active Roman Catholics per the number of total Roman Catholics has any statistical effect at all on the rates of overall societal Antisemitism, reported in the landmark ADL (2014) study on Antisemitism in 100+ countries, properly controlling for other intervening variables.

---

[2]Calculated from http://www.nationmaster.com/; http://www.catholic-hierarchy.org/; http://www.pewforum.org/2013/02/13/the-global-catholic-population/; http://www.bbc.com/news/world-21,443,313 (Download April 10, 2019).

[3]http://articles.latimes.com/1987-08-20/news/mn-3718_1_elder-brothers and http://www.nytimes.com/1986/04/14/world/text-of-pope-s-speech-at-rome-synagogue-you-are-our-elder-brothers.html?pagewanted=all (Download April 10, 2019).

[4]http://time.com/4280602/pope-john-paul-synagogue-visit/ (Download April 10, 2019).

If the end result of our statistical exercise would be that Catholicism and even active Catholicism not only do not prevent a higher societal Antisemitism but in fact are still even drivers of Antisemitism in the countries around the world, something entirely wrong must have happened with the practical realization of the good intentions of the Second Vatican Council five decades ago.

We then ask ourselves, how reliable is the support of global active Roman Catholic publics for the ideas of the bonds of brotherhood and sisterhood with Judaism, proposed by the Second Vatican Council in the already mentioned declaration *Nostra Aetate*? We will explain in our methodology section that, working with greater number of countries, other reliable and freely available Antisemitism indicators are not available to analyze the Antisemitism of the practicing Roman Catholics, and thus we have to work with the proxy indicator—*rejecting Jewish neighbors*—from the best freely available opinion research data base of the world today, the University of Michigan's *World Values Survey* project.[5] In view of the lack of availability of alternative international data and the dearth of comparative Antisemitism indices (apart from the already mentioned landmark ADL 100 study), we develop a new *Nostra Aetate Index*, which should be regarded as a new single benchmark for how well a national active Catholic community put into practice the conciliatory teachings of the Second Vatican Council on Judaism.[6] The Index starts from the following very simple basic idea: only if the Roman Catholic Church could successfully teach its faithful to accept Jewish neighbors over the last five decades,[7] only if active Roman Catholics are at the forefront of society in accepting Jewish neighbors and thus overcoming Antisemitism, and only if Catholic Antisemitism [again measured by the *World Values Survey* question item of the rejection of Jewish neighbors] decreased over time, the Second Vatican Council's document *Nostra Aetate* has had any tangible global societal success. One can argue that our indicator is terribly deficient, but still, the Second Vatican Council's document *Nostra Aetate* really had no tangible global societal success, if a country's Catholic community failed on all three items, mentioned above. In a way, we can say that our indicator measures the necessary, but not the sufficient conditions of Antisemitism, and that everybody, rejecting to have a Jewish neighbor, indeed harbors strong Antisemitic feelings.

Furthermore, we ask ourselves how strong is the support of global active Roman Catholic publics for the State of Israel, more than two decades after full diplomatic relations were finally established between the Vatican and the State of Israel. As recent research from Argentina, far too neglected by global scholarship on the subject (Bosca 2017), has shown, even the pivotal figure of the German-born Jesuit

---

[5]http://www.worldvaluessurvey.org/wvs.jsp (Download April 10, 2019).

[6]As we explain below, the correlation between the ADL 100 indicator and our own data, based on the rejection of Jewish neighbors, is sufficiently high to speak of reliable results.

[7]On the measurement of Antisemitism, see below. Our data base, the *World Values Survey*, presents only one item relevant for the study of Antisemitism, the rejection of Jewish neighbors. See also http://www.worldvaluessurvey.org/wvs.jsp (Download April 10, 2019).

Cardinal Augustin Bea, in many ways to be regarded as the architect of *Nostra Aetate* on the Catholic side, shunned away from an explicit Catholic identification with the State of Israel and rather tended to view *Nostra Aetate* as a declaration without any political consequences.[8] Bea went on record with his notable views in the Jesuit Journal *Civiltá Cattolica*, 1964, 18–IV–64, pages 105–109, for all to read. According to the Bosca (2017) study, Arab diplomatic and political influence in the Vatican at that time must be regarded as one of the factors leading to this particular turn of events.

And with the West now being confronted with large-scale Muslim immigration, how do active Roman Catholic publics really view the future trajectories of Jewish immigration, especially in Europe? Will the Roman Catholic Churches in the West be following Cardinal Bea's footsteps, and will they regard preferentially the local Jewish communities as their partner in dialogue, but will they be distant from or even be very critical of Israel, cherished by the Jewish communities worldwide as their Jewish State, built after the *Shoah*?

And is the European *culture of welcome* initiated by the German Christian Democratic Chancellor Angela Merkel limited only to Muslim refugees, and are active Catholic publics by contrast holding restrictive or even very restrictive opinions on future Jewish immigration to Europe? Is there a Catholic movement of growing rapprochement with Islam to the detriment of Catholic–Jewish relations?

This chapter attempts to evaluate all these issues by rigorous empirical means. It is based on the secondary analysis of already existing and freely available large-scale international survey data.

The present chapter is thus not an exercise in theology. It is situated well within a large and growing tradition to study *real existing* Catholicism in an empirical social scientific framework (Curran 2008; Fox et al. 2004; Jelen and Wilcox 1998; O'Collins 2008; Reese 1996; Rudolph and Piscatori 1997; Shelledy 2004; Valuer 1971). That is, we do not study what Catholics on a global level *should* think from the viewpoint of theology, but what they *do* think empirically from the viewpoint of sociology and political science (Brenner 2016; Grzymała-Busse 2015, 2016; Hanson 2014; Knippenberg 2015; Manuel et al. 2006; Norris and Inglehart 2015).

Secularization trends notwithstanding, a first look at the global map of religious denominations shows that Catholicism's huge weight in the current world still is considerable, especially in Latin America, in Latin Europe, in Ireland, in some countries of Eastern Europe, in Southern Africa, and in the Philippines. In some other countries, most notably in the United States, Canada, Germany, and Australia, it also plays an important role (Map 3.1):

There is of course a vast literature on the Roman Catholic Church and its history over the ages (Brustein 2003; Hastings 1991; Koschorke et al. 2007; Michael 2008; Perreau-Saussine 2012; Phayer 2000, 2001) and also on the legacy of Pope John

---

[8]http://www.congresojudio.org.ar/uploads/coloquio/207/MARITAIN,%20LOS%20JUDIOS%20Y%20EL%20CONCILIO%20VATICANO%20II.pdf (Download April 10, 2019).

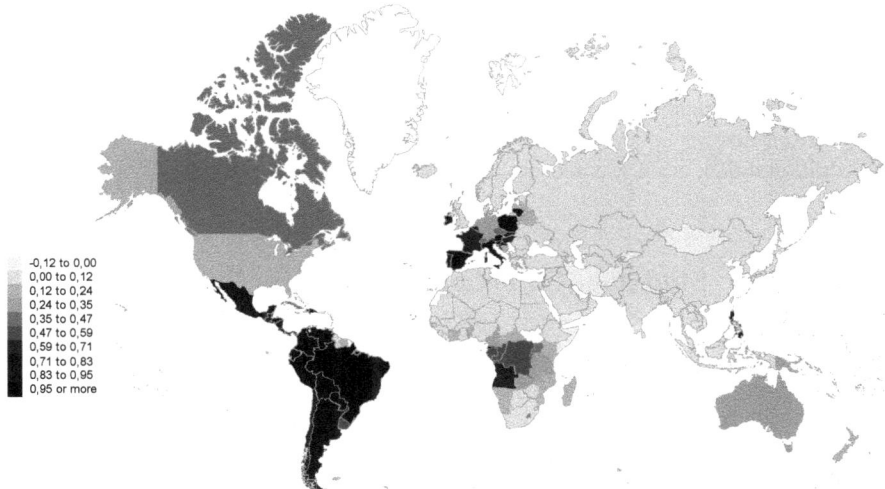

Map 3.1 The share of Roman Catholics per total population, around 2000 (based on Barro 2003a, b; scale ranging from 0.0 (0.0%) to 1.0 (100%). Highest: Malta, Colombia, Ecuador, Poland, and Venezuela. Lowest: Afghanistan, Bhutan, Iran, Kyrgyzstan, and Maldives

Paul II (Bernstein and Politi 1996; Fisher and Klenicki 1987, 1995; Kupczak 2000; Weigel 2001), who was so influential in pioneering the Judeo-Christian dialogue, and only under his Papacy, the Vatican opened diplomatic relations with the State of Israel in 1993, 45 years after Israel's declaration of independence.[9] What a difference to the times when Theodor Herzl, the founder of Zionism, already very ill and shortly before his death, met Pope Pius X in Rome in 1904 asking for the Vatican's help for the building of a Jewish State, and the Pontiff of that time famously replying then:

> We cannot prevent the Jews from going to Jerusalem—but we could never sanction it (. . .) The Jews have not recognized our Lord, therefore we cannot recognize the Jewish people[10]

How many millions of human lives could have been saved if a Jewish State already had existed at the time of the *Shoah!*

The rest of this chapter is ordered as follows: first, we present a theoretical foundation in the background section. Then, we proceed to discuss our methods

---

[9]http://mfa.gov.il/MFA/ForeignPolicy/Bilateral/Pages/Israel-Vatican_Diplomatic_Relations.Aspx (Download April 10, 2019).

[10]Quotation retrieved from http://www.bunyanministries.org (Download April 10, 2019) and the Council of Centers on Jewish-Christian Relations, Saint Joseph University, Dialogika, Texts from the History of the Relationship. Theodore Herzl: Audience with Pope Pius X (1904) (http://www.ccjr.us/dialogika-resources/primary-texts-from-the-history-of-the-relationship) (Download April 10, 2019).

and data, and then we present the results of our analysis. Finally, we draw some limited conclusions from our data. We also highlight the drivers of Antisemitism by interreligious comparison, using an OLS regression procedure applied to *World Values Survey* data and analyze the connections between general religious tolerance and Antisemitism.

Additional data are presented in the electronic Appendix.

Background: Studying (Catholic) Antisemitism

Our background section has to start from a short presentation of the ADL (2014) study, which up to now has not yet been sufficiently received in social science literature. The overall ADL Global 100 Index Score (ADL 2014) is 26%, that is to say at least 26% of the citizens of our globe—more than one billion people—are Antisemitic. This reflects the percentage of global respondents who say that at least 6 of the 11 negative stereotypes tested in the ADL (2014) study are *probably true*. In the world regions, the results are as follows (weighted percentages):

Middle East and North Africa (MENA): 74%
Eastern Europe: 34%
Western Europe: 24%
Sub-Saharan Africa: 23%
Asia: 22%
Americas: 19%
Oceania: 14%

In the mentioned study, the ADL also ran extra questions regarding awareness about the *Shoah*. Only 33% of the global population today are aware of the *Shoah* and believe it has been accurately described by history. In Oceania, it is 82%; in Western Europe, it is 77%; in Eastern Europe, it is 57%; in the Americas, this percentage is 55%; in Asia, it is 23%; and in sub-Saharan Africa, it is 12%. Notably, in the MENA region (Middle East and North Africa), it is only 8%. The data for Muslim Antisemitism in these regions corresponds to the following pattern: while fewer than 30% of Muslims in the Americas and Oceania are Antisemitic, the share of Muslims with Antisemitic attitudes in Western Europe is 29%, in Eastern Europe, it is only 20%, while in the MENA region, it is 75%. The implications of these structures for the future of Antisemitism especially in Europe can only be guessed, given the amount of a very large-scale immigration from the MENA region to Europe over recent years.

In Maps 3.2 and 3.3, we summarize the results from the ADL (2014) study and the comparison of the ADL results with per capita GDPs, as documented in Tausch (2014), in a geographical fashion in order to estimate the strength of societal Antisemitism irrespective of already achieved economic development levels.

The above materials dramatically highlight the prevalence of Antisemitism in many parts of the Muslim world. But in the entire future global parallelogram of

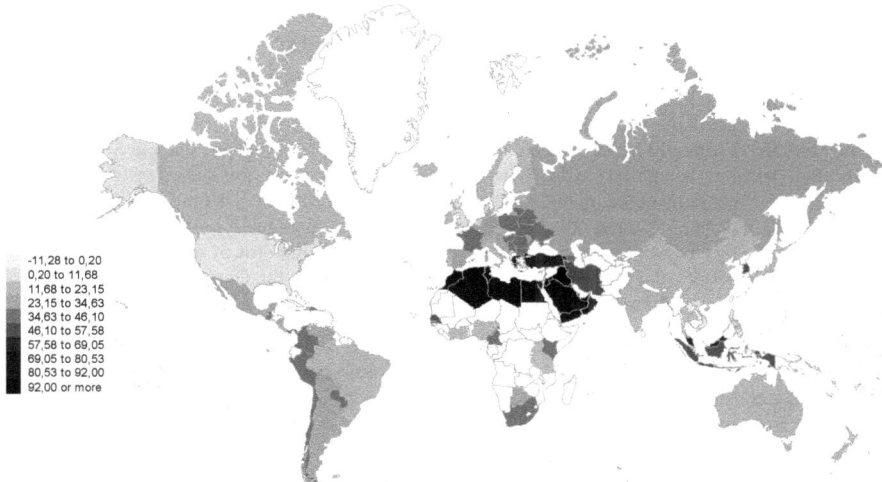

Map 3.2 The ADL 100 scores of global societal Antisemitism. Highest: Iraq, Yemen, Algeria, Libya, and Tunisia. Lowest: Laos, the Philippines, Sweden, the Netherlands, and Vietnam

Map 3.3 Societal Antisemitism irrespective of the levels of GDP per capita of a country. Highest: Yemen, United Arab Emirates, Bahrain, Kuwait, and Qatar. Lowest: the Philippines, Laos, Vietnam, Thailand, and Brazil

ideological and political forces, Roman Catholicism will still play an important role. Is the world of Roman Catholicism nowadays really so immune from Antisemitism, as the Vatican Council documents hopefully suggest? The Vatican Council's *Nostra Aetate*[11] famously stressed what it calls:

> the bond that spiritually ties the people of the New Covenant to Abraham's stock: Since the spiritual patrimony common to Christians and Jews is thus so great, this sacred synod wants to foster and recommend that mutual understanding and respect which is the fruit, above all, of biblical and theological studies as well as of fraternal dialogues. Furthermore, in her rejection of every persecution against any man, the Church, mindful of the patrimony she shares with the Jews and moved not by political reasons but by the Gospel's spiritual love, decries hatred, persecutions, displays of Antisemitism, directed against Jews at any time and by anyone.

> [. . .] No foundation therefore remains for any theory or practice that leads to discrimination between man and man or people and people, so far as their human dignity and the rights flowing from it are concerned.

> The Church reproves, as foreign to the mind of Christ, any discrimination against men or harassment of them because of their race, color, condition of life, or religion. On the contrary, following in the footsteps of the holy Apostles Peter and Paul, this sacred synod ardently implores the Christian faithful to "maintain good fellowship among the nations" (1 Peter 2:12), and, if possible, to live for their part in peace with all men, so that they may truly be sons of the Father who is in heaven.

We attempt to study Antisemitism in the framework of global value studies. This systematic social scientific study of global values and opinions, used in this chapter, has of course a long and fruitful history in the social sciences (Norris and Inglehart 2011; furthermore, on global value change Alemán and Woods 2015; Ciftci 2010; Davidov et al. 2011; Hofstede 2001; Hofstede and Minkov 2010; Hofstede et al. 2010; Minkov and Hofstede 2011, 2013).

Global value studies are made possible by the availability of systematic and comparative opinion surveys over time under the auspices of leading representatives of the social science research community, featuring the global/and or the European populations with a fairly constant questionnaire for several decades now. In each case to be represented below, the original data were made freely available to the global scientific publics and render themselves for systematic, multivariate analysis of opinion structures on the basis of the original anonymous interview data.[12] Our data are mainly from three sets of such reliable and regularly repeated global opinion surveys: The *World Values Survey* (*WVS*), the *European Social Survey* (*ESS*), and *PEW International* (see Davidov et al. 2008; Inglehart 2006; Norris and Inglehart 2015; Tausch et al. 2014).

---

[11] http://www.vatican.va/archive/hist_councils/ii_vatican_council/documents/vat-ii_decl_ 19651028_nostra-aetate_en.Html (Download April 10, 2019).

[12] http://www.worldvaluessurvey.org/wvs.jsp and http://www.europeansocialsurvey.org/ (Download April 10, 2019).

In the social sciences, there is a rich and evolving debate on the conclusions to be drawn from such comparable and freely available *omnibus surveys*. For a number of years now, also some leading economists became interested in studying global comparative opinion data, especially from the *World Values Survey* (Alesina et al. 2015). The interest of the economics profession in the relationship between religion and economic growth certainly was a factor contributing to the rise of the methodological approach, which we share with many other social scientists in this study (McCleary and Barro 2006a, b; Barro 2003a, b). Prejudice is the antithesis to societal trust; the majority of the major economic studies, using *World Values Survey* data correspondingly, concluded that trust is an important factor for long-run economic growth (Alesina et al. 2015).

In the present chapter, we feature on Roman Catholicism in the framework of what is called in political science the *civic culture* of the respective societies where the Catholics live and the role played by Catholicism in this *civic culture* (Silver and Dowley 2000). Studies on Muslim opinions were a growing focus of research in international social science since the 1990s, especially since the terror attacks of 9/11 in New York City. Compared to the now existing veritable flood of high-quality survey-based studies on Muslim communities around the globe, the available comparable opinion survey-based evidence on global Catholicism is still rather scarce (Tausch 2011, 2014, 2016a, b, c).

Sociologists, working with the unique comparative and longitudinal opinion survey data from the *World Values Survey*, have discovered inter alia that there are pretty constant and long-term patterns of change in the direction of secularization, which also affect the predominantly Roman Catholic countries (Inglehart 2006; Inglehart and Norris 2003; Norris and Inglehart 2011). Inglehart and his associates firmly believe that the ability of the Roman Catholic hierarchy to tell people how to live their lives is declining steadily (see also Morel 2003).[13]

Data and Methods in Studying Catholic Antisemitism

We are well aware that our research design is only a second-best solution, but in view of the free availability of data, we had no better choice. The analysis of Antisemitism now can look back on more than a century of fruitful studies with a vast and still growing literature (Jikeli and Allouche-Benayoun 2012; Kertzer 2007; Michael 2008; Rosenfeld 2013; von Bieberstein 1977; Wistrich 2010; see also Bauer 1993; Wistrich 2004, 2007, 2010).

Ideally, if the hallmark ADL (2014) study had included a universal global denomination variable and also a religious service attendance variable, and if—in addition—these data were freely available for global publics for further statistical

---

[13]http://ur.umich.edu/0405/Apr11_05/11.shtml (Download April 10, 2019).

analyses, our study about the Antisemitism of practicing Roman Catholics would have been a lot easier, and our additional efforts based on the *World Values Survey* would have become almost in vain. But these data do not exist. The data provided by the ADL (2014) is based on survey researched attitudes and opinions toward Jews in more than 100 countries around the world. Parameters of the survey included:

- Sample size: 53,100 total interviews among citizens aged 18 and over across 101 countries and the Palestinian Territories in the West Bank and Gaza.
- Sampling error: between ±4.4% and ±3.2%.
- Sampling methodology: all respondents were selected at random, based on random-digit dial sampling; with geographically stratified, randomly selected sampling points in each country and at the household level. Telephone interviewing was only conducted in countries where the combined telephone density exceeded 90%. Samples were adapted to the landline and mobile phone density in the total population.
- Representative samples at the national level: in an overwhelming majority of the countries and territories, the samples are fully nationally representative. In some countries (China, India, Ghana, Indonesia, Nigeria, Bangladesh, Laos, Malaysia, Mauritius, Uganda, and Vietnam), national coverage was not complete. Even there, sampling points were selected and the data was weighted to ensure the interviews from those countries reflected the national perspective.
- Index Scores and question wording: created by asking whether the negative stereotypes (11 stereotypes) are "probably true" or "probably false." Respondents who said at least 6 out of 11 statements are "probably true" are considered to hold Antisemitic attitudes.

The negative stereotypes given were:

1. Jews are more loyal to Israel than to [this country/the country they live in].
2. Jews have too much power in the business world.
3. Jews have too much power in international financial markets.
4. Jews don't care about what happens to anyone but their own kind.
5. Jews have too much control over global affairs.
6. People hate Jews because of the way Jews behave.
7. Jews think they are better than other people.
8. Jews have too much control over the United States government.
9. Jews have too much control over the global media.
10. Jews still talk too much about what happened to them in the Holocaust.
11. Jews are responsible for most of the world's wars.

Further answering the methodological issues, potentially raised by this chapter, one would be tempted to say that the *World Values Survey* theoretically is still the ideal and single best choice to be the raw data base for the scientific analysis of our theme.[14] In practice, however, it is evident that the managers of the *WVS* data base

---

[14]http://www.worldvaluessurvey.org/wvs.jsp (Download April 10, 2019).

hitherto were much more interested in issues of general sociology, the sociology of religion, and the sociology of the norms of family life and sexuality than in the hardcore issues of identifying Antisemitism. They presented only one item which we can use in our study, i.e., the rejection of Jewish neighbors. Compared to the richness of the theoretical literature, especially Wistrich (2004, 2007, 2010), this operationalization might look even primitive, but what would be the feasible global empirical alternative? We apologize to our readers for the simplicity of the *WVS* indicator used; however, we would like to remark that for the comparisons of the opinions of different denominations and different rates of religious activities in as many countries as possible, our chosen indicators are the only information available.

In order to be able to rely in any reasonable measure on our results, at least we had to look into the empirical relationship between the ADL 100 variable and our own Antisemitism rates on a country to country level, in order to calibrate our estimates. For 23 countries, we can calibrate our results accordingly and calculate at least a Pearson-Bravais correlation coefficient between the available two comparative data series on global Antisemitism, i.e., the *WVS* data on the rejection of Jewish neighbors and the ADL (2014) data. The countries with complete data for both variables are Argentina, Bangladesh, Belarus, Bosnia, Canada, Chile, the Czech Republic, Egypt, India, Iran, Iraq, Japan, Korea (South), Mexico, Moldova, Nigeria, Russia, South Africa, Spain, Uganda, the United States, Uruguay, and Venezuela, representing a fair mix of global religions and cultures. Indeed, the two measurement scales have 56.16% of the variance in common, i.e., our second-best solution using *WVS* data indeed captures more than half of the variance of the far superior measurement scale, the ADL (2014) data series. We can assume from these results that there is a constant of around 14% Antisemitism in any society around the globe, and that for every 10% of people saying that they reject Jewish neighbors according to the *WVS* data, there is an increase of 6.6% in the Antisemitism score according to the ADL (2014) criteria (Graph 3.1).

We are of course well aware of the many past valuable attempts in the growing international scientific tradition of ecumenical religious studies to arrive at theologically and social scientifically well-founded comparisons of global religions and civilizations (just to mention a few: Juergensmeyer 2000, 2011; Küng 1997, 2002; Lenoir and Tardan-Masquelier 1997; Lenoir 2008, Röhrich 2004, 2010; Sacks 1998, 2003, 2005, 2014). However, our methodology of evaluating the opinions of global publics mainly from the *World Values Survey*, the *European Social Survey*, and *PEW International* data on the beliefs of the adherents of different global religions is based on recent advances in social indicator research (Tausch et al. 2014).

The present chapter thus relies on the statistical analysis of open survey data and is based on one of the most commonly used statistical software of the world, the IBM-SPSS XXIV, utilized at many universities and research centers around the globe.[15] The program contains nearly the entire array of modern multivariate

---

[15]IBM-SPSS Statistics, http://www-03.ibm.com/software/products/en/spss-statistics (Download April 10, 2019).

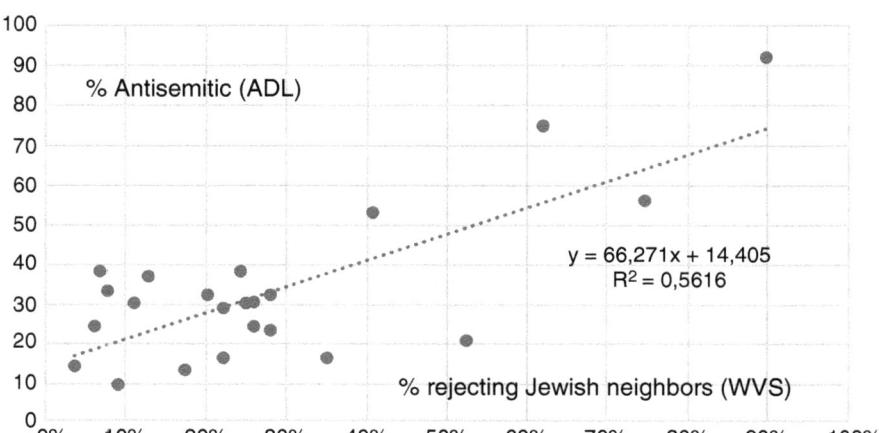

Graph 3.1 The correlation between the *WVS* data on rejecting Jewish neighbors and the ADL (2014) rates of Antisemitism. Note: *WVS* scale ranging from 0.0 (=0%) to 1.0 (=100%)

statistics, and any researcher should be able to arrive at the same results as we do here when she or he uses the same open data and the IBM-SPSS.

The data sources used are:

- The *PEW Spring 2015 Survey*.[16] The survey, conducted from March 25 to May 27, 2015, is based on 45,435 face-to-face and telephone interviews in 40 countries with adults 18 and older.[17] The Survey covers around 56% of the global citizens on earth. In our results section, we also refer to results achieved by using earlier PEW Surveys, freely available in IBM-SPSS format.[18] The *PEW Surveys* of the PEW Institute in Washington, especially the regular *Spring Surveys*, contain important informations, for example, on the opinions of global citizens on different countries around the world.

- For purposes of comparison and predictions, we especially worked with data from the *World Values Survey*. The chosen IBM-SPSS data file from the *WVS* data base is *WVS_Longitudinal_1981_2014_spss_v2015_04_18.sav*. The *World Values Survey* (*WVS*), which was started in 1981, consists of nationally repre-sentative surveys using a common questionnaire conducted in approximately 100 countries, which make up some 90% of the world's population. The *WVS* has become the largest noncommercial, cross-national, time series investigation

---

[16]*Global Attitudes and Trends*, PEW Research Center, 2017, http://www.pewglobal.org/interna tional-survey-methodology/?year_select=2015 (Download April 10, 2019). This site describes the sampling and survey methods for each country, included in the survey.

[17]*Spring Survey 2015*, PEW Research Center, 2017, http://www.pewglobal.org/2015/06/23/spring-2015-survey/ (Download April 10, 2019).

[18]http://www.pewglobal.org/category/datasets/ (Download April 10, 2019).

of human beliefs and values ever conducted. As of the time of writing this chapter, it includes interviews with almost 400,000 respondents. The countries included in the *WVS* project comprise practically all of the world's major cultural zones. At a later stage in our research, we also used earlier "waves" of the *World Values Survey* to calculate the changes of Antisemitism over time.

- Representative data from the *European Social Survey (ESS)* for 2014 (ESS7e01. sav) are available from Austria, Belgium, the Czech Republic, Denmark, Estonia, Finland, France, Germany, Ireland, the Netherlands, Norway, Poland, Slovenia, Sweden, and Switzerland. They are based on more than 28,000 representative interviews in these countries. Earlier *ESS* data also included many more additional countries, including Ukraine and Israel. As such, the *ESS* is the largest and freely available social science multivariate data base on the opinions of Europeans.[19]
- For the assessment of global opinions on Israel, we also used the *BBC Global Scan*.[20] In the version used for our secondary country-level results, a total 24,542 citizens in Argentina, Australia, Brazil, Canada, Chile, China, France, Germany, Ghana, India, Indonesia, Israel Japan, Kenya, Mexico, Nigeria, Pakistan, Peru, Russia, South Korea, Spain, Turkey, the United Kingdom, and the United States were interviewed face-to-face or by telephone between December 17, 2013, and April 28, 2014.[21] Polling was conducted for the BBC World Service in London, UK, by *GlobeScan* and its research partners in each country.

For the calculation of error margins, readers are referred to the easily readable introduction to opinion survey error margins, prepared by Cornell University Roper Center's https://ropercenter.cornell.edu/support/polling-fundamentals-total-survey-error/. Readers more interested in the details are also being referred to http://www. langerresearch.com/moe/ (Download: April 10, 2019). On the basis of the methodological literature on opinion surveys, this website makes available a direct opinion survey error margin calculator. It is important to recall that, for example, at a 5% rate of rejection of Jewish neighbors, error margins for our chosen samples of usually around 1000 representative interview partners for each country are ±1.4%; at a 10% rejection rate, the error margin is ±1.9%; and at a rejection rate of 15%, the error margin is ±2.2%; see http://www.langerresearch.com/moe/ (Download: April 10, 2019). That error margins differ according to reported rates of responses is an important fact of opinion survey research theory, often forgotten to be mentioned in the public.

Since any researcher around the globe with a proper access to the IBM-SPSS XXIV statistical program and the freely available data from the Internet should be

---

[19]http://www.europeansocialsurvey.org/data/download.html?r=7 (Download April 10, 2019).

[20]http://www.globescan.com/news_archives/bbc06-3/ (Download April 10, 2019).

[21]http://www.globescan.com/images/images/pressreleases/bbc2014_country_ratings/2014_coun try_rating_poll_bbc_globescan.pdf and https://downloads.bbc.co.uk/mediacentre/country-rating-poll.pdf (Download April 10, 2019).

able to reproduce our findings on a 1:1 basis, our presentation of the results will be rather brief, and we concentrate here on the most salient results (see below).

Our main statistical calculations relied on cross tables, comparisons of means, and bivariate and partial correlation analyses and standard multiple regressions (OLS). Keeping in line with standard traditions of empirical opinion survey research (Tausch et al. 2014), for all analyzed groups and subgroups, a minimum sample size of at least 30 respondents per country had to be available to be able to attempt reasonable predictions for general or sectoral publics.

We already mentioned at the beginning of this chapter that the Antisemitism indicator (rejection of Jewish neighbors) was analyzed for the overall population and for the practicing Roman Catholics, i.e., those Catholics who attend Sunday Mass regularly, the so-called Dominicantes. At a later stage in our project, we also used figures for the monthly religious service attendances (called by us the *Mensuantes*) among the world's major denominations (i.e., Buddhists, Hindus, Orthodox Christians, Protestants, Muslims), for whom weekly religious service attendance is not as strictly prescribed as for the Roman Catholics or not prescribed at all. We also introduced a category of people who at least sometimes still attend religious services over the years (called by us the more *seculars*), and the members of a religious denomination, who were really never attending religious services at all (called here the *completely distant*).[22] Finally, we also had to reckon with the fact that although some people do not belong (anymore) to a religious denomination, they still attend religious services. Paradoxical as this might sound at first glance, it is a social reality of our globe.

A final methodological note should be allowed on the construction of our *Nostra Aetate Index:* for the calculation of this indicator, we relied on the well-established methodology of the United Nations Human Development Programme and its *UNDP Human Development Index* (UNDP 2017a, b). Since the 1990s, the internationally recognized *Human Development Index* equally weights life expectancy, education, and real income. Life expectancy, education, and real incomes are projected onto a scale from 0 (worst value) to 1 (best value). Taking the example of the life expectancy "component" in the *Human Development Index*, let us assume that Italy nowadays, according to UNDP (2017a, b) data, has an average life expectancy of 83.3 years and Senegal 66.9 years. Let us also assume that the world's best life expectancy (currently in Hong Kong, China) is 84.2 years, and the global worst value (Central African Republic) is 51.5 years. The life expectancy component for

---

[22]For all groups and subgroups, a minimum sample of at least 30 respondents per country had to be available to be mentioned here (Tausch et al. 2014). Dealing with the PEW data, we could only distinguish publics according to their religious commitment. In our analysis, we used the PEW Spring Survey question 178 for this classification. The text of question 178 was: "Q178. How important is religion in your life—very important, somewhat important, not too important, or not at all important?" We classified as *religious* those respondents who answered question 178 by *very important* or *somewhat important*, while we classified as *secular* those respondents who answered Q178 by *not too important* or *not at all important*. The data about religious or denominational background correspond to the categories, given by PEW.

Italy then will be Italy's value minus the global worst observed value, i.e. (83.3–51.5), divided by the value of the best placed country minus the value of the worst placed country, i.e. (84.2–51.5), which results in a life expectancy component of 0.972 for Italy. The corresponding life expectancy component for Senegal would then be (66.9–51.5)/(84.2–51.5), i.e., 0.471. The simplified form of a *Human Development Index* for Italy will then be the average of its component indices for life expectancy, education, and real income, and likewise, the simplified form of a *Human Development Index* for Senegal will be the average of its component indices for life expectancy and education. Although UNDP calculation methods have become somewhat more complicated in recent years, the simple rationale remains. And our *Nostra Aetate Index* is the average of its three components: the acceptancy of Jewish neighbors by the *Dominicantes*, the degree to which *Dominicantes* better accept Jewish neighbors than the society surrounding them, and whether the acceptancy of Jewish neighbors increased or decreased over time among the *Dominicantes*. With a single number, ranging from 0.0 (worst) to 1.0 (best), our Index will then be able to tell decision-makers and our readers in general which Roman Catholic active community best adapted to the requirements of the Declaration *Nostra Aetate*.

In the following, we proceed to report our results.

Results: Toward a *Nostra Aetate* Index

The Antisemitism Among the Dominicantes *(1): 19.60% Are Openly Antisemitic*

We concentrate in the text only on the most salient results and on key trends and tendencies.

According to our results, the "real existing" global Catholicism, which emerges from our data,[23] can best be described for the aims of this study by the following global tendencies:

- *WVS* data cover 937.2 million Catholics, 84% of the global Roman Catholic population. *Dominicantes* constitute only 45% of the population-weighted total of Roman Catholics on earth.
- The top ten Catholic superpowers are the Catholic communities of Mexico, Brazil, the Philippines, the United States, Italy, Poland, Colombia, Nigeria, India, and Peru (in descending order of size) with more than ten million regular Church service attenders, which already make up more than 70% of all global *Dominicantes*. A state, transnational media corporation or a transnational center of higher learning concerned with these developments, trying to reach out in a

---

[23] http://www.catholic-hierarchy.org/country/sc1.html (Download April 10, 2019).

Table 3.1 Where the *Dominicantes* live

	Absolute number *Dominicantes*	Share of global practicing Catholics in %
Mexico	66.63	15.78
Brazil	57.60	13.64
The Philippines	43.10	10.21
The United States	29.79	7.05
Italy	20.47	4.85
Poland	20.20	4.78
Colombia	18.51	4.38
Nigeria	16.29	3.86
India	13.42	3.18
Peru	11.94	2.83
Spain	9.55	2.26
Tanzania	9.26	2.19
Uganda	8.92	2.11
Venezuela	8.34	1.97
Argentina	8.24	1.95
Guatemala	7.32	1.73
Ecuador	5.78	1.37
Germany	5.73	1.36
France	5.34	1.26
These and other smaller communities	422.27	100.00

public diplomacy effort to the world's active Catholics, would be well advised to station proper personnel in those ten key countries. *Support for the Christian-Jewish dialogue and cooperation in global Catholicism depends increasingly on the support among these strategic Catholic communities* (see Table 3.1):

- Catholicism in the Arab world, i.e., in Algeria, Comoros, Egypt, Iraq, Jordan, Kuwait, Lebanon, Libya, Mauritania, Morocco, Palestinian Territories, Sudan, Syria, Tunisia, and Yemen, amounts to only 8.7 million Roman Catholics. Catholic samples from the *World Values Survey* for this region are too small to draw any reliable conclusions for the analysis undertaken here. But the finding from the ADL 100 survey (ADL 2014) that the share of Christians with Antisemitic attitudes in the MENA region is 64% might serve as a first benchmark here.
- Inglehart is right in emphasizing the close connection between the religious factor and the level of a country's socioeconomic development. The overwhelming strength of still existing Catholic activism is to be found in the global South, while the developed countries are strongly affected by secularization [Map 3.4 and Graph 3.2; GDP per capita figures are from Tausch and Heshmati (2013)]:
- The *Catholic communities in Singapore, Malaysia, El Salvador, the United States, and Poland are still the most connected ones to the Church irrespective*

Map 3.4 *Dominicantes* in % of all Catholics—the percentages. Highest: Nigeria, Tanzania, El Salvador, Ghana, and Zimbabwe. Lowest: Finland, Sweden, the Netherlands, France, and Latvia

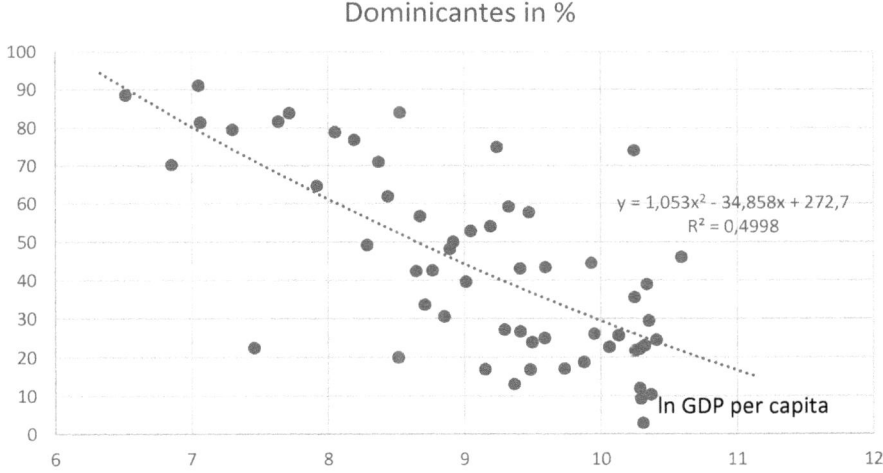

Graph 3.2 GDP per capita and Catholic religious service attendance rate

of the levels of the GDP per capita. Judging from their Church attendance rates, *they best withered the storms of secularization*, while the Catholic communities in the three postcommunist countries Moldova, Albania, and Latvia, as well as the Catholic communities in Uruguay and Finland, have the lowest Church attendance rates irrespective of their GDP per capita.

Table 3.2 Catholic Antisemitism according to *World Values Survey* data—a first overview	% *Dominicantes* rejecting Jewish neighbors
South Korea	40
South Africa	38
Slovakia	37
Nigeria	35
Bosnia	30
Venezuela	30
Spain	27
Uganda	24
Albania	24
Mexico	23
Zimbabwe	17
The Czech Republic	14
Uruguay	13
Chile	13
Belarus	12
India	8
Canada	7
The United States	6
Argentina	6

- *About one in five practicing Roman Catholics still rejects to have a Jewish neighbor, irrespective of all the Church's teaching of the Second Vatican Council.* So, rejecting Jewish neighbors is 19.60% of all *Dominicantes* in the Catholic world measured by all the available *World Values Survey* data. Catholic Antisemitism is thus a continuing and grave global problem (Table 3.2).
- *Population-weighted results from the global Catholic community also indicate that 13.40% of all Dominicantes reject people of any different religion as neighbors.* These figures are based on data covering 91.94% of all *Dominicantes* in the *World Values Survey* project and are from Albania, Argentina, Australia, Belarus, Bosnia, Brazil, Burkina Faso, Canada, Chile, Colombia, Croatia, Ecuador, El Salvador, Estonia, Finland, France, Germany, Ghana, Great Britain, Hungary, India, Indonesia, Italy, Latvia, Lebanon, Malaysia, Mexico, Moldova, the Netherlands, New Zealand, Nigeria, Peru, the Philippines, Poland, Romania, Rwanda, Serbia and Montenegro, Singapore, Slovenia, South Africa, South Korea, Spain, Sweden, Switzerland, Taiwan, Ukraine, the United States, Uruguay, Venezuela, Vietnam, Zambia, and Zimbabwe.
- Cross-checking the recent ADL figures on global Antisemitism (Tausch 2014) with the *World Values Survey* data, we even arrive at the stunning overall conclusion that the following countries with a rate of more than 30% Catholic Sunday Mass attendance also have more than 30% antisemites among the overall population: *Lebanon, Malaysia, South Korea, Indonesia, Poland, Dominican Republic, Colombia, South Africa, Ukraine, Peru, Belarus, Guatemala,*

Romania, Bosnia and Herzegovina, and Venezuela. Of course, the ADL data, as they were published, do not allow a real cross-reference with religious service attendance rates, but they indicate a certain danger that the widely existing Antisemitism in countries with a very active Catholicism also affects Catholic publics, the clergy, and possibly even the bishops or Cardinals and possibly even electors in any future Conclave to elect a new Pope eventually one day to succeed the current Pope Francis from those countries. Although watching the *papabiles* (possible candidates eventually to succeed one day Pope Francis, who is now already 82 years), from different countries is not the aim of this paper, attention should be given to the ecumenical attitudes of Catholic Church leaders from these countries, which present a mix of higher Catholic activism and higher Catholic Antisemitism, Lebanon, Malaysia, South Korea, Indonesia, Poland, Dominican Republic, Colombia, South Africa, Ukraine, Peru, Belarus, Guatemala, Romania, Bosnia and Herzegovina, and Venezuela, where Catholicism is still strong and where overall societal Antisemitism is endemic.[24] In this context, we also should mention that the current global leadership of the Roman Catholic Church seems to take a fairly liberal position on the issues of asylum and immigration,[25] which might also reflect the fact that the overwhelming majority of Roman Catholics and candidates for the priesthood now live in the global South and East and not in the secularized global North, including in countries with high rates of Antisemitism, and that an increasing share of the faithful in the rich countries and also increasingly among the clergy themselves have a so-called immigration background. Some figures recently released by the Vatican Press Office[26] dramatically highlight this view: the number of Catholic priests, diocesan and religious, from 2005 to 2014 increased by 9.381 from 406,411 to 415,792. However, this increase was not homogeneous. In Africa and Asia, there was an increase of 32.6% and 27.1%, respectively, whereas in Europe, the number declined by 8% and in Oceania by 1.7%. Candidates for the priesthood, diocesan and religious, passed from 114,439 in 2005 to 116,939 in 2014. Africa, Asia, and Oceania had a growth rate of 21, 14, and 7.2% respectively, while in Europe, there was a decline of 17.5%, and in America, especially due to a negative tendency in Latin America, there was a decrease of 7.9%. The strongest increase in seminarians was in Africa (+30.9%) and Asia (+29.4%), while Europe and the Americas registered a decrease in their numbers of 21.7% and 1.9%, respectively. From a purely organizational sociological perspective (Burrell and Morgan 1985), it is even very beneficial for Roman Catholic Church leaders to be *on*

---

[24]For readers interested in *Vaticanology*, the following list of Cardinal electors is recommended: http://www.catholic-hierarchy.org/bishop/scardc1.html (Download April 10, 2019). This list orders the Cardinals, possibly succeeding Pope Francis, by birthdate.

[25]https://www.washingtonpost.com/world/refugees-keep-streaming-into-europe-as-crisis-con tinues-unabated/2015/09/06/8a330572-5345-11e5-b225-90edbd49f362_story.html (Download April 10, 2019).

[26]https://press.vatican.va/content/salastampa/en/bollettino/pubblico/2016/03/05/160305b.html (Download April 10, 2019).

the side of immigrants, since immigrants from the global Catholic East and South now not only fill the benches of the otherwise more and more empty churches of "Northern" churches, but they also increasingly fill the theological academies and seminars in the global "North." In a way, Roman Catholic liberalism vis-à-vis mass immigration might be even a convenient counterweight to the otherwise unhalted tendencies of secularization in the rich countries.

The Antisemitism Among the Dominicantes *(2): The Spirit of* Nostra Aetate *Has Only Partially Become a Reality in the "Real Existing" Catholicism Around the World*

Although one cannot maintain in the light of available data that there is a 1:1, bivariate correlation between Catholicism and Antisemitism, a combined look at Barro's global religious adherence data (Barro 2003a, b) and the ADL (2014) study reveals that the relationship between Catholicism and Antisemitism is rather weak (some 11% of the variance in common) and curvilinear. The weakest rates of Antisemitism are to be found in societies where Roman Catholics make up some 50–55% of the total population, while societies with very few Catholics and societies with an overwhelming Catholicism tend to be more Antisemitic than the rest of global society (Graph 3.3).

In Table 3.3, we ask ourselves whether standard variables of international development accounting, gathered by the World Bank (2017) and the UNPD (2017a, b),

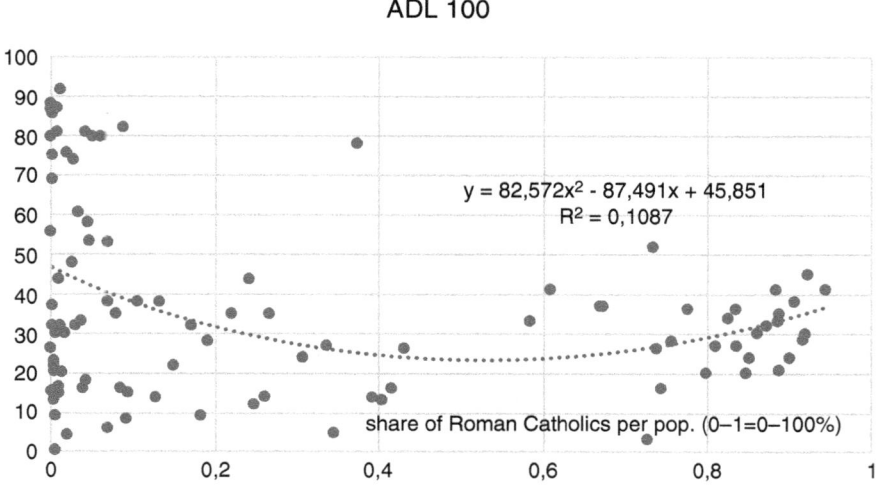

ADL 100

$$y = 82{,}572x^2 - 87{,}491x + 45{,}851$$
$$R^2 = 0{,}1087$$

share of Roman Catholics per pop. (0–1=0–100%)

Graph 3.3 The share of Roman Catholics per total population and Antisemitism [ADL 100; see ADL (2014)]

Table 3.3 The drivers of global Antisemitism (ADL 2014)—the population share of Roman Catholics is among them

	Regression coefficient B	Standard error	Standardized regression coefficient beta	T	Error p
Constant	9.131	9.674		0.944	0.348
Mean years of schooling 2013 (UNDP HDR 2014)	−1.958	1.033	−0.219	−1.896	0.062
Income 2013 (nat. logarithm of EU = 100) (World Bank 2017)	18.054	6.099	1.023	2.960	0.004
Income 2013 (nat. logarithm of EU = 100)^2 (World Bank 2017)	−1.985	0.915	−0.708	−2.170	0.033
% Roman Catholics per 2000 (Barro 2003a, b)	10.772	5.314	0.173	2.027	0.046
% Orthodox per 2000 (Barro 2003a, b)	35.687	8.588	0.318	4.155	0.000
% Muslims per 2000 (Barro 2003a, b)	54.565	5.635	0.825	9.684	0.000
Gallup poll about trust in other people (UNDP 2014)	−0.322	0.137	−0.176	−2.344	0.022

Adj. $R^2 = 69\%$; $n = 87$ countries; $F = 28.363$; error $p = 0.000$
Data from the ADL (2014), World Bank, UNDP, Robert Barro (Harvard) [As to the variable definitions and their sources. The data and a codebook are also freely available from the website https://www.academia.edu/35044095/Globalization_the_human_condition_and_sustainable_devel opment_in_the_21st_Century._Cross-national_perspectives_and_European_implications_Code book_and_EXCEL_data_file. (Download April 10, 2019). We also refer to the cross-national data for the article Tausch, available from https://www.academia.edu/37568941/Migration_from_the_ Muslim_World_to_the_West_Its_Most_Recent_Trends_and_Effects (Download April 10, 2019)]

as well as Alesina's societal trust variable (Alesina and Guiliano 2013, p. 205; Alesina and Ferrara 2000; Alesina et al. 2015) and Barro's religious adherence data (2003a, b) sufficiently well explain the global ADL (2014) Antisemitism rates. We expect that first there is an increase of Antisemitism with rising per capita incomes, leveling off at higher-income levels. Education will be an important impediment against Antisemitism, and a climate of societal trust will diminish Antisemitism. Unfortunately, it is evident that with all these other factors being constant, adherence to Catholicism, Orthodox Christianity, and Islam all are also still to be considered as significant drivers of the rate of societal Antisemitism:

The factor trust, highlighted by Alesina, is an important stabilizing factor for an open society. In our analysis, this also holds true for the determination of the absence of large-scale Antisemitism by the factor trust. The percentage of Roman Catholicism per total population and the percentages of Christian Orthodox believers and the percentages of Muslims are all significant drivers of Antisemitism. There is a

Table 3.4 On a global country to country level, Catholic "practice" even slightly increases societal Antisemitism

	Regression coefficient B	Standard error	Standardized regression coefficient beta	T	Error p
Constant	−8.311	21.285		−0.390	0.698
Mean years of schooling 2013	0.568	1.528	0.088	0.372	0.712
Income 2013 (nat. logarithm of EU = 100) (World Bank 2017)	22.494	9.646	1.757	2.332	0.025
Income 2013 (nat. logarithm of EU = 100)^2 (World Bank 2017)	−3.156	1.523	−1.580	−2.072	0.045
% Roman Catholics per 2000 (Barro 2003a, b)	3.545	7.613	0.081	0.466	0.644
% Orthodox per 2000 (Barro 2003a, b)	14.816	15.287	0.153	0.969	0.338
% Muslims per 2000 (Barro 2003a, b)	30.766	15.516	0.316	1.983	0.054
Gallup poll about trust in other people	−0.459	0.263	−0.345	−1.744	0.089
Dominicantes in %	0.027	0.130	0.043	0.212	0.834

Adj. $R^2 = 36.1\%$; $n = 48$ countries; $F = 4.317$; error $p = 0.001$

Kuznets curve (Kuznets 1976) of Antisemitism, suggesting that Antisemitism coincides with the modernization crisis experienced by semi-industrial societies at middle stages of development. In Table 3.4, we run the same multiple OLS regression as in Table 3.3, adding the Catholic Sunday religious service attendance variable from the *WVS* data base. From a liberal Catholic viewpoint, committed to the aims of the Second Vatican Council, it would be disappointing to see that the rate of Catholic Sunday religious service attendance rate even increases the ADL (2014) Antisemitism rate. What do the results of Table 3.4 then tell us? Although the influence is not significant at the 5% level, it still must be regarded as a defeat for all those who hope or had hoped that active Roman Catholicism has Antisemitism-decreasing global effect.

In the following, we analyze where the *Roman Catholic regular Sunday Mass attenders (Dominicantes)* are more rejecting to have Jewish neighbors than the totality of baptized Roman Catholics, based on *World Values Survey* data. Still best practice countries are the Czech Republic, the United States, Mexico, and Argentina (Table 3.5), while the opinions revealed by the active Catholic communities in Albania, South Africa, South Korea, Uruguay, Spain, Bosnia, Venezuela, Nigeria, Belarus, Zimbabwe, Uganda, and Canada reveal the failure of *Nostra Aetate* to gain a better foothold among their active Roman Catholics.

Table 3.5 The Antisemitism of the Catholic *Dominicantes* compared to all baptized Roman Catholics (*World Values Survey*)

Country	% Catholics—rejecting Jewish neighbors	N— Catholics in WVS	Are practicing Catholics more or less Antisemitic? (%)	% practicing Catholics— rejecting Jewish neighbors	N— Dominicantes in WVS	% rate of catholic practice
The Czech Republic	21	340	−7	14	51	15.000
The United States	10	280	−4	6	145	51.786
Mexico	25	2703	−2	23	1369	50.647
Argentina	7	2589	−1	6	607	23.445
Chile	14	2374	0	13	666	28.054
Slovakia	36	325	0	37	147	45.231
India	8	40	0	8	38	95.000
Canada	5	721	1	7	219	30.374
Uganda	22	356	2	24	283	79.494
Zimbabwe	15	171	2	17	132	77.193
Belarus	11	161	2	12	49	30.435
Nigeria	32	220	3	35	193	87.727
Venezuela	26	990	3	30	321	32.424
Bosnia	25	154	5	30	84	54.545
Spain	23	2214	5	27	671	30.307
Uruguay	9	735	5	13	128	17.415
South Korea	36	166	5	40	89	53.614
South Africa	32	337	5	38	210	62.315
Albania	18	580	6	24	119	20.517

Lamentably enough, *Nostra Aetate* seems to have had no effect in several African states, in several Latin American countries, on the Balkans, etc. This is also evident from Table 3.6. The case of Catholic South Korean Antisemitism is really extreme. It might be categorized as *Antisemitism without Jews*, since there is hardly any Jewish presence on the Korean Peninsula. In South Korea, South Africa, the Slovak Republic, Nigeria, Bosnia, and Venezuela, Antisemitism among the *Dominicantes* is 30% or higher:

The case of Argentina on the other hand is especially noteworthy, considering that it is the home country of the current Pontiff, Pope Francis. Does the case of Argentina then correspond to a *Bergoglio effect*? Argentina, together with the United States, Canada, and India, has the lowest rejection rate of Jewish neighbors among the global practicing Roman Catholics (*Dominicantes*).

Summing up our analysis of the Antisemitism of the active Roman Catholics and the partial failure of *Nostra Aetate* so far, we can say:

Freedom from overt forms of Antisemitism: More than 10% of *Dominicantes* rejecting to have a Jewish neighbor are marked in bold.

1. The United Kingdom	19. **Italy**
2. The Netherlands	20. **Latvia**
3. The United States	21. **Belgium**
4. Argentina	22. **Zimbabwe**
5. Germany	23. **Malta**
6. Canada	24. **Croatia**
7. India	25. **Mexico**
8. France	26. **Lithuania**
9. Austria	27. **Albania**
10. **Hungary**	28. **Uganda**
11. **Portugal**	28. **Slovenia**
12. **Belarus**	30. **Poland**
13. **Luxembourg**	31. **Spain**
14. **Ireland**	32. **Bosnia and Herzegovina**
15. **Uruguay**	33. **Venezuela**
16. **Chile**	34. **Nigeria**
17. **Romania**	35. **Slovakia**
18. **The Czech Republic**	36. **South Africa**
	37. **South Korea**

Table 3.6 Antisemitism among the *Dominicantes*

Country	% Catholics—rejecting Jewish neighbors	N—Catholics in WVS	Are practicing Catholics more or less Antisemitic? (%)	% practicing Catholics—rejecting Jewish neighbors	N Dominicantes in WVS	% rate of catholic practice
South Korea	36	166	5	40	89	53.614
South Africa	32	337	5	38	210	62.315
Slovakia	36	325	0	37	147	45.231
Nigeria	32	220	3	35	193	87.727
Bosnia	25	154	5	30	84	54.545
Venezuela	26	990	3	30	321	32.424
Spain	23	2214	5	27	671	30.307
Uganda	22	356	2	24	283	79.494
Albania	18	580	6	24	119	20.517
Mexico	25	2703	−2	23	1369	50.647
Zimbabwe	15	171	2	17	132	77.193
The Czech Republic	21	340	−7	14	51	15.000
Uruguay	9	735	5	13	128	17.415
Chile	14	2374	0	13	666	28.054
Belarus	11	161	2	12	49	30.435
India	8	40	0	8	38	95.000
Canada	5	721	1	7	219	30.374
The United States	10	280	−4	6	145	51.786
Argentina	7	2589	−1	6	607	23.445

Where Dominicantes are less or more Antisemitic than the rest of society. Catholic communities whose Antisemitism is stronger than in the rest of society are marked in bold.

1. The Czech Republic	19. **Germany**
2. The United States	20. **France**
3. The United Kingdom	21. **Belarus**
4. Mexico	22. **Zimbabwe**
5. Argentina	23. **Lithuania**
6. India	24. **Uganda**
7. Hungary	25. **Luxembourg**
8. Chile	26. **Romania**
9. Malta	27. **Venezuela**
10. Poland	28. **Nigeria**
11. Slovakia	29. **Uruguay**
12. **Canada**	30. **Spain**
13. **Austria**	31. **Bosnia and Herzegovina**
14. **Portugal**	32. **South Africa**
15. Ireland	33. **South Korea**
16. **Italy**	34. **Croatia**
17. **Belgium**	35. **Albania**
18. **The Netherlands**	36. **Slovenia**
	37. **Latvia**

Maps 3.5 and 3.6 further summarize our results achieved so far.

Tables 3.7 and 3.8 reveal another, even more intriguing, aspect of the partial failure of the *Nostra Aetate* process: only in Slovakia, Slovenia, Portugal, the Czech Republic, Austria, Chile, Belgium, Germany, and the Netherlands, there was a reduction in the rate of Antisemitism over time, while in Spain, Malta, Mexico, Poland, Ireland, the United Kingdom, Italy, Argentina, the United States, France, and Canada, Antisemitism among the *Dominicantes* increased over time (Tables 3.7 and 3.8):

This yields the following per decade rates of change of Antisemitism.

We now summarize our analysis of the changes of the Antisemitism of the *Dominicantes* over time.

Reduction or increase of Antisemitism over time: Catholic communities where Antisemitism increased are marked in bold.

1. Slovakia
2. Slovenia
3. Portugal
4. The Czech Republic
5. Austria
6. Chile
7. Belgium
8. Germany

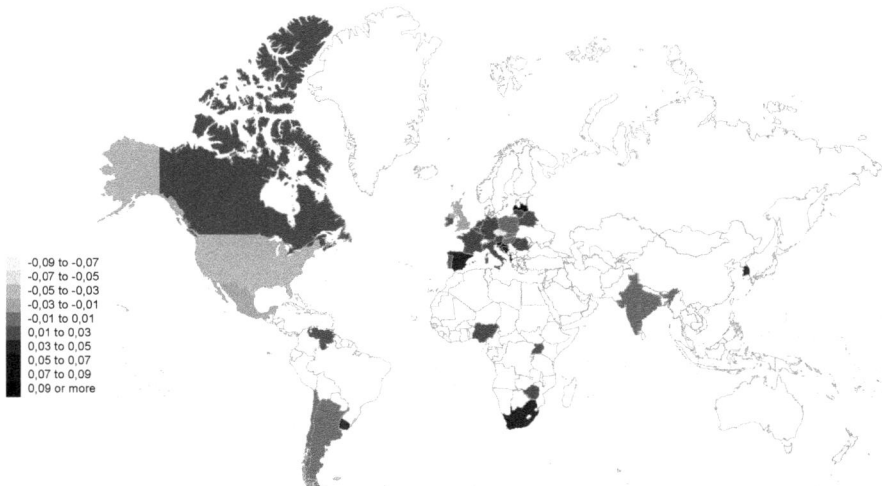

Map 3.5 Where practicing Catholics are less antisemitic (light gray) or more antisemitic (dark gray and black) than the baptized Roman Catholics. Best: the Czech Republic, the United States, the United Kingdom, Mexico, and Argentina. Worst: Latvia, Albania, Croatia, Slovenia, and Bosnia and Herzegovina

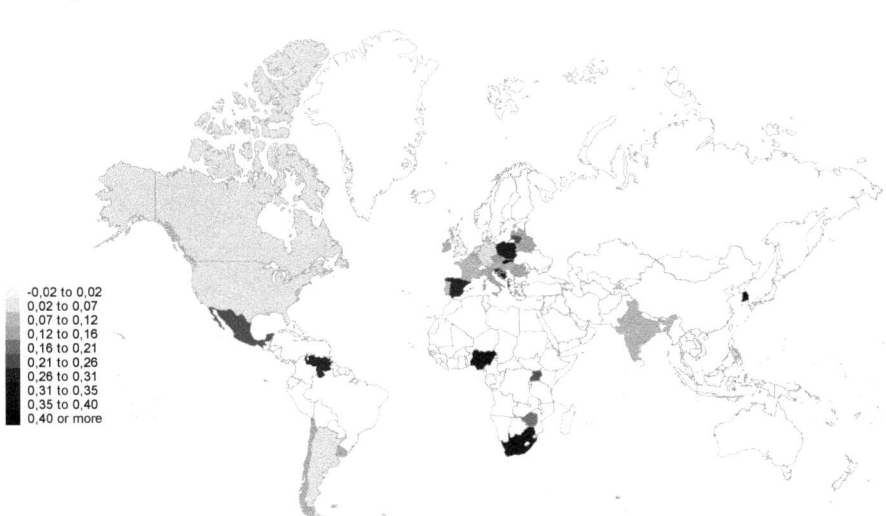

Map 3.6 The Antisemitism of the *Dominicantes*—where practicing Catholics are strongly antisemitic (dark gray) or less antisemitic (light gray)—percentages of people rejecting Jewish neighbors (0–100%, i.e., 0.00–1.00 in our map). Best: the United Kingdom, the Netherlands, Argentina, the United States, and Germany. Worst: South Korea, South Africa, Slovakia, Nigeria, and Bosnia and Herzegovina

Table 3.7 Is there a *Nostra Aetate* effect over time?—Average rejection rate of Jewish neighbors (0 no Antisemitism, 1 Antisemitism)

	n	Antisemitism Catholic *practicantes*
Argentina (1991)	166	0.035
Argentina (1995)	191	0.090
Argentina (1999)	225	0.059
Austria (1990)	282	0.158
Austria (1999)	298	0.100
Belgium (1990)	594	0.161
Belgium (1999)	236	0.129
Canada (1990)	251	0.063
Canada (2000)	240	0.070
Chile (1990)	226	0.154
Chile (1996)	131	0.155
Chile (2000)	225	0.096
The Czech Republic (1990)	44	0.137
The Czech Republic (1991)	118	0.224
The Czech Republic (1999)	121	0.032
France (1990)	82	0.079
France (1999)	90	0.091
Germany (1990)	376	0.096
Germany (1999)	93	0.061
Great Britain (1990)	64	0.000
Great Britain (1999)	42	0.023
Ireland (1990)	731	0.070
Ireland (1999)	555	0.122
Italy (1990)	648	0.118
Italy (1999)	665	0.146
Malta (1991)	316	0.073
Malta (1999)	643	0.215
Mexico (1990)	490	0.176
Mexico (1996)	570	0.264
The Netherlands (1990)	81	0.080
The Netherlands (1999)	40	0.048
Northern Ireland (1990)	66	0.096
Northern Ireland (1999)	227	0.124
Poland (1990)	511	0.188
Poland (1999)	466	0.266
Portugal (1990)	334	0.251
Portugal (1999)	313	0.116
Slovakia (1990)	93	0.367
Slovakia (1991)	216	0.308
Slovakia (1999)	421	0.127
Slovenia (1992)	123	0.382

(continued)

Table 3.7 (continued)

	n	Antisemitism Catholic *practicantes*
Slovenia (1999)	123	0.259
Spain (1990)	691	0.110
Spain (1990)	322	0.187
Spain (1999)	246	0.143
Spain (2000)	175	0.394
The United States (1990)	273	0.042
The United States (1999)	140	0.054

Table 3.8 The rate of change of Antisemitism among practicing Roman Catholics per decade

Starting period	Period of change of rate of Antisemitism	Rate of change of Antisemitism in %	Rate of change of Antisemitism in % per decade
Slovakia (1990)	1990–1999	−24	−27
Slovenia (1992)	1992–1999	−12	−18
Portugal (1990)	1990–1999	−14	−15
The Czech Republic (1990)	1990–1999	−11	−12
Austria (1990)	1990–1999	−6	−6
Chile (1990)	1990–2000	−6	−6
Germany (1990)	1990–1999	−4	−4
Belgium (1990)	1990–1999	−3	−4
The Netherlands (1990)	1990–1999	−3	−4
Canada (1990)	1990–2000	1	1
France (1990)	1990–1999	1	1
The United States (1990)	1990–1999	1	1
Great Britain (1990)	1990–1999	2	3
Argentina (1991)	1991–1999	2	3
Italy (1990)	1990–1999	3	3
Northern Ireland (1990)	1990–1999	3	3
Ireland (1990)	1990–1999	5	6
Poland (1990)	1990–1999	8	9
Mexico (1990)	1990–1996	9	15
Malta (1991)	1990–1999	14	16
Spain (1990)	1990–2000	26	26

9. The Netherlands
10. **Canada**
11. **France**
12. **The United States**
13. **Argentina**
14. **Italy**
15. **The United Kingdom**
16. **Ireland**
17. **Poland**
18. **Mexico**
19. **Malta**
20. **Spain**

These results also yield Map 3.7.

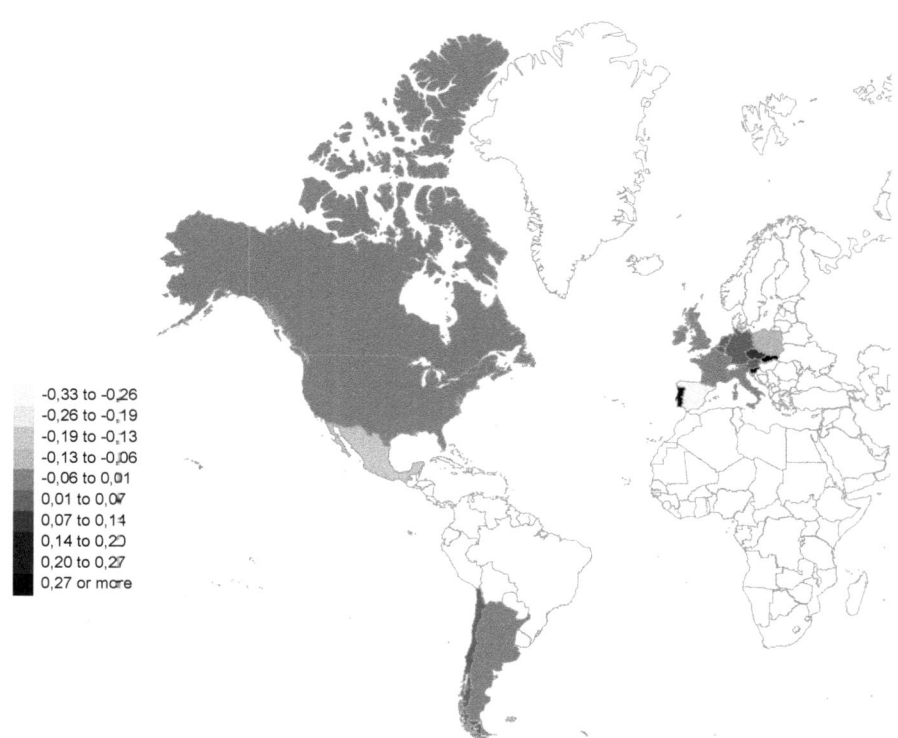

Map 3.7 Reduction of Antisemitism among *Dominicantes* in % per decade (0% to ±100%, i.e., 0.00 to ±1.00 in our map). Greatest reduction: Slovakia, Slovenia, Portugal, the Czech Republic, and Austria. Lowest reduction or even increase: Spain, Malta, Mexico, Poland, and Ireland

Now, it is time to summarize our results at one glance. Our *Nostra Aetate* Index, concretely and even bluntly tells decision-makers and our overall readership how well active Roman Catholics, attending Church services each Sunday, first accepted Jewish neighbors, second, whether active Roman Catholics more accepted Jewish neighbors than the society surrounding them, and third, whether the acceptancy of Jewish neighbors increased or decreased over time.

Our data also show that among the world's top performing Roman Catholic, we find active communities in the Czech Republic, the United States, the United Kingdom, Portugal, and Argentina, while among world's Catholicism worst *Nostra Aetate* performers, we find the active Catholic communities in Spain, Poland, Malta, Slovenia, Mexico, and Slovakia. In those countries, social realities among the active Catholic faithful could not be more distant from the ideas and perspectives, expressed in *Nostra Aetate*.

The results of Table 3.9 are also summarized in Map 3.8.

Table 3.9 *Nostra Aetate* Index

	Nostra Aetate Index
The Czech Republic	0.793
The United States	0.711
The United Kingdom	0.709
Portugal	0.630
Argentina	0.622
The Netherlands	0.601
Austria	0.589
Germany	0.588
Chile	0.586
Canada	0.574
France	0.528
Belgium	0.518
Ireland	0.492
Italy	0.488
Slovakia	0.487
Mexico	0.409
Slovenia	0.383
Malta	0.366
Poland	0.361
Spain	0.122

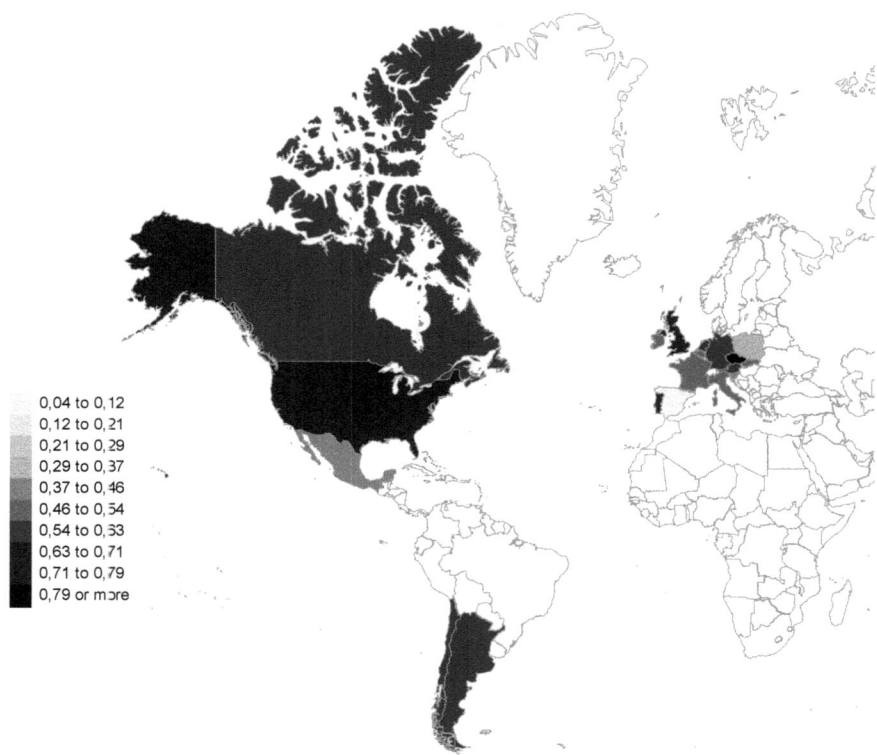

Map 3.8 *Nostra Aetate* Index. Highest values: the Czech Republic, the United States, the United Kingdom, Portugal, and Argentina. Lowest values: Spain, Poland, Malta, Slovenia, and Mexico

The Antisemitism Among the Dominicantes *(3): "Antizionism" Is Becoming Increasingly a Problem for Catholic–Jewish Relations*

Comparative international opinion survey data about the phenomena, which we will now discuss, are even more scarce than about the phenomena, described above. So, one might say that we did not "collect" data on "Antizionism" and active Catholicism, but we rather had to "scramble together" what there was available in terms of international survey data to yield at least some reliable proxy results.

In Western society at large, more and more, "Antizionism" is a new name for "Antisemitism," a fact, which was already discovered by the great American political scientist Seymour Martin Lipset in a prophetic essay, published in 1969 (Lipset 1969). Can we draw any conclusions for the global practicing Roman Catholics? In

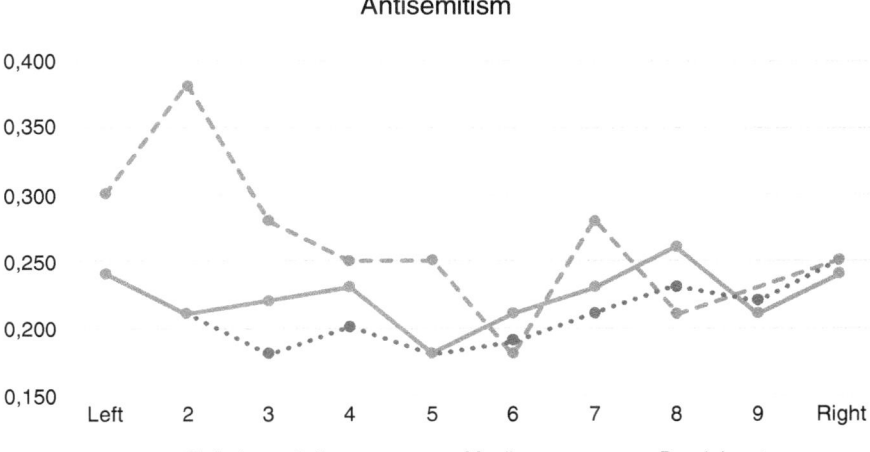

Graph 3.4 Antisemitism according to political ideology around the world according to *World Values Survey* data—global population, *Dominicantes*, Muslims. Global population with complete *WVS* data: $n = 35,611$. Muslim population with complete *WVS* data: $n = 3003$. *Dominicantes* with complete *WVS* data: $n = 4487$. All *WVS* respondents received an equal weight regardless of country size, and for that reason, our results must be regarded as preliminary

Graphs 3.4 and 3.5, we show preliminarily the connection between self-professed political ideology on a 10-point left to right scale, religious denomination, and Antisemitism according to *World Values Survey* data, which in a way is a background to "Antizionism," because both political parties of the extreme left and the extreme right nowadays are very critical of the State of Israel. The highest global propensity for someone to be Antisemitic is to be found among the Hindu right and Hindu left, the Buddhist left and Buddhist right, and the Muslim left, while among the *Dominicantes*, it is to be noted that both among the active Catholic left and the active Catholic far right also higher propensities toward Antisemitism are to be found.

While global Catholic *Dominicantes* from all political self-identifications can be presumed to be less Antisemitic than Buddhists and Hindus, most political camps among the global Orthodox and Protestant believers as well as center-right Muslims are probably less Antisemitic than Catholic *Dominicantes*.

The electronic Appendix Table 3.9 further highlights these aspects, with a first international comparison of political party support and Antisemitism across the globe on the basis of our analyzed *World Values Survey* data. Generally speaking, this electronic Appendix Table 3.9 is a *Who is Who* of international Antisemitism along political party support line, comprising supporters of Muslim parties, left-wing parties, right-wing parties, and regionalist parties (Basque National Party in Spain) but also supporters of some Christian democratic parties, in Belarus, Bosnia, Bulgaria, Bulgaria, Germany, Greece, India, Iraq, Japan, Macedonia, Mexico,

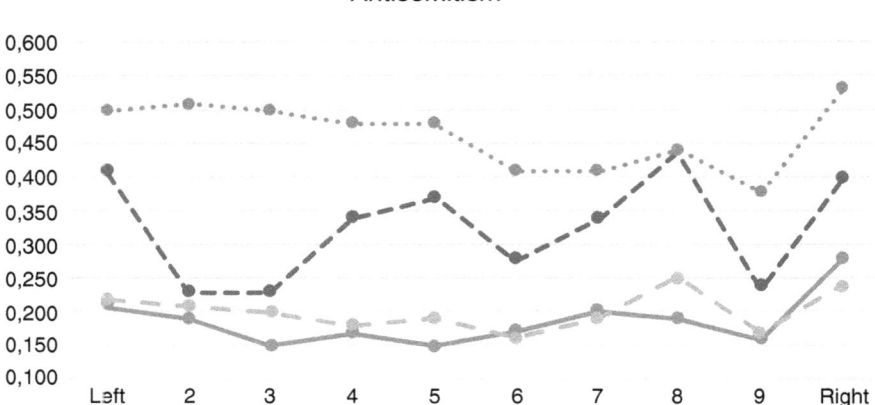

Graph 3.5 Antisemitism according to political ideology around the world according to *World Values Survey* data—Buddhists, Hindus, Orthodox, and Protestants. Buddhist population with complete *WVS* data: $n = 507$. Hindu population with complete *WVS* data: $n = 1901$. Orthodox population with complete *WVS* data: $n = 3175$. Protestant population with complete *WVS* data: $n = 3222$. All *WVS* respondents received an equal weight regardless of country size, and for that reason, our results must be regarded as preliminary

Moldova, Nigeria, Poland, Romania, Slovakia, Slovenia, Spain, and Venezuela. Lamentably enough, the supporters of practically all major political parties in Turkey are among the global constituencies whose average rate of Antisemitism is 0.300 or higher on the 0.0–1.0 scale. Without going into the details, many of these mentioned political parties "excel" each other in their Israel-hating agenda.

Before we discuss some possible hints about opinions on Israel by Christians/ Roman Catholics, which we can deduct from the PEW Spring 2013 Survey, we have to present some general evidence on opinions about Israel and the relationship these opinions have with Antisemitism.

First of all, we should mention the results of the BBC world poll *BBC World Scan*. The BBC world poll, which is based on representative surveys in Argentina, Australia, Brazil, Canada, Chile, China, France, Germany, Ghana, India, Indonesia, Israel Japan, Kenya, Mexico, Nigeria, Pakistan, Peru, Russia, South Korea, Spain, Turkey, the United Kingdom, and the United States, shows that on a population-weighted basis, only 23% of the citizens of our globe now say that Israel mainly has a positive influence, while some 41% say that the Jewish State has mainly a negative influence. The countrywide support rates for Israel in a way reflect the PEW-based evidence, discussed in this study. Only in the United States and in some sub-Saharan African countries, Israel still enjoys some degrees of support which are higher than the percentages of people with negative opinions on the State of Israel. The results for key Western allies are devastating, with only 8% of all Germans, who forever will bear the collective responsibility of the most terrible crime in human history, the *Shoah*, are saying that Israel wields a generally positive or very positive influence. It should be noted that our PEW data were collected in 2013, while the BBC World data were collected 1 year later in 2014. Israel-positive attitudes in Western democracies with a considerable Catholic heritage are:

The United States	51%
Chile	29%
Canada	25%
France	21%
Peru	16%
Australia	16%
Poland	15%
Brazil	15%
The United Kingdom	14%
Mexico	13%
Germany	8%
Spain	4%

Only in the United States, Ghana, and Kenya, positive attitudes outweigh negative attitudes. In Germany, the pro-opinions (8%) are exceeded to the tune of 59% by the negative opinions (67%).

That Antizionism and Antisemitism are but two sides of the same coin was already documented in the path-breaking empirical article by Edward H. Kaplan and Charles A. Small in the *Journal of Conflict Resolution* more than a decade ago (Kaplan and Small 2006), which concluded that indeed extreme criticisms of Israel (e.g., Israel is an apartheid state, the Israel Defense Forces deliberately targeting Palestinian civilians), coupled with extreme policy proposals (e.g., boycott of Israeli academics and institutions, divest from companies doing business with Israel), are motivated by nothing else than blatant Antisemitic sentiments. This finding acquires special importance at a time when the BDS (boycott-divest-sanction) movement against the Jewish State becomes stronger in many Western countries. Based on a survey of 500 citizens in each of 10 European countries, the authors asked whether those individuals with extreme anti-Israel views are more likely to be Antisemitic in their general attitudes. Even after statistically controlling for numerous factors, they found that anti-Israel sentiments consistently predicted the probability that an individual is indeed Antisemitic, with the likelihood of measured Antisemitism increasing with the extent of anti-Israel sentiment observed. A similarly important quantitative analysis (Jacobs et al. 2011) under the title *The impact of the conflict in Gaza on Antisemitism in Belgium* came to a similar mathematical-statistical conclusion that complaints about Antisemitism in Belgium indeed showed a statistically significant increase during the Israeli military operation Cast Lead (2008–2009) against Hamas in Gaza. The article made use of a data base of complaints to the *Centrum voor gelijkheid van kansen en voor racismebestrijding* (Center of Equal Opportunities and Opposition to Racism), which is a Belgium federal anti-racism agency, and of an analysis of political claims making in the written press.

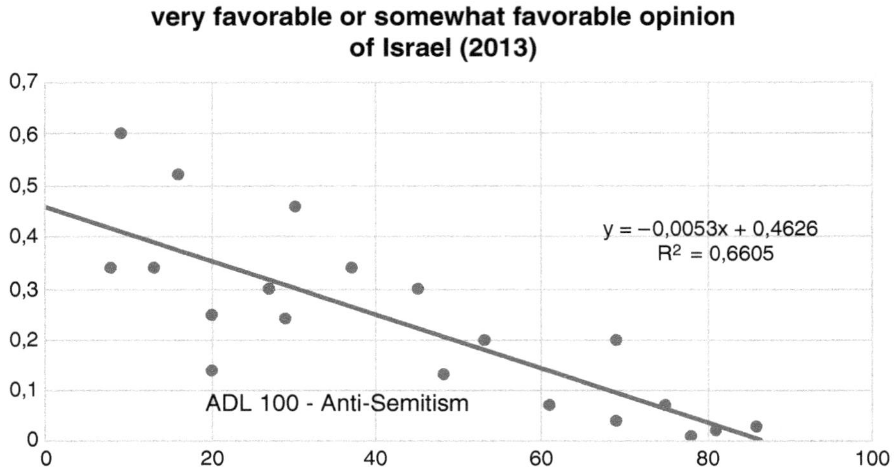

**very favorable or somewhat favorable opinion
of Israel (2013)**

$$y = -0.0053x + 0.4626$$
$$R^2 = 0.6605$$

ADL 100 - Anti-Semitism

Graph 3.6 The clear negative correlation between country rates of Antisemitism (ADL 100) (*x*-axis) and (very) favorable opinion of Israel

Graph 3.6 shows the 66% negative correlation between favorable opinions on Israel according to PEW data and Antisemitism according to the ADL study.

Table 3.10 shows that support for Israel—apart from the United States and Nigeria—is only voiced by minorities in the respective countries, and especially in key Western allies with a stronger Catholic tradition, this support is now very low.

Table 3.11 documents the erosion of support for the Jewish State among the adherents of different political parties in Europe (EU/European NATO members). Generally, one can say that center-right and center-left parties, especially in Eastern Europe, still provide the most solid basis of support for the Jewish State in Europe, while both among extreme left-wing and extreme right-wing European parties, we witness the most rapid erosion of support for Israel.[27] Interestingly enough, rejection of the Jewish State is by far most pronounced among the adherents of the different political parties in the EU-member candidate state and NATO-member country Turkey, while adherents of Christian Democratic European parties still are more inclined to support Israel.

---

[27]For an analysis of the especially dark chapter of lacking German solidarity with Israel during the finest hour of the Jewish State during the Yom Kippur War of 1973, see https://www.welt.de/politik/deutschland/article116955753/Wie-Willy-Brandt-den-Nahost-Frieden-verspielte.html and https://www.welt.de/geschichte/article121069722/Fuer-Erdoel-setzte-Bonn-1973-das-Buendnis-aufs-Spiel.html (Download April 10, 2019). As the analysis of formerly secret documents now released shows, the government of the German "Peace Chancellor" Willy Brandt denied the use of German airports for US planes sending badly needed military hardware to the beleaguered Jewish State, attacked by the advancing Egyptian and Syrian armies just 28 years after the end of the *Shoah*.

Table 3.10 Country support rates for Israel, PEW 2013

	Very favorable or somewhat favorable opinion of Israel (2013) (%)
The United States	60
Nigeria	52
Russia	46
France	34
Britain	34
The Czech Republic	34
Poland	30
Germany	30
Italy	25
Spain	24
Greece	20
Senegal	20
China	14
Indonesia	13
Egypt	7
Malaysia	7
Pakistan	4
Turkey	4
Palestinian territories	3
Tunisia	3
Jordan	2
Lebanon	1

To round up our analysis of the support rates for Israel, we also present PEW-based data on the intensity of religious practice and religious denomination in conjunction with international Israel support rates. Our data analysis documents that not only (with a few exceptions) Muslims but also Oriental Christians show very low rates of support for Israel or rather even an outright rejection of the Jewish State. Only in the Czech Republic, more religiously active Catholics show a higher support for Israel than their more secular counterparts, while in Italy and Poland, the more religious Catholics support Israel less than their more secular counterparts. Opposition against Israel among Lebanese Christians—in their majority Roman Catholic Maronite Christians—is especially strong. Also, Christians in Egypt—in their great majority Coptic Christians—are very much opposed to the State of Israel. The most negative opinions on Israel in the entire sample of analyzed groups were to be found among secular Lebanese Christians (Table 3.12).

Table 3.11 Support for Israel according to political parties (calculated from PEW data)

Country	Party supporters of …	Sample size	(Very) favorable opinion of Israel (%)
The Czech Republic	Top 09	70	57
France	L'Union des Démocrates Indépendants (UDI) de Jean-Louis Borloo	62	45
France	UMP	261	43
The United Kingdom	UK Independence Party (UKIP)	101	43
The United Kingdom	Conservative Party	193	42
Poland	Platforma Obywatelska RP—PO	119	39
Spain	PP	190	38
France	Parti Socialiste	249	38
Spain	UPyD	57	37
The Czech Republic	ODS	66	36
Germany	FDP	36	36
Poland	Sojusz Lewicy Demokratycznej—SLD	39	36
Germany	SPD	231	33
France	Mouvement démocrate—Modem	37	32
Germany	CDU\CSU	303	32
Germany	Bündnis 90, Die Grünen	168	32
The United Kingdom	Labour Party	291	31
The Czech Republic	CSSD	148	30
Italy	Partito Democratico (PD)	168	29
The United Kingdom	Liberal Democrats	69	29
France	Front National	90	28
Poland	Prawo i Sprawiedliwosc—PiS	98	26
Greece	New Democracy (N.D.)	107	24
Germany	Piratenpartei	33	24
France	Lutte Ouvrière, NPA	36	22
Germany	Die Linke	41	22
The Czech Republic	KSCM	56	21
Greece	Coalition of Radical Left—Unitary Social Front (SY.RIZ.A)	96	21
Italy	Movimento 5 stelle	202	21
Italy	Popolo della Libertà (PDL)	108	19
Spain	PSOE	203	19
Greece	Communist Party of Greece (K.K.E)	42	19
France	Europe Ecologie/Les verts	79	19

(continued)

Table 3.11 (continued)

Country	Party supporters of ...	Sample size	(Very) favorable opinion of Israel (%)
France	Parti de Gauche de Jean-Luc Mélenchon	87	16
Spain	IU/EU Izquierda Unida	101	13
The United Kingdom	Green Party	34	12
Greece	Golden Dawn	63	11
Turkey	Cumhuriyet Halk Partisi (CHP) (Kemal Kýlýçdaroðlu)	140	6
Turkey	Barýþ ve Demokrasi Partisi (BDP) (Selahattin Demirtaþ/Gültan Kýþanak)	36	6
Turkey	Adalet ve Kalkýnma Partisi (AKP) (R.T. Erdogan)	420	4
Turkey	Milliyetçi Hareket Partisi (MHP) (Devlet Bahçeli)	85	4

The Antisemitism Among the Dominicantes (4): Mixed Attitudes on Jewish Immigration

The *European Social Survey*, an important biannual survey instrument, co-financed by the European Commission in Brussels, offers important insights into European xenophobia and racism. One does not have to invoke Ye'or's bleak scenario (*Eurabia*) of an evolving alliance of Islam, anti-Americanism, and Antisemitism in Europe (Ye'or 2005) to ask the simple question whether or not Jewish immigration is accepted by different denominational groups, including the Catholic *Dominicantes*, and how this acceptancy or rejection is related to that of other immigrant groups.

As Fig. 3.1 shows, at first sight, the data for 2014 seem to confirm that only the *Dominicantes* in the Netherlands, the Czech Republic, and France are more positively oriented toward Jewish immigration than the totality of the baptized Roman Catholics in the country, while *Dominicantes* in Slovenia, Poland, Ireland, Switzerland, Belgium, and Austria by and large reject Jewish immigration in dismal proportions and also fall behind the more secular Catholics in their respective country in their meager support of Jewish immigration. One also finds that only in Germany, a more significant proportion of persons (all denominations and secular and religious groups among them) was in strong favor of Jewish immigration at all.

Table 3.13 shows the rankings of average support for Jewish immigration to European countries by the different denominational groups, with the active Roman Catholics being compared with European Muslims (wherever data were available) and overall society. The best-placed Roman Catholic *Dominicantes* sample (from Germany) is placed behind the results for overall society in Sweden and Germany and behind Sweden's Muslim community (2014).

Table 3.12 Our evaluation of the PEW data on the support for Israel according to religious denomination and religious practice[a]

Country	Religious/cultural background	Average opinion on Israel: 1—very good to 4—very bad	N	Standard deviation
Nigeria—religious	Christian	1.800	305	0.906
Russia—religious	Orthodox	2.470	336	0.795
The Czech Republic—religious	Roman Catholic	2.480	65	0.850
Russia secular	Orthodox	2.500	159	0.856
Poland secular	Catholic	2.590	96	0.674
Poland—religious	Catholic	2.680	338	0.670
Russia—religious	Muslim	2.680	22	0.894
Nigeria—religious	Muslim	2.780	178	1.015
China secular	Buddhist	2.840	154	0.715
The Czech Republic secular	Roman Catholic	2.930	29	0.753
Senegal—religious	Muslim	2.930	339	0.896
Italy secular	Catholic	2.940	161	0.793
Italy—religious	Catholic	3000	539	0.825
China—religious	Buddhist	3.020	91	0.666
China—religious	Christian	3.040	28	0.881
Greece—religious	Orthodox	3.050	589	0.754
China——religious	Muslim	3.090	23	0.668
Greece secular	Orthodox	3.110	151	0.767
Malaysia—religious	Hindu	3.200	25	1.000
Senegal—religious	Christian	3.230	31	0.956
Greece secular	Atheist/not believer	3.250	20	0.786
Indonesia—religious	Muslim	3.380	579	0.783
Malaysia—religious	Buddhist	3.410	49	0.610
Pakistan—religious	Muslim	3.610	327	0.692
Egypt—religious	Christian	3.650	78	0.753
Turkey secular	Muslim	3.660	29	0.670
Malaysia—religious	Muslim	3.670	328	0.632
Turkey—religious	Muslim	3.760	563	0.521
Lebanon secular	Muslim	3.770	30	0.504
Egypt—religious	Muslim	3.820	660	0.578
Egypt secular	Muslim	3.820	28	0.548
Lebanon—religious	Druze	3.830	64	0.380
Palestinian Territories—religious	Muslim	3.830	503	0.535
Tunisia—religious	Muslim	3.870	474	0.487

(continued)

Table 3.12 (continued)

Country	Religious/cultural background	Average opinion on Israel: 1—very good to 4—very bad	N	Standard deviation
Lebanon— religious	Christian	3.920	319	0.296
Lebanon— religious	Muslim	3.920	483	0.337
Jordan—religious	Muslim	3.940	689	0.360
Jordan secular	Muslim	3.960	28	0.189
Lebanon secular	Christian	4.000	28	0.000

[a]In our analysis, we used the PEW Spring Survey question 178 for the classification of publics according to their religious commitment. The text of question 178 is: "Q178. How important is religion in your life—very important, somewhat important, not too important, or not at all important?" We classified as "religious" those respondents who answered question 178 by "very important" or "somewhat important," while we classified as "secular" those respondents who answered Q178 by "not too important" or "not at all important." The data about religious or denominational background correspond to the categories, given by PEW

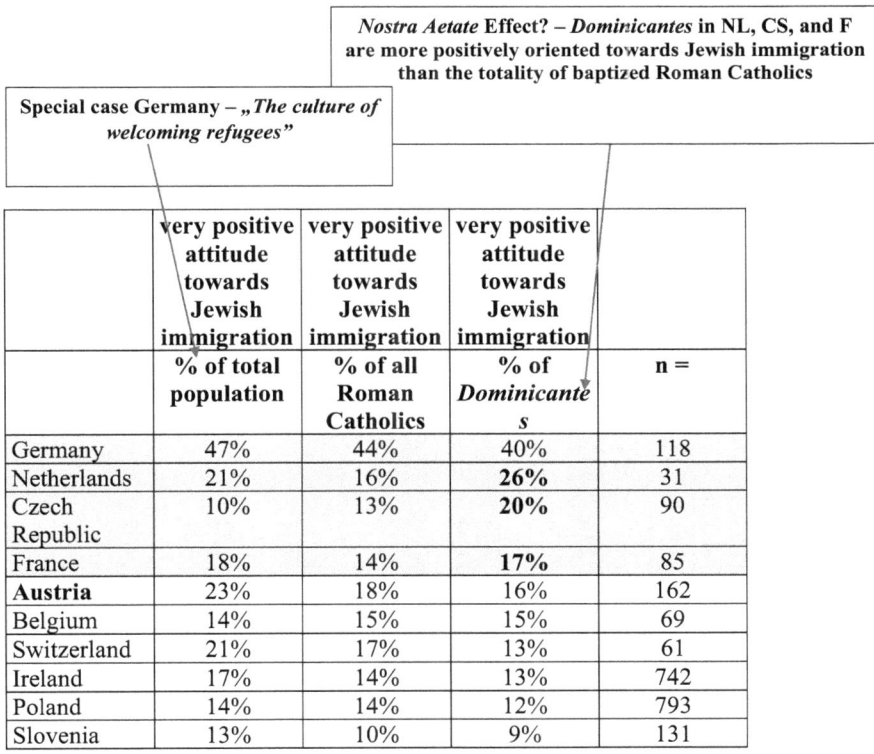

Fig. 3.1 The denominational landscape of the acceptancy of Jewish immigration in Europe

Table 3.13 The denominational and immigration political landscape of the rejection of Jewish immigration in Europe (4—high rejection; 1—full acceptance)

	Country	Allow many/few immigrants of different race/ethnic group from majority	Allow many/few immigrants from poorer countries in Europe	Allow many/few immigrants from poorer countries outside Europe	Allow many or few Jewish people to come and live in country	Allow many or few Muslims to come and live in country	Allow many or few Gypsies to come and live in country	Rejection of Jewish immigrants—rejection of Muslim immigrants
Dominicantes	Slovenia	2.62	2.60	2.77	2.71	2.88	3.10	−0.17
Overall society	The Czech Republic	2.99	xx	2.98	2.62	3.40	3.50	−0.78
Euro Islam	Switzerland	2.16	2.28	2.34	2.58	2.05	2.53	0.53
Dominicantes	Poland	2.48	2.35	2.54	2.56	3.06	2.94	−0.50
Euro Islam	Belgium	2.25	2.27	2.23	2.47	2.01	2.83	0.46
Dominicantes	Ireland	2.58	2.59	2.76	2.45	2.84	3.29	−0.39
Overall society	Poland	2.39	2.27	2.48	2.45	2.96	2.87	−0.51
Overall society	Slovenia	2.33	2.39	2.56	2.43	2.57	2.85	−0.14
Overall society	Ireland	2.47	2.50	2.69	2.36	2.68	3.09	−0.32
Dominicantes	Switzerland	2.34	2.34	2.54	2.36	2.76	2.90	−0.40
Dominicantes	Austria	2.62	2.62	2.71	2.36	2.80	2.82	−0.44
Dominicantes	Belgium	2.52	2.31	2.61	2.36	2.81	2.97	−0.45
Dominicantes	The Czech Republic	2.84	xx	2.89	2.36	3.20	3.29	−0.84
Overall society	Belgium	2.44	2.38	2.56	2.30	2.56	2.84	−0.26
Overall society	Finland	2.49	2.54	2.71	2.29	2.69	2.84	−0.40

Overall society	Estonia	2.59	2.63	2.93	2.29	3.11	3.34	-0.82
Euro Islam	The Netherlands	2.04	2.15	2.21	2.27	2.11	2.41	0.16
Overall society	Austria	2.50	2.55	2.63	2.26	2.62	2.72	-0.36
Euro Islam	Denmark	1.90	2.23	2.26	2.17	2.06	2.66	0.11
Overall society	France	2.38	2.39	2.56	2.13	2.35	2.58	-0.22
Overall society	The Netherlands	2.24	2.39	2.49	2.13	2.47	2.60	-0.34
Euro Islam	Germany	2.09	2.30	2.19	2.11	1.93	2.40	0.18
Overall society	Switzerland	2.29	2.27	2.41	2.10	2.45	2.66	-0.35
Euro Islam	Austria	2.07	2.26	2.31	2.09	1.87	2.41	0.22
Dominicantes	The Netherlands	2.32	2.40	2.41	2.05	2.42	2.53	-0.37
Dominicantes	France	2.43	2.29	2.57	2.05	2.45	2.60	-0.40
Overall society	Denmark	2.30	2.38	2.57	1.94	2.41	2.78	-0.47
Euro Islam	France	2.09	2.22	2.25	1.93	1.79	2.30	0.14
Overall society	Norway	2.03	2.08	2.18	1.93	2.24	2.60	-0.31
Dominicantes	Germany	2.12	2.07	2.24	1.82	2.25	2.58	-0.43
Euro Islam	Sweden	1.55	1.67	1.58	1.69	1.53	1.83	0.16
Overall society	Germany	2.01	2.07	2.19	1.68	2.10	2.33	-0.42
Overall society	Sweden	1.66	1.74	1.76	1.61	1.84	1.90	-0.23

Table 3.13 also shows that *Dominicantes* in Slovenia, overall society in the Czech Republic, Euro Islam in Switzerland, and *Dominicantes* in Poland all voice a rejection of Jewish immigration greater or equal than 2.50 on the 4-point acceptancy scale.

Almost eight decades after the beginning of the Second World War, it is also interesting to note which denominational groups give greater or lesser support to Jewish immigration (Jewish immigration = 100) in preference or rejection of the immigration of other groups to Europe. Table 3.13 informs us, for example, that *Dominicantes* in Slovenia prefer the immigration of people from a different race/ethnic group from the majority and for immigrants from poorer countries in Europe over Jewish immigration to Europe, while *Dominicantes* in Slovenia slightly prefer Jewish immigration over immigrants from poorer countries outside Europe, Muslims, and Gypsies coming and living in Slovenia.

Muslim respondents in all surveyed European countries give clear preference to further Muslim immigrants over further Jewish immigration to Europe. The *Dominicantes* in Slovenia, Poland, Switzerland, and Belgium all preferred some other immigrant groups over Jewish immigrants. More and more, the preferred immigrant groups mentioned by the *Dominicantes* in Slovenia, Poland, Switzerland, and Belgium resemble the preferences voiced by European Muslims—all to the detriment of further Jewish immigration (Tables 3.14 and 3.15).

To proceed with the presentation of our results, we also analyze the ranking of the European rejection of Jewish Immigration according to religious denomination and religious service attendance. The rejection front is being led by the *Mensuantes* (monthly religious service attenders) among Roman Catholics in Slovenia, Poland, and Ireland, followed by Belgium Muslim monthly regular Mosque attenders, the total baptized Roman Catholic population of Slovenia, the monthly Catholic religious service attenders in Belgium, etc. Only Protestant and secular populations in the Nordic countries, the Netherlands, and Germany and active Roman Catholics in Germany really welcomed Jewish immigration to Europe (average answers < 2.0). In the light of *Nostra Aetate*, the rejection of Jewish immigration from the more active Catholic communities in Austria, Belgium, Ireland, Poland, Slovenia, and Switzerland (greater than 2.0) is especially disappointing. It is an irony that Austrian Catholic *Mensuantes* even have a more negative average opinion on further Jewish immigration to Austria 80 years after the *Anschluss* in 1938 than the Austrian Muslims.

The Antisemitism Among the Dominicantes (5): The Drivers of the Antisemitism of the Dominicantes by International Ecumenical Comparison (for Specialists Only)

In the following paragraph, written for the specialists in the social science profession, we attempt to compare how different religious attitudes and practices and also

Table 3.14 How do different publics in Europe reject different immigrant groups (rejection of Jewish immigration $= 1$)

	Country	Allow many/few immigrants of different race/ethnic group from majority	Allow many/few immigrants from poorer countries in Europe	Allow many/few immigrants from poorer countries outside Europe	Allow many or few Jewish people to come and live in country	Allow many or few Muslims to come and live in country	Allow many or few Gypsies to come and live in country
Dominicantes	Slovenia	96.68	95.94	102.21	100.00	106.27	114.39
Overall society	The Czech Republic	114.12	xx	113.74	100.00	129.77	133.59
Euro Islam	Switzerland	83.72	88.37	90.70	100.00	79.46	98.06
Dominicantes	Poland	96.88	91.80	99.22	100.00	119.53	114.84
Euro Islam	Belgium	91.09	91.90	90.28	100.00	81.38	114.57
Dominicantes	Ireland	105.31	105.71	112.65	100.00	115.92	134.29
Overall society	Poland	97.55	92.65	101.22	100.00	120.82	117.14
Overall society	Slovenia	95.88	98.35	105.35	100.00	105.76	117.28
Overall society	Ireland	104.66	105.93	113.98	100.00	113.56	130.93
Dominicantes	Switzerland	99.15	99.15	107.63	100.00	116.95	122.88
Dominicantes	Austria	111.02	111.02	114.83	100.00	118.64	119.49
Dominicantes	Belgium	106.78	97.88	110.59	100.00	119.07	125.85
Dominicantes	The Czech Republic	120.34	xx	122.46	100.00	135.59	139.41
Overall society	Belgium	106.09	103.48	111.30	100.00	111.30	123.48
Overall society	Finland	108.73	110.92	118.34	100.00	117.47	124.02
Overall society	Estonia	113.10	114.85	127.95	100.00	135.81	145.85
Euro Islam	The Netherlands	89.87	94.71	97.36	100.00	92.95	106.17

(continued)

Table 3.14 (continued)

	Country	Allow many/few immigrants of different race/ethnic group from majority	Allow many/few immigrants from poorer countries in Europe	Allow many/few immigrants from poorer countries outside Europe	Allow many or few Jewish people to come and live in country	Allow many or few Muslims to come and live in country	Allow many or few Gypsies to come and live in country
Overall society	Austria	110.62	112.83	116.37	100.00	115.93	120.35
Euro Islam	Denmark	87.56	102.76	104.15	100.00	94.93	122.58
Overall society	France	111.74	112.21	120.19	100.00	110.33	121.13
Overall society	The Netherlands	105.16	112.21	116.90	100.00	115.96	122.07
Euro Islam	Germany	99.05	109.00	103.79	100.00	91.47	113.74
Overall society	Switzerland	109.05	108.10	114.76	100.00	116.67	126.67
Euro Islam	Austria	99.04	108.13	110.53	100.00	89.47	115.31
Dominicantes	The Netherlands	113.17	117.07	117.56	100.00	118.05	123.41
Dominicantes	France	118.54	111.71	125.37	100.00	119.51	126.83
Overall society	Denmark	118.56	122.68	132.47	100.00	124.23	143.30
Euro Islam	France	108.29	115.03	116.58	100.00	92.75	119.17
Overall society	Norway	105.18	107.77	112.95	100.00	116.06	134.72
Dominicantes	Germany	116.48	113.74	123.08	100.00	123.63	141.76
Euro Islam	Sweden	91.72	98.82	93.49	100.00	90.53	108.28
Overall society	Germany	119.64	123.21	130.36	100.00	125.00	138.69
Overall society	Sweden	103.11	108.07	109.32	100.00	114.29	118.01

Table 3.15 The ranking of the European rejection of Jewish Immigration (1—very positive to 4—very negative) according to religious denomination and religious service attendance (*Mensuantes* = religious service)

		Religion or denomination belonging to at present	Mean	N	Standard deviation
Mensuantes	Slovenia	Rimokatoliška (Roman Catholic)	2.640	213	0.882
Mensuantes	Poland	Roman Catholic Church	2.510	975	0.897
Mensuantes	Poland	Catholic (denomination not specified)	2.480	80	0.906
Mensuantes	Ireland	Roman Catholic	2.430	1040	0.873
Mensuantes	Belgium	Muslim	2.430	54	1.002
Total population	Slovenia	Rimokatoliška (Roman Catholic)	2.390	64	0.953
Mensuantes	Belgium	(Rooms) Katholiek (Roman Catholic)	2.350	150	0.860
Mensuantes	Austria	Römisch-katholische Kirche (Roman Catholic)	2.320	355	0.898
Mensuantes	Switzerland	Roman Catholic	2.270	142	0.818
Mensuantes	Finland	Lutheran	2.240	181	0.884
Mensuantes	The Netherlands	Rooms Katholiek (Roman Catholic)	2.220	83	0.741
Total population	Poland	Roman Catholic	2.220	68	0.908
Total population	Finland	Lutheran	2.160	212	0.872
Total population	Belgium	(Rooms) Katholiek (Roman Catholic)	2.140	293	0.764
Total population	The Netherlands	Rooms Katholiek (Roman Catholic)	2.080	252	0.733
Mensuantes	Austria	Islamische Glaubensgemeinschaft in Österreich (Muslim)	2.070	41	0.919
Total population	Switzerland	Roman Catholic	2.060	102	0.818
Total population	Austria	Römisch-katholische Kirche (Roman Catholic)	2.050	228	0.927
Total population	Ireland	Roman Catholic	2.030	239	0.961
Total population	Switzerland	Protestant reformed	2.020	85	0.740
Mensuantes	The Netherlands	Protestantse Kerk in Nederland (PKN) (Protestant reformed)	1.960	59	0.814
Mensuantes	Switzerland	Protestant reformed	1.930	74	0.816
Mensuantes	Norway	Den norske Kirke (Lutheran)	1.870	78	0.795
Total population	Norway	Den norske Kirke (Lutheran)	1.830	172	0.693
Mensuantes	Germany	Römisch-Katholisch	1.710	287	0.768
Total population	Germany	Evangelisch/Protestantisch (EKD, without Freikirchen) (Lutheran)	1.650	218	0.738
Total population	Germany	Römisch-Katholisch (Roman Catholic)	1.560	176	0.698

(continued)

Table 3.15 (continued)

		Religion or denomination belonging to at present	Mean	N	Standard deviation
Total population	Sweden	Svenska kyrkan (Lutheran)	1.540	153	0.628
Mensuantes	Germany	Evangelisch/Protestantisch (EKD, without Freikirchen) (Lutheran)	1.500	174	0.606
Mensuantes	Sweden	Svenska kyrkan (Lutheran)	1.500	68	0.586
Mensuantes	Germany	Evangelische Freikirche (Evangelical Protestant)	1.260	33	0.446

phobias led the global *Dominicantes* to reject Jewish neighbors by comparison with the adherents of other religious denominations around the globe on the basis of the *World Values Survey* data.

The electronic Appendix Table 3.10 informs about the world-level correlations between the rejection of Jewish neighbors and the other phobia data from the *World Values Survey*.

We also wanted to know, for example, how religious service attendance increases or decreases Antisemitism among global Muslims, Buddhists, *Dominicantes*, etc. and, also, how the professed *importance of G'd* to the *WVS* respondents increased or decreased Antisemitism among global Muslims, Buddhists, *Dominicantes*, etc. These informations are contained in the electronic Appendix Tables 3.7 and 3.8. They rely on the statistical method of partial correlation analysis.

The independent variables are highest educational level attained, how often do you attend religious services, how important is G'd in your life, age, and sex. The dependent variable is rejecting to have a Jewish neighbor.

The end result of our analysis is the following:

- Catholic, Orthodox, nonreligious, Protestant, and Hindu nonattendance of religious services tends to decrease Antisemitism, while Buddhist and Muslim nonattendance of religious services tends to increase Antisemitism. That is to say, people staying away from frequent religious service attendance among the global Catholics, Orthodox, people not belonging to denominational groups, Protestants, and Hindus all tend to be less Antisemitic than their less secular counterparts, while secular Buddhists and Muslims, not regularly attending religious services, are more Antisemitic than their more religious counterparts.

In Appendix Table 3.8, the independent variables again are highest educational level attained, how often do you attend religious services, how important is G'd in your life, age, and sex. The dependent variable is rejecting to have a Jewish neighbor.

The end result of this analysis is that Catholic, Buddhist, nonreligious, and Protestant G'd centered spirituality tend to decrease Antisemitism, while Orthodox, Hindu, and Muslim G'd centered spirituality tend to increase Antisemitism.

In Appendix Tables 3.12, 3.13 and 3.14, readers find various multiple regression analyses on how the rejection of various groups of people as neighbors is statistically related to the rejection of Jews as neighbors. We wanted to know, for example, how different is the effect of the rejection of foreign workers as neighbors on the Antisemitism of Buddhists, Hindus, Muslims, etc., all compared to the Antisemitism of the Catholic *Dominicantes*.

To analyze the statistical relationships between the rejection of Jewish neighbors and other forms of xenophobia and racism with the *World Values Survey* data base, we entered the following variables:

- Homophobia (rejection of homosexuals as neighbors)
- Racism (rejection of people of another race as neighbors)
- Xenophobia against immigrants/foreign workers (rejection of immigrants/foreign workers as neighbors)
- Xenophobia against Muslims (rejection of Muslims as neighbors)

as determinants in a multiple OLS standard regression, predicting each time the rejection of Jewish neighbors for the following global samples:

1. Buddhists
2. Catholics
3. *Dominicantes*
4. Global population
5. Hindus
6. Muslims
7. Orthodox
8. People without denomination
9. Protestants

The following graphs tell us about the size of the standardized regression coefficients (beta weights) predicting Antisemitism for each chosen sample (Buddhists, Catholics, *Dominicantes*, global population, Hindus, Muslims, Orthodox, people without denomination, Protestants) by their respective homophobia, racism, xenophobia against immigrants/foreign workers, and xenophobia against Muslims.

Our methodology allows us to compare, for example, whether xenophobia against Muslims is a stronger driver of Antisemitism among, say, Hindus than among Protestants.

Our results tell us that, nowhere, the Antisemitism of the *Dominicantes* was to be predicted in a stronger fashion by any of these phobias than among the other analyzed global denominations.

- Homophobia was the strongest driver of Antisemitism among Muslims, while it was the weakest driver of Antisemitism among Buddhists.
- Xenophobia against immigrants was the strongest driver of Antisemitism among global Hindus, while this phobia was the weakest driver of Antisemitism among Buddhists.
- Xenophobia against Muslims was the strongest driver of Antisemitism among Buddhists and—quite expectedly—the weakest driver among Muslims.

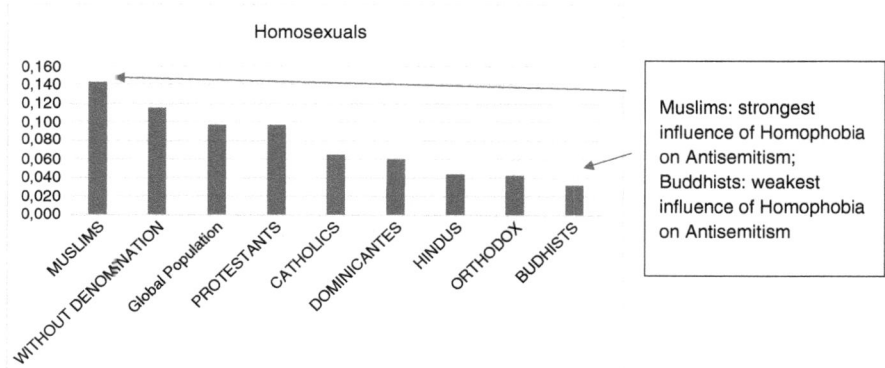

Graph 3.7 Homophobia as a driver of Antisemitism among the different global denominations (beta weights)

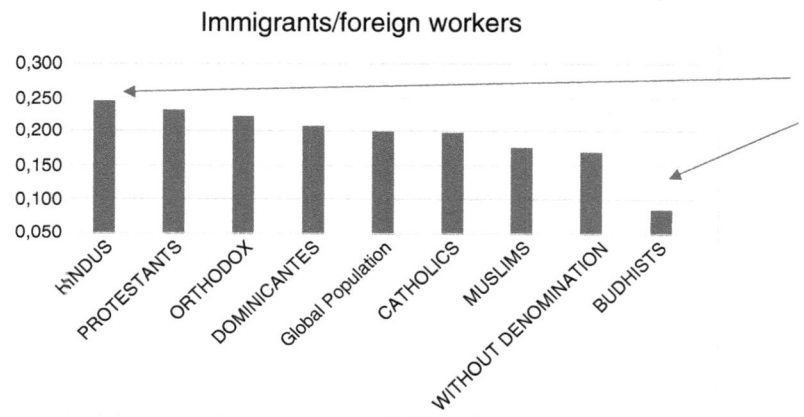

Graph 3.8 Xenophobia against immigrants/foreign workers as a driver of Antisemitism among the different global denominations (beta weights)

- The rejection of people of another race as neighbors was the strongest driver of Antisemitism among the Orthodox and the weakest driver of Antisemitism among global Hindus.

Nowhere, the phobias of the *Dominicantes* are stronger predictors of Antisemitism than the phobias among other global denominations. Our Graphs tell us how the adherents of different denominations around the globe are susceptible to combine Antisemitism with other phobias, lamentably prevalent among their global rank and file. Graph 3.7 tells us, for example, that Muslims, people without denomination, the global population, Protestants, and Catholics associate their Antisemitism in a stronger fashion with homophobia than Buddhists, Orthodox, Hindus, and Catholic *Dominicantes*. In a similar fashion, Graphs 3.8, 3.9, and 3.10

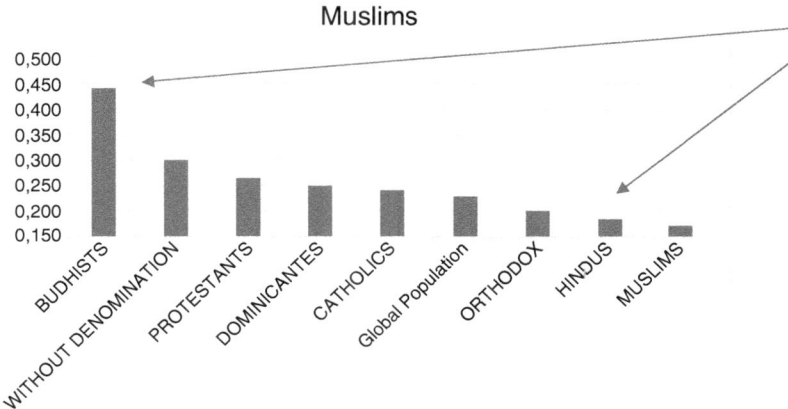

Graph 3.9 Xenophobia against Muslims as a driver of Antisemitism among the different global denominations (beta weights)

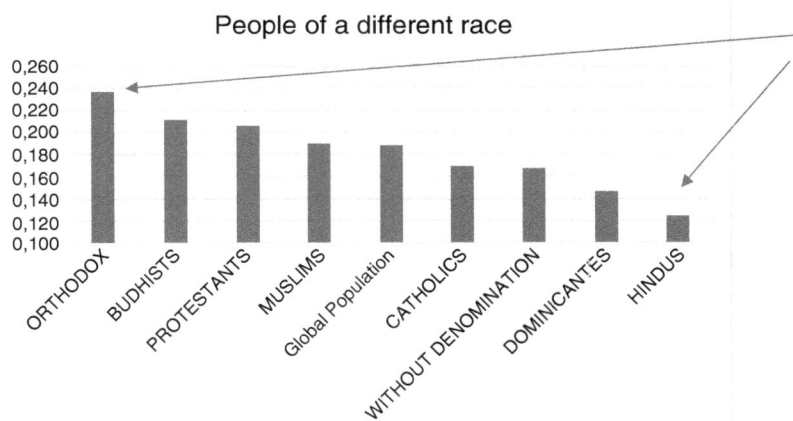

Graph 3.10 Racism as a driver of Antisemitism among the different global denominations (beta weights)

inform readers about the susceptibility of the adherents of the major global denominations and the nondenominational groups to associate their Antisemitism with xenophobia against immigrants/foreign workers, xenophobia against Muslims, and racism.

Graph 3.7 shows the beta weights of the Antisemitism-predictor *reject homosexuals as neighbors* for the different global denominations. Among global Muslims, rejection of homosexual neighbors wields the highest influence on the rejection of Jewish neighbors, while among the global Buddhists, this effect is weakest.

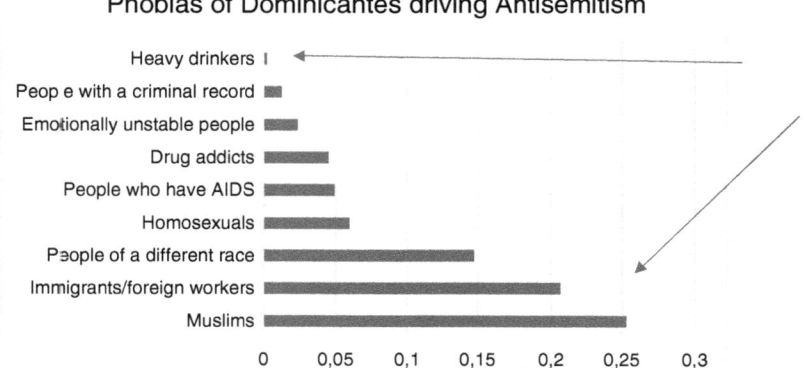

Graph 3.11   The rejection of ... as neighbors driving the rejection of Jewish neighbors among the global *Dominicantes*. Results of OLS multiple regression analysis with *World Values Survey* data—*beta* weights

Analogously, xenophobia against immigrants/foreign workers as a predictor of Antisemitism has the strongest effect among global Hindus and the weakest effect among global Buddhists.

Islamophobias defined as the rejection of Muslim neighbors has the strongest effect as a predictor of Antisemitism among global Buddhists, while among global Hindus, this effect is weakest (not counting Muslim self-hatred).

Among all the compared global denominations, the connection between racism (rejection of a neighbor of a different race) and Antisemitism is strongest among the global Orthodox Christians and weakest among the global Hindus.

Finally, we also analyze the results of our electronic Appendix Tables 3.12, 3.13 and 3.14 concerning the hierarchy of phobias among the global *Dominicantes*, statistically related to the Antisemitism of the *Dominicantes*. While racism among the global Orthodox believers is a far stronger statistical determinant of Antisemitism than among the *Dominicantes* (Graph 3.10), we can also say that the rejection of Muslim neighbors has the strongest statistical relationship with the Antisemitism of the *Dominicantes*. Interestingly enough, it also emerges that Muslim self-hatred and Muslim unwillingness to live side by side with fellow Muslims is also an important motive for Muslims to reject Jewish neighbors (Graph 3.11). The effect of Muslim homophobia, i.e., the rejection of homosexual neighbors by Muslims, is the strongest statistical relationship of the homophobia variable on any Antisemitism rate than among all compared religious denominations (Graphs 3.7 and 3.12).

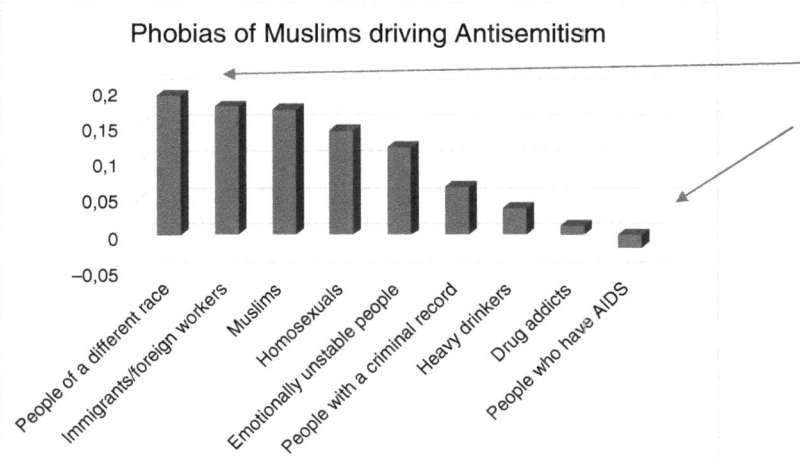

Graph 3.12 The rejection of ... as neighbors driving the rejection of Jewish neighbors among the global Muslims. Results of OLS multiple regression analysis with *World Values Survey* data—*beta weights*

Conclusions and Prospects from This Chapter

In Table 3.16, we summarize our rather bleak final result of our *World Values Survey*-based investigation. Only the *Dominicantes* in Argentina and the United States were among the world's top 10% performers in overcoming Antisemitism, while the *Dominicantes* in Venezuela, Bosnia, Nigeria, Slovakia, South Africa, and South Korea were among the world's bottom 2/3 of communities in overcoming Antisemitism.

We can finally say that our results about the anchoring of *Nostra Aetate* in the hearts and minds of global Catholics are rather pessimistic. We are afraid that on the Catholic side, the zenith of goodwill and understanding, reached during the pontificates of Popes John Paul II, Benedict XVI, and Francis, has already been reached and that the global Catholic rank and file increasingly threatens to be infected by the rising rates of global Antisemitism and hate of the Jewish State. Let us never forget that only three full decades ago, full diplomatic relations were finally established between the Vatican and the State of Israel and that—as we have shown in this work—even the pivotal figure of Cardinal Augustin Bea shunned away from a Catholic identification with the State of Israel and rather tended to view *Nostra Aetate* as a declaration without any political consequences. At a time of growing international migration, even in the rich Western countries, where support for *Nostra Aetate* was stronger, new generations of Catholic clergy and faithful, whose home countries did not share the experience of the reckoning and mea culpa of Christianity after the *Shoah* and the Second World War, slowly enter into positions of leadership and power in the Catholic Church. This could be combined with a more general climate of enmity against the Jewish State, brought about by a growing Antisemitism

Table 3.16 The *Dominicantes'* performance in overcoming Antisemitism—a global comparison, based on *World Values Survey* data

Rank in overcoming Antisemitism	Sample	Country/ region	Antisemitism (average rejection of Jewish neighbors, scale 0–1)	N	Percentile performance
1	Protestants	Uruguay	0.000	30	1.14
2	Protestants	Canada	0.020	336	2.27
3	Protestants	Argentina	0.020	44	3.41
4	Countrywide	Canada	0.040	1931	4.55
5	Countrywide	Argentina	0.060	3361	5.68
6	*Dominicantes*	Argentina	0.060	607	6.82
7	*Dominicantes*	The United States	0.060	145	7.95
8	Orthodox	Belarus	0.060	1145	9.09
9	Countrywide	Belarus	0.070	2092	10.23
10	*Dominicantes*	Canada	0.070	219	11.36
11	Protestants	The United States	0.070	313	12.50
12	Countrywide	Uruguay	0.080	2000	13.64
13	*Dominicantes*	India	0.080	38	14.77
14	Muslims	Russia	0.080	104	15.91
15	Countrywide	The United States	0.090	1200	17.05
16	Orthodox	Kyrgyzstan	0.100	78	18.18
17	Countrywide	Russia	0.110	4001	19.32
18	Orthodox	Russia	0.110	1525	20.45
19	Protestants	Albania	0.110	180	21.59
20	*Dominicantes*	Belarus	0.120	49	22.73
21	Countrywide	Chile	0.130	3700	23.86
22	*Dominicantes*	Chile	0.130	666	25.00
23	*Dominicantes*	Uruguay	0.130	128	26.14
24	*Dominicantes*	The Czech Republic	0.140	51	27.27
25	*Dominicantes*	Zimbabwe	0.160	131	28.41
26	Countrywide	Albania	0.170	1000	29.55
27	Muslims	South Africa	0.170	84	30.68
28	Countrywide	The Czech Republic	0.180	924	31.82
29	Protestants	Uganda	0.180	443	32.95
30	Countrywide	Zimbabwe	0.190	1002	34.09
31	Muslims	Bangladesh	0.190	1378	35.23
32	Orthodox	Macedonia	0.190	627	36.36
33	Orthodox	Chile	0.190	139	37.50
34	Orthodox	Mexico	0.190	37	38.64
35	Protestants	Venezuela	0.190	75	39.77
36	Countrywide	Bangladesh	0.200	1500	40.91

(continued)

Table 3.16 (continued)

Rank in overcoming Antisemitism	Sample	Country/region	Antisemitism (average rejection of Jewish neighbors, scale 0–1)	N	Percentile performance
37	Countrywide	Macedonia	0.200	1055	42.05
38	Countrywide	Kyrgyzstan	0.200	1043	43.18
39	Muslims	Macedonia	0.200	266	44.32
40	Protestants	The Czech Republic	0.200	51	45.45
41	Protestants	Zimbabwe	0.210	273	46.59
42	Countrywide	Spain	0.220	2719	47.73
43	Countrywide	Uganda	0.220	1002	48.86
44	Hindus	South Africa	0.220	54	50.00
45	*Dominicantes*	Mexico	0.230	1369	51.14
46	Muslims	Kyrgyzstan	0.230	775	52.27
47	Countrywide	South Africa	0.240	3000	53.41
48	*Dominicantes*	Uganda	0.240	283	54.55
49	*Dominicantes*	Albania	0.240	119	55.68
50	Protestants	South Africa	0.240	1048	56.82
51	Buddhists	Japan	0.250	272	57.95
52	Countrywide	Moldova	0.250	1008	59.09
53	Orthodox	Moldova	0.250	878	60.23
54	Protestants	Chile	0.250	62	61.36
55	Countrywide	Mexico	0.260	3895	62.50
56	Countrywide	Venezuela	0.260	1200	63.64
57	*Dominicantes*	Spain	0.270	671	64.77
58	Protestants	Nigeria	0.270	211	65.91
59	Countrywide	Bosnia	0.280	1200	67.05
60	Countrywide	Japan	0.280	1011	68.18
61	Muslims	Bosnia	0.280	485	69.32
62	*Dominicantes*	Venezuela	0.300	321	70.45
63	*Dominicantes*	Bosnia	0.300	84	71.59
64	Protestants	Mexico	0.310	158	72.73
65	Protestants	Slovakia	0.330	40	73.86
66	Countrywide	Slovakia	0.340	466	75.00
67	Countrywide	Nigeria	0.350	1001	76.14
68	*Dominicantes*	Nigeria	0.350	193	77.27
69	Muslims	Uganda	0.350	169	78.41
70	Protestants	South Korea	0.350	284	79.55
71	Hindus	Bangladesh	0.360	107	80.68
72	Orthodox	Bosnia	0.360	248	81.82
73	*Dominicantes*	Slovakia	0.370	147	82.95
74	*Dominicantes*	South Africa	0.380	210	84.09
75	*Dominicantes*	South Korea	0.400	89	85.23
76	Countrywide	South Korea	0.410	1200	86.36

(continued)

Table 3.16 (continued)

Rank in overcoming Antisemitism	Sample	Country/ region	Antisemitism (average rejection of Jewish neighbors, scale 0–1)	N	Percentile performance
77	Muslims	Nigeria	0.410	248	87.50
78	Orthodox	Nigeria	0.430	176	88.64
79	Buddhists	South Korea	0.440	250	89.77
80	Countrywide	India	0.530	2500	90.91
81	Hindus	India	0.530	2206	92.05
82	Countrywide	Egypt	0.620	3000	93.18
83	Muslims	Egypt	0.620	2830	94.32
84	Muslims	India	0.640	138	95.45
85	Countrywide	Iran	0.750	2657	96.59
86	Muslims	Iran	0.750	2614	97.73
87	Countrywide	Iraq	0.900	4924	98.86
88	Muslims	Iraq	0.900	4874	100.00

among the global political far right and political far left and the ever more present thought patterns imported by rising Muslim migration to the rich Western countries.

As we have shown in this work on the basis of ADL data, only 33% of the global population today are aware of the *Shoah* and believe it has been accurately described by history. In Oceania, it is 82%; in Western Europe, it is still 77%; in Eastern Europe, it is 57%; and in Asia, it is dismally low at 23%, not to talk about sub-Saharan Africa (12%). Notably, in the MENA (Middle East and North Africa) region, it was even only 8%. These structures will also have their repercussions for the Roman Catholic Church at a time of the increased global migration of the Catholic clergy and the Catholic faithful from regions with a low *Shoah* awareness to Europe, North America, and Australia/New Zealand.

And yet, Catholicism is just too important to be left drifting in our globe. Efforts of public diplomacy by states, transnational media corporations, and transnational centers of higher learning concerned with these developments must be undertaken. *Nostra Aetate*, by and large, was primarily an offspring of Roman Catholicism in the Atlantic arena. But as we have also shown in this work, the days of the European Church and Catholic Europe are definitively over. Bringing the spirit of *Nostra Aetate* to the Catholic communities in Latin America, Africa, and Asia would be an important task for public diplomacy in the twenty-first century. Add to this that already today the top ten active Catholic communities of our globe are located in Mexico, Brazil, the Philippines, the United States, Italy, Poland, Colombia, Nigeria, India, and Peru (in descending order of size) with more than ten million regular Church service attenders each, which already make up more than 70% of all global *Dominicantes*. Support for the Christian-Jewish dialogue and cooperation in global Catholicism depends increasingly on the support among these strategic Catholic communities.

Literature

Alemán, J., & Woods, D. (2015). Value orientations from the *World Values Survey*. How comparable are they cross-nationally? *Comparative Political Studies*, 0010414015600458.

Alesina, A., & Ferrara, E. L. (2000). *The determinants of trust* (No. w7621). National Bureau of Economic Research.

Alesina, A., & Guiliano P. (2013). *Culture and institutions* (NBER Working Paper Series, Working Paper 19750). Download April 10, 2019, from http://scholar.harvard.edu/alesina/publications

Alesina, A., Algan, Y., Cahuc, P., & Giuliano, P. (2015). Family values and the regulation of labor. *Journal of the European Economic Association, 13*(4), 599–630.

Anti-Defamation League (ADL). (2014). *ADL 100 Index*. Download April 10, 2019, from http://global100.adl.org/

Barro, R. J. (1991). Economic growth in a cross-section of countries. *Quarterly Journal of Economics., 106*(2), 407–443.

Barro, R. J. (1996). Democracy and growth. *Journal of Economic Growth, 1*(1), 1–27.

Barro, R. J. (1998). *Determinants of economic growth: A cross-country empirical study*. Lionel Robbins Lectures (1st ed.). Cambridge, MA: MIT Press.

Barro, R. J. (2003a). Economic growth in a cross section of countries. *International Library of Critical Writings in Economics, 159*(1), 350–386.

Barro, R. J. (2003b). *Religion adherence data*. Harvard University, Department of Economics. https://scholar.harvard.edu/Barro/publications/religion-adherence-data

Barro, R. J. (2004). Spirit of capitalism religion and economic development. *Harvard International Review, 25*(4), 64–67.

Barro, R. J. (2012). *Convergence and modernization revisited*. Department of Economics, Harvard University.

Barro, R. J., & McCleary, R. M. (2003). Religion and economic growth across countries. *American Sociological Review, 68*(5), 760–781.

Barro, R. J., & Sala-i-Martin, X. (1992). Convergence. *Journal of Political Economy, 100*(2), 223–251.

Barro, R. J., & Sala-i-Martin, X. (2003). *Economic growth* (2nd ed.). Cambridge, MA: MIT Press.

Barro, R. J., & Ursúa, J. F. (2008, Spring). Macroeconomic crises since 1870. *Brookings Papers on Economic Activity*, 255–335. Download April 10, 2019, from http://www.people.fas.harvard.edu/~jfursua/papers/bpea.pdf

Barro, R. J., Sala-i-Martin, X., et al. (1991). Convergence across states and regions. *Brookings Papers on Economic Activity, 1*, 107–182.

Bauer, Y. (1993). Antisemitism as a European and world problem. *Patterns of Prejudice, 27*(1), 15–24.

Bea, A. (1966). *The church and the Jewish people; a commentary on the Second Vatican Council's Declaration on the relation of the Church to non-Christian religions*. New York: Harper & Row.

Bergson, H. L. (1935). *The two sources of religion and morality* (R. Ashley Andrà & C. Brereton with the assistance of W. Horsefall Carter, Trans.). New York: Henry Holt.

Bernstein, C., & Politi, M. (1996). *His Holiness: John Paul II and the hidden history of our time*. New York: Doubleday.

Bosca, R. (2017). *Maritain, Los Judios y el Concilio Vaticano II*. Universidad Austral, Buenos Aires, Argentina. Download April 10, 2019, from http://congresojudio.org/uploads/coloquio/207/MARITAIN,%20LOS%20JUDIOS%20Y%20EL%20CONCILIO%20VATICANO%20II.pdf

Bowker, J. (2000). *The concise Oxford dictionary of world religions*. Oxford: Oxford University Press.

Brenner, P. S. (2016). Cross-national trends in religious service attendance. *Public Opinion Quarterly*, nfw016.

Browne, M. W. (2001). An overview of analytic rotation in exploratory factor analysis. *Multivariate Behavioral Research, 36*(1), 111–150.

Brustein, W. (2003). *Roots of hate: Anti-Semitism in Europe before the Holocaust.* Cambridge: Cambridge University Press.

Burleigh, M. (2000). *The third Reich: A new history.* Basingstoke: Pan Macmillan.

Burns, G. (1990). The politics of ideology: The papal struggle with liberalism. *American Journal of Sociology,* 1123–1152.

Burrell, G., & Morgan, G. (1985). *Sociological paradigms and organisational analysis: Elements of the sociology of corporate life.* Aldershot: Gower.

Bytwerk, R. L. (2015). Believing in "Inner Truth": The protocols of the elders of Zion in Nazi Propaganda, 1933–1945. *Holocaust and Genocide Studies, 29*(2), 212–229.

Ciftci, S. (2010). Modernization, Islam, or social capital: What explains attitudes toward democracy in the Muslim world. *Comparative Political Studies, 43*(11), 1442–1470.

Ciftci, S. (2012). Islamophobia and threat perceptions: Explaining anti-Muslim sentiment in the west. *Journal of Muslim Minority Affairs, 32*(3), 293–309. https://doi.org/10.1080/13602004. 2012.727291.

Ciftci, S. (2013). Secular-Islamist cleavage, values, and support for democracy and Shari'a in the Arab world (December 26, 2012). *Political Research Quarterly, 66*(4), 781–793. Available at SSRN: https://ssrn.com/abstract=2920382.

Ciftci, S., & Bernick, E. M. (2015). Utilitarian and modern: Clientelism, citizen empowerment, and civic engagement in the Arab world (August 8, 2014). *Democratization, 22*(7), 1161–1182. Available at SSRN: https://ssrn.com/abstract=2920373.

Connelly, J. (2012). *From enemy to brother: The revolution in Catholic teaching on the Jews, 1933–1965.* Cambridge, MA: Harvard University Press.

Conway, M. (2008). *Catholic politics in Europe, 1918–1945.* New York: Routledge.

Coordination Forum for Countering Antisemitism. (2015). Download April 10, 2019, from http:// antisemitism.org.il/?lang=en

Corrin, J. P. (2002). *Catholic intellectuals and the challenge of democracy.* Notre Dame: University of Notre Dame Press.

Coughlin, J. J. (2003). Pope John Paul II and the dignity of the human being. *Harvard Journal of Law & Public Policy, 27*(65), 1–17.

Cunningham, P. A. (2015). *Seeking shalom: The journey to right relationship between Catholics and Jews.* Grand Rapids, MI: William B. Eerdmans.

Curran, C. E. (2008). *Catholic moral theology in the United States: A history.* Washington, DC: Georgetown University Press.

D'Costa, G. (2014). *Vatican II: Catholic Doctrines on Jews and Muslims.* Oxford: Oxford University Press.

Davidov, E., Schmidt, P., & Schwartz, S. H. (2008). Bringing values back in the adequacy of the *European Social Survey* to measure values in 20 countries. *Public Opinion Quarterly, 72*(3), 420–445.

Davidov, E., Schmidt, P., & Billiet, J. (2011). *Cross-cultural analysis: Methods and applications.* New York: Routledge.

Doney, K. (1993). *Freemasonry in France during the Nazi occupation and it's rehabilitation after the end of the Second World War.* Ph.D. thesis, University of Aston, Birmingham.

Eisenstadt, S. N. (1968). *The protestant ethic and modernization: A comparative view.* New York: Basic Books.

Elzinga, K. G. (1999). Economics and religion. In *Religion and economics: Normative social theory* (pp. 131–139). Dordrecht: Springer.

Etzioni, A. (1998). *The active society: A theory of societal and political processes.* London/New York: Collier-Macmillan/Free Press.

Fisher, E. J., & Klenicki, L. (1987). *Pope John Paul II on Jews and Judaism: 1979–1986 (No. 151).* Washington, DC: USCCB.

Fisher, E. J., & Klenicki, L. (Eds.). (1995). *Spiritual pilgrimage: Texts on Jews and Judaism, 1979–1995*. New York: Herder & Herder.

Fox, J. (2000). *A world survey of religion and the state*. New York: Cambridge University Press.

Fox, J., Sandler, S., & Sandier, S. (2004). *Bringing religion into international relations* (pp. 9–10). New York: Palgrave Macmillan.

Francis, P. (2014). *The church of mercy: A vision for the church*. Chicago, IL: Loyola Press (Journal for the Sociological Integration of Religion and Society, 5 (1)).

Gillis, C. (2016). *Political Papacy: John Paul II, Benedict XVI, and their influence*. New York: Routledge.

Giroux, H. A. (2016). Donald Trump and neo-fascism in America. *Arena Magazine (Fitzroy, Vic), 140*, 31.

Glahe, F., & Vorhies, F. (1989). Religion, liberty and economic development: An empirical investigation. *Public Choice, 62*(3), 201–215.

Goldhagen, D. J. (2007). *A moral reckoning: The role of the Church in the Holocaust and its unfulfilled duty of repair*. New York: Vintage.

Gorsuch, R. L. (1983). *Factor analysis*. Hillsdale, NJ: Erlbaum.

Grim, B. J. (2014). Growing religion and growing religious restrictions: A global overview. *International Area Studies Review, 17*(2), 134–145. https://doi.org/10.1177/2233865914537054.

Grümme, B. (1997). Ein schwieriges Verhältnis: Karl Rahner und die Juden. *Zeitschrift für katholische Theologie*, 265–283.

Grzymała-Busse, A. (2015). *Nations under G'd: How churches use moral authority to influence policy*. Princeton, NJ: Princeton University Press.

Grzymala-Busse, A. (2016). Weapons of the Meek. *World Politics, 68*(01), 1–36.

Guiso, L., Sapienza, P., & Zingales, L. (2003). People's opium? Religion and economic attitudes. *Journal of Monetary Economics, 50*(1), 225–282.

Habermas, J. (2010). Leadership and Leitkultur. *New York Times, 28*, 10.

Hann, C. (2015). The fragility of Europe's Willkommenskultur. *Anthropology Today, 31*(6), 1–2.

Hanson, E. O. (2014). *The Catholic church in world politics*. Princeton, NJ: Princeton University Press.

Harman, H. H. (1976). *Modern factor analysis* (3rd ed.). Chicago, IL: University of Chicago Press.

Harrison, E., & Mitchell, S. M. (2014). *The triumph of democracy and the eclipse of the West* (1st ed.). New York: Palgrave Macmillan.

Hastings, A. (1991). *Modern Catholicism: Vatican II and after*. New York: Oxford University Press.

Hastings, D. (2009). *Catholicism and the roots of Nazism: Religious identity and national socialism*. Oxford: Oxford University Press.

Heinemann, J., et al. (2007). Antisemitism. In M. Berenbaum & F. Skolnik (Eds.), *Encyclopaedia Judaica* (Vol. 2, pp. 206–246, 2nd ed.). Detroit: Macmillan (Gale Virtual Reference Library).

Heschel, A. J. (1966). No religion is an island. *Union Theological Seminary Quarterly Review, 21*(2), 1.

Hofstede, G. (2001). *Culture's consequences: Comparing values, behaviors, institutions, and organizations across nations*. Thousand Oaks, CA: Sage.

Hofstede, G., & Minkov, M. (2010). Long- versus short-term orientation: New perspectives. *Asia Pacific Business Review, 16*(4), 493–504.

Hofstede, G.; Hofstede, G. J., & Minkov, M. (2010). *Cultures and organizations: Software of the mind* (Rev. and Expanded 3rd ed.). New York: McGraw-Hill.

Hogan, J., & Haltinner, K. (2015). Floods, invaders, and parasites: Immigration threat narratives and right-wing populism in the USA, UK and Australia. *Journal of Intercultural Studies, 36*(5), 520–543.

Hollifield, J., Martin, P., & Orrenius, P. (2014). *Controlling immigration: A global perspective*. Stanford, CA: Stanford University Press.

Holmes, D. L. (2006). *The faiths of the founding fathers*. Oxford: Oxford University Press.

Hoppenbrouwers, F. (2004). The principal victim: Catholic antisemitism and the holocaust in Central Europe. *Religion, State and Society, 32*(1), 37–51.

Houellebecq, M. (2015). *Soumission*. Paris: Flammarion.

Huntington, S. P. (1993). *The third wave: Democratization in the late twentieth Century* (Vol. 4). Norman: University of Oklahoma Press.

Huntington, S. P. (2000). The clash of civilizations? In *Culture and politics* (pp. 99–118). New York: Palgrave Macmillan.

Inglehart, R. F. (1988). The renaissance of political culture. *American Political Science Review, 82* (04), 1203–1230.

Inglehart, R. F. (1990). *Culture shift in advanced industrial countries*. Princeton, NJ: Princeton University Press.

Inglehart, R. F. (2000). Globalization and postmodern values. *Washington Quarterly, 23*(1), 215–228.

Inglehart, R. F. (2006). Mapping global values. *Comparative Sociology, 5*(2), 115–136.

Inglehart, R. F. (2008). Changing values among western publics from 1970 to 2006. *West European Politics, 31*(1–2), 130–146.

Inglehart, R. F. (2015). *The silent revolution: Changing values and political styles among Western publics*. Princeton, NJ: Princeton University Press.

Inglehart, R. F., & Baker, W. E. (2000). Modernization, cultural change, and the persistence of traditional values. *American Sociological Review, 65*(1), 19–51. Download April 10, 2019, from http://my.fit.edu/~gabrenya/cultural/readings/Inglehart-Baker-2000.pdf

Inglehart, R. F., & Norris, P. (2003). *Rising tide: Gender equality and cultural change around the world*. New York: Cambridge University Press.

Inglehart, R. F., & Norris, P. (2009, November 4). The true clash of civilizations. *Foreign Policy*. Available at: http://foreignpolicy.com/2009/11/04/the-true-clash-of-civilizations/

Inglehart, R. F., & Norris, P. (2012). The four horsemen of the apocalypse: Understanding human security. *Scandinavian Political Studies, 35*(1), 71–95.

Inglehart, R. F., & Norris, P. (2016). *Trump, Brexit, and the rise of populism: Economic have-nots and cultural backlash*. Download April 10, 2019, from SSRN: http://ssrn.com/abstract=2818659. HKS Working Paper No. RWP16-026.

Inglehart, R. F., & Welzel, C. (2003). Political culture and democracy: Analyzing cross-level linkages *Comparative Politics, 36*(1), 61–79.

Inglehart, R. F., & Welzel, C. (2009, March, April). How development leads to democracy. What we know about modernization. *Foreign Affairs*. Download April 10, 2019, from http://www.foreignaffairs.com/articles/64821/ronald-inglehart-and-christian-welzel/how-development-leads-to-democracy

Inglehart, R. F., & Welzel, C. (2010). Changing mass priorities: The link between modernization and democracy. *Perspectives on Politics, 8*(02), 551–567.

Inglehart, R. F., Ponarin, E., & Inglehart, R. C. (2017). Cultural change, slow and fast: The distinctive trajectory of norms governing gender equality and sexual orientation. *Social Forces, 95*(4), 1313–1340.

Institute for Economics and Peace. (2014). *Global terrorism index 2014*. Institute for Economics and Peace. Download April 10, 2019, from http://www.visionofhumanity.org/sites/default/files/Global%20Terrorism%20Index%20Report%202014_0.pdf

Jacobs, D., et al. (2011). The impact of the conflict in Gaza on antisemitism in Belgium. *Patterns of Prejudice, 45*(4), 341–360. https://doi.org/10.1080/0031322X.2011.605845.

Jelen, T. G., & Wilcox, C. (1998). Context and conscience: The Catholic Church as an agent of political socialization in Western Europe. *Journal for the Scientific Study of Religion,* 28–40.

Jerusalem Fost. (2015). *Israel is standing By Europe, Europe must stand By Israel*. Download January 1, 2016, from http://www.jpost.com/Israel-News/Politics-And-Diplomacy/Netanyahu-Israel-is-standing-by-Europe-Europe-must-stand-by-Israel-387083

Jikeli, G., & Allouche-Benayoun, J. (Eds.). (2012). *Perceptions of the Holocaust in Europe and Muslim communities: Sources, comparisons and educational challenges* (Vol. 5). New York: Springer.

John Paul II. (1994). *Catechism of the Catholic church*. Rome: Urbi Et Orbi Communications. Download April 10, 2019, from http://www.vatican.va/archive/ENG0015/_INDEX.HTM

Juergensmeyer, M. (2000). *Terror in the mind of G'd: The global rise of religious violence*. Berkeley: University of California Press.

Juergensmeyer, M. (2011). *The Oxford handbook of global religions (Oxford handbooks)*. Oxford: Oxford University Press.

Kaplan, E. H., & Small, C. A. (2006). Anti-Israel sentiment predicts Antisemitism in Europe. *Journal of Conflict Resolution, 50*(4), 548–561.

Kappler, S., Hancock, K., & Plante, T. G. (2013). Roman Catholic gay priests: Internalized homophobia, sexual identity, and psychological well-being. *Pastoral Psychology, 62*(6), 805–826.

Kasper, W. (2015). *Pope Francis' revolution of tenderness and love*. New York: Paulist Press.

Kertzer, D. I. (2007). *The Popes against the Jews: The Vatican's role in the rise of modern Antisemitism*. New York: Vintage.

Kimelman, R. (2004). Rabbis Joseph B. Soloveitchik and Abraham Joshua Heschel on Jewish-Christian relations. *Modern Judaism, 24*(3), 251–271.

Knippenberg, H. (2015). Secularization and transformation of religion in post-war Europe. In *The changing world religion appendix map* (pp. 2101–2127). Dordrecht: Springer.

Koschorke, K., Ludwig, F., & Delgado, M. (2007). *A history of Christianity in Asia, Africa, and Latin America, 1450–1990: A documentary sourcebook*. Grand Rapids, MI: William B. Eerdmans.

Küng, H. (1997). *A global ethic for global politics and economics* (J. Bowden, Trans. from the German). London: SCM Press.

Küng, H. (2002). *Tracing the way: Spiritual dimensions of the world religions*. New York: Continuum.

Kupczak, J. (2000). *Destined for liberty: The human person in the philosophy of Karol Wojtyla/John Paul II*. Washington, DC: Catholic University of America Press.

Kuznets, S. (1976). *Modern economic growth: Rate, structure and spread*. New Haven, CT: Yale University Press.

Laqueur, W. (1997). *Fascism: Past, present, future*. Oxford: Oxford University Press.

Lasswell, H. D. (1948). The structure and function of communication in society. In L. Bryson (Ed.), *The communication of ideas. A series of addresses* (pp. 32–51). New York: Harper and Row.

Lebl, L. S. (2010). Radical Islam in Europe. *Orbis, 54*(1), 46–60.

Lebl, L. S. (2013). The sons of pigs and apes: Muslim Antisemitism and the conspiracy of silence. *Middle East Quarterly, 20*(3), 95.

Lebl, L. S. (2014a). The EU, the Muslim brotherhood and the organization of Islamic cooperation. *Orbis, 57*(1), 101–119.

Lebl, L. S. (2014b). The Islamist threat to European security. *Middle East Quarterly, 21*, 3. Download April 10, 2019, from http://webcache.googleusercontent.com/search?q=cache:bL4E40YEtWQJ:www.meforum.org/3837/the-islamist-threat-to-european-security+&cd=1&hl=de&ct=clnk&gl=at

Lehner, U. L., & Printy, M. (2010). *A companion to the Catholic enlightenment in Europe*. Boston: Brill.

Lenoir, F. (2008). *Le Christ philosophe*. Paris: Plon.

Lenoir, F., & Etchegoin, M.-F. (2009). *La Saga des francs-maçons*. Paris: Robert Laffont.

Lenoir, F., & Tardan-Masquelier, Y. (1997). *Encyclopédie des religions*. Paris: Bayard.

Lewy, G. (2009). *The Catholic church and Nazi Germany*. Boston: Da Capo Press.

Lipset, S. M. (1959). Some social requisites of democracy: Economic development and political legitimacy. *American Political Science Review, 53*(01), 69–105.

Lipset, S. M. (1969, December). The socialism of fools—The left, the Jews and Israel. *Encounter*, 24.

Mainwaring. S. (2003). *Christian democracy in Latin America: Electoral competition and regime conflicts*. Stanford, CA: Stanford University Press.

Manuel, P. C., Reardon, L. C., & Wilcox, C. (2006). *The Catholic church and the nation-state: Comparative perspectives*. Washington, DC: Georgetown University Press.

Maritain, J. (1936). *Humanisme integral. Problemes temporels et spirituels d'une nouvelle chretiente*. Paris: Aubier (1936). 334 S. 8°. Aubier.

Maritain, J. (2012). *Christianity and democracy, the rights of man and natural law*. San Francisco, CA: Ignatius Press.

McCleary, R. M., & Barro, R. J. (2006a). Religion and economy. *The Journal of Economic Perspectives, 20*(2), 49–72.

McCleary, R. M., & Barro, R. J. (2006b). Religion and political economy in an international panel. *Journal for the Scientific Study of Religion, 45*(2), 149–175.

McDonough, P., Barnes, S. H., & Pina, A. L. (1986). The growth of democratic legitimacy in Spain. *American Political Science Review, 80*(03), 735–760.

Michael, R. (2008). *A history of Catholic antisemitism: The dark side of the church*. New York: Springer.

Minkov, M. (2014). The K factor, societal hypometropia, and national values: A study of 71 nations. *Personality and Individual Differences, 66*, 153–159.

Minkov, M.. & Hofstede, G. (2011). *Cultural differences in a globalizing world*. Bingley: Emerald.

Minkov, M.. & Hofstede, G. (2013). *Cross-cultural analysis: The science and art of comparing the world's modern societies and their cultures*. Los Angeles: Sage.

Minkov, M., & Hofstede, G. (2014). Nations versus religions: Which has a stronger effect on societal values? *Management International Review, 54*(6), 801–824.

Moaddel, M., & Karabenick, S. A. (2013). *Religious fundamentalism in the Middle East: A cross-national, inter-faith, and inter-ethnic analysis*. Amsterdam: Brill.

Montesquieu, C.-L. de Secondat (1989 [1689–1755]). *The spirit of the laws* (A. M. Cohler & B. C. Miller, Trans. and Eds.) Harold Samuel Stone. Cambridge: Cambridge University Press (Cambridge texts in the history of political thought).

Morel, J. S. J. (2003). *Radikale Kirchenreform. Für eine mutige Erneuerung*. Innsbruck: Tyrolia.

Moyser, G. (2005). European religion in comparative perspective. *Political Theology, 6*(3), 325–342.

Muller, E. N., & Seligson, M. A. (1994). Civic culture and democracy: The question of causal relationships. *American Political Science Review, 88*(03), 635–652.

Müller, A., Tausch, A., Zulehner, P. M., & Wickens, H. (Eds.). (2000). *Global capitalism, liberation theology, and the social sciences: An analysis of the contradictions of modernity at the turn of the millennium*. Hauppauge, NY: Nova Science.

Nelsen, B. F., & Guth, J. L. (2003, August). Roman Catholicism and the founding of Europe: How Catholics shaped the European Communities. In Prepared for delivery at the Annual Meeting of the American Political Science Association, Philadelphia, PA (pp. 28–31).

Norris, P., & Inglehart, R. F. (2002). Islamic culture and democracy: Testing the 'clash of civilizations' thesis. *Comparative Sociology, 1*(3), 235–263.

Norris, P., & Inglehart, R. F. (2011). *Sacred and secular: Religion and politics worldwide*. New York: Cambridge University Press.

Norris, P., & Inglehart, R. F. (2012). Muslim integration into Western cultures: Between origins and destinations. *Political Studies, 60*(2), 228–251.

Norris, P., & Inglehart, R. F. (2015). Are high levels of existential security conducive to secularization? A response to our critics. In *The changing world religion map* (pp. 3389–3408). Dordrecht: Springer.

Novak, M. (1984). *Catholic social thought and liberal institutions: Freedom with justice*. New Brunswick, NJ: Transaction Publishers.

Novak, M. (1991a). *The spirit of democratic capitalism*. Totowa, NJ: Rowman, & Littlefield.

Novak, M. (1991b). *Will it liberate? Questions about liberation theology.* New York: Madison Books.

Oates, S., & Moe, W. W. (2016, August). *Donald Trump and the 'Oxygen of publicity': Branding, social media, and mass media in the 2016 Presidential primary elections.* In American Political Science Association Annual Meeting.

O'Collins, G. (2008). *Catholicism: A very short introduction* (Vol. 198). Oxford: Oxford University Press.

Office of the Prime Minister, the State of Israel. (2015). Download April 10, 2019, from http://www.pmo.gov.il/English/MediaCenter/Speeches/Pages/speechfunreal130115.aspx

Oishi, S., Diener, E. F., Lucas, R. E., & Suh, E. M. (1999). Cross-cultural variations in predictors of life satisfaction: Perspectives from needs and values. *Personality and Social Psychology Bulletin, 25*(8), 980–990.

Park, J. (2015). *Europe's migration crisis.* New York: Council of Foreign Relations. Download April 10, 2019, from http://www.cfr.org/refugees-and-the-displaced/europes-migration-crisis/p32874

Paz, R. (2015). The Islamist perspective. In B. Rubin & J. C. Rubin (Eds.), *The loathing of America: Anti-Americanism old and new.* Global Research in International Affairs (GLORIA) Center, Interdisciplinary Center Herzliya, PO Box 167, Herzliya, 46150, Israel

Perreau-Saussine, E. (2012). *Catholicism and democracy: An essay in the history of political thought.* Princeton, NJ: Princeton University Press.

Petrella, I. (2004). *The future of liberation theology: An argument and manifesto.* Aldershot: Gower.

PEW Research Center, Global Attitudes and Trends. (2015). Download April 10, 2019, from http://www.pewglobal.org/category/datasets/

Phayer, M. (2000). *The Catholic church and the Holocaust, 1930–1965.* Bloomington, IN: Indiana University Press.

Phayer, M. (2001). Totalitarianism: Questions about Catholic Resistance. *Church History: Studies in Christianity and Culture, 70*(02), 328–344.

Philpott, D. (2004). The Catholic wave. *Journal of Democracy, 15*(2), 32–46.

Pollard, J. (2007). 'Clerical Fascism': Context, overview and conclusion. *Totalitarian Movements and Political Religions, 8*(2), 433–446.

Popper, K. S. (2012). *The open society and its enemies.* New York: Routledge.

Porta, R. L., Lopez-De-Silane, F., Shleifer, A., & Vishny, R. W. (1996). *Trust in large organizations* (No. w5864). National Bureau of Economic Research.

Post, S. G. (2005). Altruism, happiness, and health: It's good to be good. *International Journal of Behavioral Medicine, 12*(2), 66–77.

Putnam, R. D. (1993). *Making democracy work: Civic traditions in modern Italy.* Princeton, NJ: Princeton University Press.

Rahner, K. (1963). *The Christian commitment: Essays in pastoral theology.* New York: Sheed and Ward.

Reese, T. J. (1996). *Inside the Vatican: The politics and organization of the Catholic church* (p. 164). Cambridge, MA: Harvard University Press.

Rich, D. (2017). *The left's Jewish problem. Jeremy Corbyn, Israel and Antisemitism.* London: Biteback Publishing.

Rittner, C., & Roth, J. K. (Eds.). (2016). *Pope Pius XII and the Holocaust.* London: Bloomsbury.

Röhrich, W. (2004). *Die Macht der Religionen: Glaubenskonflikte in der Weltpolitik.* München: Beck.

Röhrich, W. (2010). *Rückkehr der Kulturen: die neuen Mächte in der Weltpolitik.* Baden-Baden: Nomos.

Rosenfeld, A. H. (2013). *Resurgent Antisemitism: Global perspectives.* Bloomington, IN: Indiana University Press.

Rubin, B. (1998). The geopolitics of Middle East conflict and crisis. *Middle East Review of International Affairs, 2*(3), 40–45.

Rubin, B., & Rubin, J. C. (2004). *Anti-American terrorism and the Middle East: A documentary reader*. Oxford: Oxford University Press.

Rudolph, S H., & Piscatori, J. P. (Eds.). (1997). *Transnational religion and fading states*. Boulder, CO: Westview Press.

Runciman, D. (2015). *The confidence trap: A history of democracy in crisis from World War I to the present* (Second printing, first paperback printing, with a new afterword by the author, 2015). Princeton, NJ: Princeton University Press.

Sacks, J. (1998). Morals and markets: Seventh annual IEA Hayek Memorial Lecture given in London on Tuesday, 2 June 1998). London: Institute of Economic Affairs, 1999.

Sacks, J. (2003). *The dignity of difference: How to avoid the clash of civilizations*. New York: Continuum.

Sacks, J. (2005). *To heal a fractured world: The ethics of responsibility*. Montreal: McGill-Queens University Press.

Sacks, J. (2014). *The religious other: Hostility, hospitality, and the hope of human flourishing*. Lanham, MD: Lexington Books.

Sapienza, P.; Zingales L., & Guiso L. (2006). *Does culture affect economic outcomes?* (No. w11999). National Bureau of Economic Research.

Scannone, J. C. (2016). Pope Francis and the theology of the people. *Theological Studies, 77*(1), 118–135.

Sengupta, S. (2015, September 30). Refugee crisis in Europe prompts Western engagement in Syria. *New York Times*.

Shelledy, R. B. (2004). The Vatican's role in global politics. *SAIS Review of International Affairs, 24*(2), 149–162.

Sigmund, P. E. (1987). The Catholic tradition and modern democracy. *The Review of Politics, 49*(04), 530–548.

Silver, B. D., & Dowley, K. M. (2000). Measuring political culture in multiethnic societies reaggregating the *World Values Survey*. *Comparative Political Studies, 33*(4), 517–550.

SPSS (IBM-SPSS). (2007). *Statistical package for the social sciences*. User Guide. Version 14, August 2007.

Tausch, A. (2011). El Papa ¿Cuántas Divisiones Tiene? Sondeo Global del Catolicismo Mundial Según el '*World Values Survey*' y el '*European Social Survey*'. E-Book N° 49 Centro Argentino de Estudios Internacionales (in Spanish) [English Title: 'The Pope—How Many Divisions Does He Have?' a First Global Survey of World Catholicism Based on the '*World Values Survey*' and the '*European Social Survey*']. Download April 10, 2019, from http://www.caei.com.ar/es/irebooks.htm

Tausch, A. (2013, Fall). A look at international survey data about Arab opinion. *Middle East Review of International Affairs, 17*(3).

Tausch, A. (2014, Fall). The new global Antisemitism: Implications from the recent Adl-100 data. *Middle East Review of International Affairs, 18*(3).

Tausch, A. (2015a). *Documentation for books and articles*. Download April 10, 2019, from http://uibk.academia.edu/ArnoTausch/Documentation-for-books-and-articles

Tausch, A. (2015b, Spring). Estimates on the global threat of Islamic state terrorism in the face of the 2015 Paris and Copenhagen attacks. *Middle East Review of International Affairs, 19*(1).

Tausch, A. (2015c). Europe's refugee crisis. Zur aktuellen politischen Ökonomie von Migration, Asyl und Integration in Europa. (Europe's Refugee Crisis. On the Current Political Economy of Migration, Asylum and Integration in Europe), October 22, 2015. Download April 10, 2019, from SSRN http://ssrn.com/abstract=2677645 or https://doi.org/10.2139/ssrn.2677645

Tausch, A. (2015d, Spring). Further insight into global and Arab Muslim opinion structures: Statistical reflections on the 2013 Pew Report "The World's Muslims". *Middle East Review of International Affairs, 18*(1).

Tausch, A. (2016a, September). Islamism and Antisemitism. Preliminary evidence on their relationship from cross-national opinion data. *Social Evolution and History, 15*(2), 50–99 (Uchitel

Publishing House, Moscow), and *Journal of Globalization Studies*, 7, 2, November 2016: 137–170 (Uchitel Publishing House, Moscow).

Tausch, A. (2016b). Muslim immigration continues to divide Europe: A quantitative analysis of *European Social Survey* Data. *Middle East Review of International Affairs, 20*(2).

Tausch, A. (2016c). The civic culture of the Arab world: A comparative analysis based on *World Values Survey* data. *Middle East Review of International Affairs*, Rubin Center, Research in International Affairs, IDC Herzliya, Israel, (April 2016). Download April 10, 2019, from https://papers.ssrn.com/sol3/papers.cfm?abstract_id=2827232

Tausch, A. (2017a). Global Catholicism in the age of mass migration and the rise of populism: Comparative analyses, based on recent *World Values Survey* and *European Social Survey* Data (September 20, 2017). Download April 10, 2019, from SSRN: https://papers.ssrn.com/sol3/papers.cfm?abstract_id=2875289

Tausch, A. (2017b). *Occidentalism, terrorism, and the Shari'a State: New multivariate perspectives on Islamism based on International Survey Data* (January 12, 2017). Download April 10, 2019, from SSRN: https://ssrn.com/abstract=2731640 or https://doi.org/10.2139/ssrn.2731640

Tausch, A., & Heshmati, A. (2013). *Globalization, the human condition, and sustainable development in the twenty-first century: Cross-national perspectives and European implications*. London: Anthem Press.

Tausch, A., & Heshmati, A. (2016). Islamism and gender relations in the Muslim world as reflected in recent *World Values Survey* Data (IZA Discussion Paper No. 9672). Download April 10, 2019, from SSRN: http://ssrn.com/abstract=2725033

Tausch, A., & Moaddel, M. (2009). *What 1.3 billion Muslims really think. An answer to a recent Gallup study, based on the 'World Values Survey'*. Hauppauge, NY: Nova Science.

Tausch, A., Heshmati, A., & Karoui, H. (2014). *The political algebra of global value change: General models and implications for the Muslim world*. Hauppauge, NY: Nova Science.

Tessler, M. (2015). *Islam and politics in the Middle East: Explaining the views of ordinary citizens*. Bloomington, IN: Indiana University Press.

Todorov, T. (2014). *The inner enemies of democracy*. Cambridge: Polity.

Toft, M. D., Philpott, D., & Shah, T. S. (2011). *God's century: Resurgent religion and global politics*. W. W. Norton.

UNDP. (2014). *Human development report*. New York: Oxford University Press.

UNDP. (2017a). *Human development data (1990–2015)*. Download April 10, 2019, from http://hdr.undp.org/en/data

UNDP. (2017b). *Human development report*. New York: Oxford University Press.

Valkenberg, P., & Cirelli, A. (2016). *Nostra Aetate: Celebrating 50 Years of the Catholic Church's dialogue with Jews and Muslims*. Washington, DC: Catholic University of America Press.

Valuer, I. (1971). The Roman Catholic church: A transnational actor. *International Organization, 25*(03), 479–502.

von Bieberstein, J. R. (1977). The story of the Jewish-Masonic conspiracy, 1776–1945. *Patterns of Prejudice, 11*(6), 1–21.

Wallstreet Journal. (2015). *Immigration and Islam: Europe's crisis of faith*. Download April 10, 2019, from http://www.wsj.com/articles/europe-immigration-and-islam-europes-crisis-of-faith-1421450060

Ward, J. M. (2013). *Priest, politician, collaborator: Jozef Tiso and the making of fascist Slovakia*. Ithaca, NY: Cornell University Press.

Weigel, G. (2001). *Witness to hope: The biography of Pope John Paul II*. New York: Harper Collins.

Weigel, G. (2010). *The end and the beginning: Pope John Paul II – The victory of freedom, the Last Years, the legacy*. New York: Image.

Wejnert, B. (2014). *Diffusion of democracy: The past and future of global democracy*. New York: Cambridge University Press.

Weltalmanach, F. (2013). *Der Fischer Weltalmanach*. Frankfurt am Main: Fischer.

Whitehead, L. (1996). *The international dimensions of democratization: Europe and the Americas.* New York: Oxford University Press.

Wills, G. (2016). *The future of the Catholic church with Pope Francis.* New York: Penguin Books.

Wippermann, W. (1983). *Europäischer Faschismus im Vergleich (1922–1982).* Frankfurt am Main: Suhrkamp.

Wistrich, R. S. (1991). *Antisemitism: The longest hatred.* New York: Pantheon Books.

Wistrich, R. S. (2004). Anti-Zionism and anti-Semitism. *Jewish Political Studies Review, 2004,* 27–31.

Wistrich, R. S. (2007). *Anti-Semitism and multiculturalism: The uneasy connection.* Vidal Sassoon International Center for the Study of Anti-Semitism, The Hebrew University of Jerusalem.

Wistrich, R. S. (2010). *A lethal obsession: Antisemitism from antiquity to the global Jihad.* New York: Random House.

World Bank. (2017). *World bank open data.* Washington, DC: World Bank: data.worldbank.org.

World Values Survey. (2017). Download April 10, 2019, from http://www.worldvaluessurvey.org/wvs.jsp

Wright, C. F. (2015). Why do states adopt liberal immigration policies? The policymaking dynamics of skilled visa reform in Australia. *Journal of Ethnic and Migration Studies, 41*(2), 306–328.

Ye'or, B. (2005). *Eurabia: The Euro-Arab axis.* Madison, NJ: Fairleigh Dickinson University Press.

Yeşilada, B. A., & Noordijk, P. (2010). Changing values in Turkey: Religiosity and tolerance in comparative perspective. *Turkish Studies, 11*(1), 9–27.

Zak, P. J., & Knack, S. (2001). Trust and growth. *The economic Journal, 111*(470), 295–321.

Zhirkov, K., Verkuyten, M., & Weesie, J. (2014). Perceptions of world politics and support for terrorism among Muslims: Evidence from Muslim countries and Western Europe. *Conflict Management and Peace Science, 31*(5), 481–501.

Zussman, A (2014). The effect of political violence on religiosity. *Journal of Economic Behavior, & Organization, 104*(2014), 64–83.

Chapter 4
Global Catholicism, Civil Society, Democracy, and Mass Migration

Introduction

The current leadership of the Roman Catholic Church, headed by Pope Francis, takes an especially liberal and conciliatory view of migration and refugee issues (Kasper 2015; Scanone 2016), which is in stark contrast to the restrictive attitudes taken by populist politicians like Mr. Donald Trump in America or the current Hungarian Prime Minister Viktor Orban in Europe. Do Roman Catholics, practicing their faith, today follow the advice of their Church leaders on issues of migration and xenophobia, and is the Roman Catholic Church really a bastion of the democratic center in the West?

In this chapter, we would like to reflect then in a detached and empirical way on the role of the active, global Catholics in the formation of global values, using advanced methods of comparative social science research. We are not interested here in the question of which asylum and migration policies are correct or which path should be followed in this respect by the developed, rich, Western democracies. We are only interested in what the active Roman Catholics—in comparison with overall society—think about the most pressing issues of our time, including migration. So, the question resembles the old question *how many divisions the Pope has?* by the Soviet dictator Joseph Stalin.[1] Again, the present chapter is thus well within a large and growing tradition to study *real existing* Catholicism in an empirical social scientific framework, mentioned earlier. Global secularization trends notwithstanding the Roman Catholic Church still command not only the fellowship of more than 1.3 billion global citizens,[2] but it also continues to be a highly significant actor in international relations. Today, important studies on the Church do not exclude the

---

[1]On the words used by Joseph Stalin, see Tausch (2011).

[2]http://www.nationmaster.com/; http://www.catholic-hierarchy.org/; http://www.pewforum.org/2013/02/13/the-global-catholic-population/; http://www.bbc.com/news/world-21443313 (Download April 10, 2019).

© Springer Nature Switzerland AG 2020
A. Tausch, S. Obirek, *Global Catholicism, Tolerance and the Open Society*,
https://doi.org/10.1007/978-3-030-23239-9_4

Roman Catholic Papacy (Gillis 2016), nor the overall role of the Roman Catholic Church in international relations (Napolitano 2015).

Needless to say that, in view of the current global migration and political processes, which suggest a sharp polarization in the Western countries on the issues of migration, such solid social scientific information is ever more necessary.

There are also immediate and pressing current world affairs reasons suggesting that it is time to write such an analysis. In this chapter, we share the realist hypothesis of an important contemporary Jewish thinker, Rabbi Pinchas Goldschmidt, president of the Conference of European Rabbis, about two trains of extremism in the West now about to collide. What is to be understood by this?

> Speaking to the European Parliament [...], Rabbi Pinchas Goldschmidt said that Jews in Europe feel as if they are standing on a train track with two "trains coming at each other with ever increasing speed." "One train is the train of radical Islam and Islamic terrorism... The other train is the Antisemitism of old Europe, the extreme right," Goldschmidt said [...] the recent terror wave has made the public realize there is an "existential problem for the very fabric of Europe." A [...] unit should be created to protect the outer borders of the EU to "rein in the waves of millions of immigrants ... flooding Europe and threatening the future character of the European continent," he said. In order to do so, Goldschmidt highlighted the need to "integrate them into the European value system." Making an explicit effort to distance himself from anti-Islamic rhetoric common among Europe's far-right parties, Goldschmidt emphasized that "Islam is not our enemy. The moderate Muslims are the victims of radical Islam like we Jews are and every other European is."[3]

Where do global and where do European Roman Catholics really stand in this context regardless of what the Church officially pronounces in its *magisterium*?[4]

Background: Studying Catholicism in the Age of Populism

As in Chap. 3, the availability of systematic and comparative opinion surveys over time under the auspices of leading representatives of the social science research community, featuring the global and/or the European populations with a fairly constant questionnaire for several decades now, also made possible the empirical study of this chapter. The original data were again made freely available to the global scientific publics and render themselves for systematic, multivariate analysis of opinion structures on the basis of the original anonymous interview data.[5] Our data, as in Chap. 3, are mainly from two sets of such reliable and regularly repeated global opinion surveys: the *World Values Survey* (*WVS*) and the *European Social Survey* (*ESS*).

---

[3]http://www.haaretz.com/world-news/europe/1.745507 (Download April 10, 2019).

[4]The body of official declarations, like papal ex cathedra pronouncements and papal encyclicals but also episcopal letters by bishops, etc.

[5]http://www.worldvaluessurvey.org/wvs.jsp and http://www.europeansocialsurvey.org/ (Download April 10, 2019).

The *World Values Survey* (*WVS*) was already described at length in Chap. 3 of this work. We also recall here that representative data from the *European Social Survey* (*ESS*) for 2014 are available from Austria, Belgium, Czech Republic, Denmark, Estonia, Finland, France, Germany, Ireland, the Netherlands, Norway, Poland, Slovenia, Sweden, and Switzerland. They are based on more than 28,000 representative interviews in these countries. Earlier ESS data also included many more additional countries, including Ukraine and Israel.

An important starting point in the choice of the values under study here is that ever since the end of Communism in Eastern Europe and the Soviet Union, there were scholars in the West who thought that now the definitive hour of the triumph of democracy and the market economy has arrived (Fukuyama 2006). Many saw—with justification—the positive role played by the Roman Catholic Church in the victory of democracy and the market economy in Eastern Europe in the time period between 1989 and 1991 (Novak 1984, 1991a, b; Weigel 2010).

Classical political science research on the *civic culture* of countries and even entire global cultures teaches us important lessons today. Here, one encounters the full legacy of the twentieth-century modern political scientist Gabriel Abraham Almond (1911–2002): with his deep understanding of the normative aspects of human society, he perhaps came closest to capturing the dilemmas of Western and non-Western and non-Muslim and Muslim contemporary societies of today, as they emerge from the empirical data. He did so especially by pointing out the many adverse trends in the civic culture in leading Western democracies themselves brought about by the current contemporary erosion of social capital and a declining civic engagement and civic trust (Almond 1996). As causes of this contemporary decline in civic engagement, Almond cites in reference to the work of the political scientist Robert D. Putnam the weakening of the family (Putnam 1993). A second major factor that Almond cites is the transformation of leisure by the electronic media. This tidal wave of value decay has begun to affect the Catholic communities in Africa, Asia, Latin America, and Oceania as well. The civic culture approach presupposes that a political culture congruent with a stable democracy involves a high degree of consensus concerning the legitimacy of democratic institutions and the content of public policy (for a survey of the relevant literature, see Tausch 2016a).

Inglehart by contrast developed an interpretation of global value change that rests on a well-known two-dimensional scale of global values and global value change. It is based on the statistical technique of factor analysis of up to some 20 key *World Values Survey* variables. The two Inglehart dimensions are (1) the traditional/secular-rational dimension and (2) the survival/self-expression dimension. These two dimensions explain more than 70% of the cross-national variance in a factor analysis of ten indicators, and each of these dimensions is strongly correlated with scores of other important variables. For Inglehart and Baker (2000), all of the preindustrial societies show relatively low levels of tolerance for abortion, divorce, and homosexuality; tend to emphasize male dominance in economic and political life, deference to parental authority, and the importance of family life; are relatively authoritarian; and mostly place strong emphasis on religion. Advanced industrial societies tend to have the opposite characteristics (Tausch et al. 2014).

Inglehart, therefore, predicted a more or less generalized global increase in human security in parallel with the gradual waning of the religious phenomenon in the majority of countries across the globe. Inglehart spells out what tendencies are brought about by the waning of the religious element in advanced Western democracies: higher levels of tolerance for abortion, divorce, and homosexuality; the erosion of parental authority; the decrease of the importance of family life, etc. When survival is uncertain, cultural diversity seems threatening. When there isn't *enough to go around*, foreigners are seen as dangerous outsiders who may take away one's sustenance. People cling to traditional gender roles and sexual norms and emphasize absolute rules and familiar norms in an attempt to maximize predictability in an uncertain world. Conversely, when survival begins to be taken for granted, ethnic and cultural diversity become increasingly acceptable—indeed, beyond a certain point, diversity is not only tolerated, but it may even be positively valued because it is seen as interesting and stimulating. In advanced industrial societies, people seek out foreign restaurants to taste new cuisines; they pay large sums of money and travel long distances to experience exotic cultures. Changing gender roles and sexual norms no longer seem threatening. Recalculating results from different waves of the *World Values Survey* data, Tausch et al. (2014) however claim to have discovered a large-scale implosion of the self-expression values, deemed by Inglehart and his followers to be so vital for the future of democracy in the wake of the global economic crisis of 2008. Arguing in the framework of Inglehart's theory, Tausch et al. (2014) would imply that now setbacks in the further development of an Open Society in leading Western countries could happen more frequently.

In view of the implosion of trust by majority of populations in Western democracies in their respective political systems, we are inclined to mention here as well Ronald Inglehart's most recent theory of *cultural evolution* (Inglehart 2018). In this book, Inglehart still argues that people's values and behavior are shaped by the degree to which survival is secure, repeating his argument that it was precarious for most of history, which encouraged heavy emphasis on group solidarity, rejection of outsiders, and obedience to strong leaders. Still, high levels of existential security encourage openness to change, diversity, and new ideas. The unprecedented prosperity and security of the postwar era brought cultural change, the environmentalist movement, and the spread of democracy. But, Inglehart now admits, in recent decades, diminishing job security and rising inequality have led to an authoritarian reaction. In the perspective of Inglehart's theory, growing unease with *multiculturalism* and *migration* coincides with rising inequality in many countries of the Western world.[6]

---

[6]For most recent time series data about inequality, see University of Texas Inequality Project, available at https://utip.lbj.utexas.edu/data.html (Download April 10, 2019).

Sociologists, working with the unique comparative and longitudinal opinion survey data from the *World Values Survey*, have discovered that there are pretty constant and long-term patterns of change in the direction of secularization, which also affect the predominantly Roman Catholic countries (Inglehart 2006; Inglehart and Norris 2003; Norris and Inglehart 2011). Inglehart and his associates firmly believed and still believe that the ability of the Roman Catholic hierarchy to tell people how to live their lives is declining steadily.[7] This opinion was shared among others also by the late Jesuit father and professor of sociology at Innsbruck University, Julius Morel (1927–2003; Morel 1972, 1977, 1986, 1997, 1998, 2003), who in many ways must be regarded as the most important sociologist of religion among the influential Catholic order of the Jesuits of the twentieth century.

For Inglehart, such phenomena as bribery, corruption, tax evasion, cheating the state to get government benefits for which one wouldn't be entitled, but also the countervailing healthy activism of citizens in volunteer organizations, already described by Etzioni (1998), hardly exist, while the rich data base of the *World Values Survey* provides ample evidence about these phenomena and their occurrence in world societies. The economics profession, that is, mathematical, quantitative economics, already began to make large-scale use of the *World Values Survey* data, integrating the *WVS* country-level results into international economic growth accounting (Alesina and Guiliano 2013; Barro and McCleary 2003). Thus, the art of *growth accounting* received a new and important input (Barro 1991, 1998, 2004, 2012; Barro and Sala-i-Martin 1992, 2003; Guiso et al. 2003). Following Hayek, we think that values like hard work—which brings success—and competition, which is the essence of a free market economy together with the private ownership of business, play an overwhelming role in the twenty-first-century capitalism and cannot be overlooked in empirical global value research.

As highlighted earlier, the issue of immigration now polarizes more and more opinions in the developed Western democracies. This sharp polarization in Germany and other European countries about the future of immigration policy gathered pace especially since Chancellor Angela Merkel's policy of invitation and welcoming refugees in late summer 2015 (Carrera et al. 2015; Park 2015; Sengupta 2015; Tausch 2015a, b).[8] Also, in other Western countries, there seems to be a strong backlash against liberal immigration policy. Prominent examples would be the case of the United States and Australia (Albertson and Gadarian 2016; Fry 2016; Giroux 2016; Hogan and Haltinner 2015; Hollifield et al. 2014; Inglehart and Norris 2016; Oates and Moe 2016; Wright 2015). For the first time since 1945, the chance is real that far-right wing parties and candidates could gain power at the ballot boxes in many Western countries, if they did not do so already. Asylum and migration greatly

---

[7]http://ur.umich.edu/0405/Apr11_05/11.shtml (Download April 10, 2019).

[8]http://ec.europa.eu/echo/refugee-crisis_en; https://www.theguardian.com/world/2016/sep/07/angela-merkel-defends-german-immigration-policy-elections-afd; http://www.ibtimes.com/germany-wants-christian-migrants-not-muslims-angela-merkels-party-wants-refugees-2413054; https://www.theguardian.com/world/2016/aug/17/refugees-did-not-bring-terrorism-to-germany-says-angela-merkel (Download April 10, 2019).

polarize the political landscape everywhere. In a way, Roman Catholic liberalism vis-à-vis mass immigration might be even a convenient counterweight to the otherwise unhalted tendencies of secularization in the rich countries (Norris and Inglehart 2011, 2015).

Further developing the argument, already hinted at in Chap. 3, one can say: the data contained in the recent PEW Study on Global Catholicism make clear that the days of the European Church and Catholic Europe are definitively over.[9] In 1910, Catholics comprised about half (48%) of all Christians and 17% of the world's total population. A century later, Catholics still comprise about half (50%) of Christians worldwide and 16% of the total global population. But in 1910, Europe was home to about two-thirds of all global Roman Catholics, and nearly nine-in-ten lived either in Europe (65%) or in Latin America (24%). By 2010, by contrast, only about a quarter of all Catholics (24%) lived in Europe. The largest share (39%) lived in Latin America and the Caribbean.

Pope Francis'[10] open and liberal positions on the European refugee crisis (Berryman 2016; de Maio et al. 2016; Francis 2014; Wills 2016) are clear and to be seen in the framework of the current Pontiff's overall commitment to a moderate non-Marxist and nonviolent version of Latin American liberation theology (Petrella 2004). As it is well known:

> Pope Francis criticized the "self interests" prompting European Union leaders to enforce stringent immigration policies that shut out desperate refugees during his acceptance speech for the Charlemagne Prize—an award to promote European unification [. . .]

> "I dream of a Europe where being a migrant is not a crime, but a summons to a greater commitment on behalf of the dignity of every human being," Francis said. "I dream of a Europe that promotes and protects the rights of everyone, without neglecting its duties toward all. I dream of a Europe of which it will not be said that its commitment to human rights was its last utopia."

The clash with the majority of the world's right-wing politicians, often speaking about *Christian Europe* or *Christian West*, could not be greater. Viktor Orban, the Hungarian Prime Minister and the most vociferous critic of Chancellor Angela Merkel's *open door* refugee policy, went on the record of saying[11] that Europe is in the grip of madness over immigration and refugees and argued that he was defending European Christianity against a Muslim influx. "Everything which is now taking place before our eyes threatens to have explosive consequences for the whole of Europe," Orban wrote in Germany's *Frankfurter Allgemeine Zeitung*. His argument is simply that "Europe's response [to the global refugee crisis] is madness. We must acknowledge that the European Union's misguided immigration policy is

---

[9]http://www.pewforum.org/2013/02/13/the-global-catholic-population/

[10]https://thinkprogress.org/in-powerful-speech-pope-francis-condemns-eu-leaders-efforts-to-shut-out-refugees-c990c573a25e#.wvhfpdato (Download April 10, 2019).

[11]https://www.theguardian.com/world/2015/sep/03/migration-crisis-hungary-pm-victor-orban-europe-response-madness (Download April 10, 2019).

responsible for this situation."[12] He added: "Those arriving have been raised in another religion, and represent a radically different culture. Most of them are not Christians, but Muslims." "This is an important question, because Europe and European identity is rooted in Christianity." And here, the true clash of worldviews of the Pope also with Republican President Elect Donald Trump could not be sharper: Pope Francis was even questioning Trump's *Christianity*, rebuking him on his views on Islam and violence, and Donald Trump called the Pope's remarks as *disgraceful.*[13]

Considering the current polarization in Europe on immigration policy (Tausch 2016a, b), it is entirely conceivable that the old structure of the European political party systems, dominated for decades by Christian democratic, social democratic, liberal, and green parties, has ultimately been transformed into a structure dominated by a sharp polarization between pro- and anti-immigration parties. Migration policy variables play a major role in our empirical analyses of the *European Social Survey* data. It is entirely feasible that the empirical data will show that Roman Catholic rank and file active Church members are as deeply divided on the issues of immigration as the rest of society.

Data and Methods in Studying Catholicism and the Open Society

The methodology of this chapter, resembling in many ways the methodology of Chap. 3, was determined by the following points:

1. *Basic literature*: As in Chap. 3, the methodological guiding post is the firmly established methodology of *World Values Survey*-based comparative opinion research (Davidov et al. 2008; Inglehart 2006; Norris and Inglehart 2015; Tausch et al. 2014).
2. *Comparative Catholicism research*: The aim is to study Roman Catholicism in the framework of comparative and opinion survey-based political science (Basáñez and Inglehart 2016; Brenner 2016; Hanson 2014; Knippenberg 2015; Manuel et al. 2006; Norris and Inglehart 2015).
3. *Ecumenical religion studies*: We recognize the importance of theologically and social scientifically well-founded comparisons of global religions and civilizations in the growing international scientific tradition of ecumenical religion studies (Juergensmeyer 2000, 2011; Küng 1997, 2002; Lenoir and Tardan-

---

[12]https://www.theguardian.com/world/2015/sep/03/migration-crisis-hungary-pm-victor-orban-europe-response-madness (Download April 10, 2019).

[13]https://www.theguardian.com/us-news/2016/feb/18/donald-trump-pope-francis-christian-wall-mexico-border and http://time.com/4436759/pope-francis-trump-radical-islam/ (Download April 10, 2019).

Masquelier 1997; Lenoir 2008; Röhrich 2004, 2010; Sacks 1998, 2003, 2005, 2014) but prefer to rely on sociological data.

4. *IBM-SPSS XXIV analysis of open individual-level data*: As in Chap. 3, our statistical calculations were again performed by the routine and standard IBM-SPSS statistical program (IBM-SPSS XXIV),[14] available at many academic research centers around the world.

5. *Factor analysis*: Our methodology of evaluating the global opinion survey data is based on recent advances in mathematical statistical factor analysis (Basilevsky 2009; Cattell 2012; Hedges and Olkin 2014; Kline 2014; McDonald 2014; Mulaik 2009; Tausch et al. 2014; Thompson 2004). Factor analysis allows to investigate the underlying structures of the relationships between the variables.

6. *Oblique factor rotation*: We used oblique rotation of the factors, underlying the correlation matrix (Abdi 2003; Browne 2001; Dunlap and York 2008; Kim 2010). The IBM-SPSS routine chosen in this context was the so-called *promax* rotation of factors (Basáñez et al. 2014; Braithwaite and Law 1985; Browne 2001; Fabrigar et al. 1999; Minkov 2014; Suhr 2012; Yeşilada and Noordijk 2010). which in many ways must be considered to be the best-suited rotation of factors in the context of our research.[15]

7. *Factor scores*: We analyzed the country data, resulting from factor analysis (factor scores) (see also Tausch et al. 2014, furthermore Clauß and Ebner 1970; Dien et al. 2005; Dziuban and Shirkey 1974; Finch 2006; Gorsuch 1983; Hotelling 1933; Jolliffe 2002; Kieffer 1998; McLeod et al. 2001; Rummel 1970; Tabachnick and Fidell 2001).

8. *Who are the active Roman Catholics?* We evaluated the democratic civil society commitment of the overall population and of the practicing Roman Catholics, i.e., those Catholics who attend Sunday Mass regularly, the so-called Dominicantes.

9. *What to do with denominational comparisons?* Again, as in Chap. 3, and due to too small country sample sizes for the weekly religious service attenders of most major global denominations (i.e., like Buddhists, Hindus, Orthodox Christians, Protestants, Muslims, Buddhists, Hindus, etc.), for whom weekly religious service attendance is not as strictly prescribed as for the Roman Catholics, we used figures for monthly religious service attendances (called by us the *Mensuantes*).

10. *What to do with the secularly oriented respondents?* We introduced a category of people who at least sometimes still attend religious services over the years (called by us the more *seculars*) and the members of a religious denomination,

---

[14]https://www-01.ibm.com/software/at/analytics/spss/ (Download April 10, 2019).

[15]Older approaches often assumed that there is no correlation between the factors, best representing the underlying dimensions of the variables. But, for example, in attempting to understand the recent pro-Brexit vote in the United Kingdom, it would be ridiculous to assume that, say, there is no correlation between anti-immigration attitudes and anti-European Union attitudes.

who were really never attending religious services at all (called here the *completely distant*).

11. *Minimum of compared subsamples*: For all analyzed groups and subgroups, a minimum sample of at least 30 respondents per country had to be available in the original data sets to attempt reasonable predictions for the general or sectoral publics to be analyzed, thus keeping in line with standard traditions of empirical opinion survey research (Tausch et al. 2014).

12. *Validity*: Since both our data and the statistical methods used are available around the globe, any researcher can repeat our research exercise with the available open data and should be able to reproduce the same results as we did.

In our study using the *European Social Survey* data, we hoped to arrive at an index of nationwide European voter liberalism, based on factor analysis, and we compared this liberalism of practicing Roman Catholics with that of the overall European population. Norris and Inglehart, in their study on the problems under scrutiny here, use similar variables, but their methodological approach was different. The ESS dimensions used in our research endeavor were the following:

- Allowing immigration from poorer countries inside and outside Europe
- Allowing immigration of different race or the same race
- Allowing immigration of Gypsies, Jews, and Muslims
- Attitudes on antidiscrimination policy
- Attitudes on European integration
- Attitudes on gays and lesbians
- Attitudes on racism
- Contact with people of a different race
- Effects of immigration on the countries' culture, crime situation, and economy
- Position on the left/right political spectrum
- Religiosity

Our analysis of the *World Values Survey* data works with the following scales and data:

- Attitudes on democracy
- Attitudes on gender equality
- Background data like age, gender, state of health, feeling of happiness, and feeling of security
- Confidence in economic and political institutions
- Global citizenship
- Interest in politics
- Positions on the market economy, like competition, inequality, and private enterprise
- What is important in life
- What is justifiable and what is not justifiable
- Work ethics
- Xenophobia

The rollout of the data, freely downloaded from the *WVS* website, for this chapter was   *G:\Analyses   2016\WVS_Longitudinal_1981_2014_spss_v2015_04_18.sav.* Again, we took great care in assuring that the variable names reflect the highest numerical values in the questionnaire, and thus, they might differ from the original variable label in the *WVS*.

In the following, we shortly present our main research results, which rather caution us against the view that the Catholic global rank and file will follow the Church's substantially weakened leadership in endorsing a liberal asylum and migration policy.

Results: Catholicism and the Open Society: What We Really Know from Global and European Surveys

Result 1: Roman Catholic Dominicantes and the Open Society

We have made our full results in our electronic Appendix. In this chapter, we concentrate here on the most salient results and on key trends and tendencies, as they emerge from the results. In presenting our results, we best should remind our readers first that already Almond (1948), emphasizing the possible contribution of Christian democracy to the future of an Open Society (Popper 2012), was well aware of the challenge of democracy to the Church (Almond 1948; Burns 1990; Corrin 2002; Coughlin 2003; Glahe and Vorhies 1989; Philpott 2004; Sigmund 1987).

According to our results, the "real existing" global Catholicism, which emerges from our data[16] and our distillation of the available surveys today, can best be described by the following main tendencies:

- *48.05% of all Dominicantes in the world are in favor of strict limits in migration policy or even would like to prevent people from coming,* as indicated by the population-weighted figures from Albania, Argentina, Australia, Belarus, Bosnia, Brazil, Burkina Faso, Canada, Chile, Croatia, Czech Republic, Dominican Republic, Estonia, Finland, Germany, Ghana, Guatemala, Hungary, India, Indonesia, Italy, Japan, Latvia, Lithuania, Malaysia, Mexico, Moldova, New Zealand, Nigeria, Peru, Philippines, Poland, Puerto Rico, Romania, Rwanda, Serbia and Montenegro, Singapore, Slovakia, Slovenia, South Africa, South Korea, Spain, Sweden, Switzerland, Taiwan, Tanzania, Uganda, Ukraine, the United States, Uruguay, Venezuela, Vietnam, Zambia, and Zimbabwe, which together cover 91.08% of all *Dominicantes* in the *WVS* project.

---

[16]http://www.catholic-hierarchy.org/country/sc1.html (Download April 10, 2019).

Result 2: European Catholics Are Not the Forefront of European Tolerance: Evidence, Based on the European Social Survey

Our electronic Appendix Tables 1, 2, and 3 and electronic Appendix Graphs 1–8 now portray the results of our first factor analytical investigation. Our first factor analytical model, based on *European Social Survey* data, explains 59.41% of the total variance. It combines background variables about education and religiosity or a secular lifestyle with variables of trust and attitudes on migration. The trust variables also contain items on European integration and European institutions.

Our electronic Appendix data (Appendix Table 4.2) show the factor loadings after the *promax* rotation of principal components, which explain the underlying correlation matrix between the variables. We show how we interpret the results in terms of the processes "trust," "xenophobia," "secularism," and "European antiracism." We also document the strong correlation between these dimensions (electronic Appendix Table 4.3). They all correspond to the theoretical expectations confirming the close relationship between pro-immigration sentiments, Euro-multi-culturalism, the rejection of racism, personal multicultural experience, and the rejection of right-wing culturalism. It should be emphasized that these factors correspond to different dimensions, although they are closely correlated with each other.

Based on our factor analytical criteria, it is fair to suggest that the following Catholic *Dominicantes* political cultures are the most liberal and the most anti-liberal to be encountered in Europe (see Table 4.1). The Voter Liberalism Index is an *Eigenvalue*-weighted combination of the five-factor analytical dimensions:

- Pro-immigration
- Euro-multiculturalism
- Reject racism
- Personal multicultural experience
- No right-wing culturalism

Table 4.1 Voter liberalism in Europe

Country	Voter Liberalism Index—total population	Voter Liberalism Index—Catholic *Dominicantes*	Voter liberalism of Roman Catholic *Dominicantes* compared to the total population
Belgium	−1.6669	−2.3102	−0.6433
Austria	−1.7220	−2.7882	−1.0662
Poland	−1.3291	−2.4404	−1.1112
France	−0.5685	−1.8634	−1.2949
Germany	3.0722	1.6273	−1.4449
Ireland	−2.0655	−4.0909	−2.0254
Switzerland	0.0201	−2.5012	−2.5214
Slovenia	0.2321	−3.6861	−3.9182

Table 4.2 Liberal Catholicism in Europe

Country	Voter Liberalism Index—Catholic *Dominicantes*
Germany	1.6273
France	−1.8634
Belgium	−2.3102
Poland	−2.4404
Switzerland	−2.5012
Austria	−2.7882
Slovenia	−3.6861
Ireland	−4.0909

In not a single European country, practicing Catholics were more liberal in their attitudes on migration than overall society. Only in Germany, there was any relevant active Catholic support for liberal attitudes on migration, as measured by our index, while opposition to them was especially strong in Ireland, Slovenia, and Austria. In other words, active Catholic publics in Europe could be open to the "populist anti-immigration virus" just as their fellow Roman Catholics in the November 8, 2016, election in the United States (Table 4.2).[17]

The factor scores for the Index components are as follows (Tables 4.3 and 4.4):

Result 3: The Global Evidence Based on the World Values Survey also Indicate that Only in a Limited Number of Countries, Catholic Dominicantes Are at the Forefront of a Democratic, Open Society

Our pessimistic European analysis in many ways is reflected also in our global analysis. Electronic Appendix Tables 4–10 as well as the choropleth map electronic Appendix Map 4.7 to 41 highlight the results. Limited publication space again dictates that we highlight here only the most salient results. Our analysis of the *World Values Survey* data was derived from the following factor analytical scales which are well compatible with the large social scientific literature on the *Open Society*:

1. The law-abiding society (Tyler and Darley 1999)
2. Democracy movement (Huntington 1993)
3. Climate of personal nonviolence (APA 1993)
4. Trust in institutions (Alesina and Ferrara 2000; Fukuyama 1995)
5. Happiness, good health (Post 2005)
6. No redistributive religious fundamentalism (Huntington 2000)

---

[17]https://www.pewresearch.org/fact-tank/2016/11/09/how-the-faithful-voted-a-preliminary-2016-analysis/ (Download April 10, 2019).

Table 4.3 European general publics

Country	Pro-immigration	Euro-multiculturalism	Reject racism	Personal multicultural experience	No right-wing culturalism	Voter Liberalism Index
Austria	−1.236	−0.595	−0.166	−0.109	0.385	−1.722
Belgium	−1.534	−0.162	−0.085	0.051	0.064	−1.667
France	−0.892	0.014	−0.011	0.099	0.222	−0.568
Germany	2.753	0.101	0.002	0.057	0.159	3.072
Ireland	−1.700	−0.021	−0.177	−0.031	−0.137	−2.065
Poland	−1.023	0.461	−0.203	−0.765	0.201	−1.329
Slovenia	−0.219	0.046	−0.202	0.027	0.580	0.232
Switzerland	0.111	0.030	−0.344	0.123	0.100	0.020

Table 4.4 European Catholic *Dominicantes*

Country	Pro-immigration	Euro-multiculturalism	Reject racism	Personal multicultural experience	No right-wing culturalism	Voter Liberalism Index
Austria	−1.967	−0.616	−0.125	−0.424	0.343	−2.788
Belgium	−1.406	0.021	−0.312	−0.724	0.111	−2.310
France	−1.046	−0.232	−0.354	−0.139	−0.093	−1.863
Germany	2.065	0.104	−0.159	−0.328	−0.054	1.627
Ireland	−2.864	−0.181	−0.480	−0.338	−0.227	−4.091
Poland	−1.655	0.279	−0.288	−0.926	0.150	−2.440
Slovenia	−2.690	−0.122	−0.644	−0.388	0.158	−3.686
Switzerland	−1.373	−0.073	−0.561	−0.592	0.098	−2.501

7. Accepting the market economy (Elzinga 1999; Glahe and Vorhies 1989; von Hayek 2012; Novak 1991a, b)
8. Feminism (Ferber and Nelson 2009)
9. Involvement in politics (Lipset 1959)
10. Optimism and engagement (Oishi et al. 1999)
11. No welfare mentality, acceptancy of the Calvinist work ethics (Giorgi and Marsh 1990)

Our index construction was based on the following weighting of our factor scores as suggested by the *Eigenvalues*:

1. The law-abiding society	[The violent and lawless society −4.263]
2. Democracy movement	2.574
3. Climate of personal nonviolence	[Climate of personal violence −2.260]
4. Trust in institutions	[Lack of trust in institutions −1.929]
5. Happiness, good health	[Unhappiness, poor health −1.864]
6. No redistributive religious fundamentalism	[Redistributive religious fundamentalism −1.554]
7. Accepting the market economy	[Rejecting the market economy −1.434]
8. Feminism	1.245
9. Involvement in politics	[Distance to politics −1.197]
10. Optimism and engagement	[Nihilism −1.141]
11. No welfare mentality, acceptancy of the Calvinist work ethics	[Welfare mentality, rejection of the Calvinist work ethics −1.075]

Here, we also list the "factor loadings," which have 10% or more of the variance in common with the variables of the analysis. Such a detailed listing shows that there is indeed nothing arbitrary in the naming of the factors and that they indeed correspond to the theoretical expectations of the social scientific literature, quoted earlier. Each factor has already been named according to the literature, and the signs of the loadings were reverted where it was necessary. Following Tyler and Darley (1999), we think that a society accepting lawlessness is absolutely incompatible with an Open Society. Factor 1, for example, originally had to be named as the violent and lawless society. In such a society, a great number of people feel that it is okay avoiding a fare on public transport, stealing property, claiming government benefits without proper entitlements, accepting a bribe, using violence against other people, and for a man to beat his wife. Among the countries with complete data, such a social climate is unfortunately most heavily present in South Africa, India, Philippines, Mexico, and Algeria. And it is least present in Azerbaijan, Georgia, Jordan, Yemen, and Tunisia. The Roman Catholic *Dominicantes*, most inclined to be affected by such a syndrome, are to be encountered in South Africa, Philippines, Mexico, Peru, and Lebanon, and the Roman Catholic active communities, most resistant against this syndrome of lawlessness, are located in Germany, Trinidad and Tobago, Ghana, Rwanda, and Australia.

Attempting the factor analytical measurement of an Open Society suggests that a vital component of an Open Society is a society based on nonviolence and law abidance. Thus, Factor 1 must be reverted and then can be further used for the index construction for a factor analytical measurement of the Open Society. The "law-abiding society" is a society in which people strongly reject avoiding a fare on public transport, strongly reject stealing property, refrain from claiming government benefits without proper entitlements, would never accept a bribe, would not be using violence against other people, and think it is absolutely unjustified for a man to beat his wife. Such a social climate is most present in Azerbaijan, Georgia, Jordan, Yemen, and Tunisia and least present in South Africa, India, Philippines, Mexico, and Algeria. The Roman Catholic active communities, most characterized by such a climate of the respect of the law, are to be found in Germany, Trinidad and Tobago, Ghana, Rwanda, and Australia; and the Roman Catholic *Dominicantes*, whose thinking is least characterized by this factor, are to be encountered in South Africa, Philippines, Mexico, Peru, and Lebanon.

The Law-Abiding Society

Justifiable: Avoiding a fare on public transport   −0.7960
Justifiable: Stealing property   −0.7650
Justifiable: Claiming government benefits   −0.7600
Justifiable: Someone accepting a bribe   −0.7320
Justifiable: Violence against other people   −0.5600
Justifiable: For a man to beat his wife   −0.4510

Following Huntington (1993), a "real existing" democracy movement is a vital element in any Open Society, worth its name derived from Popper (2012) and Bergson (1935). The strongest support for democracy, vital for an Open Society, rests on three elements: an understanding of democracy as an institution for the furthering of civil rights to protect people's liberty against oppression, an institution in which people choose their leaders in free elections, and democracy as a guarantee that women have the same rights as men.

Democracy Movement

Democracy: Civil rights protect people's liberty against oppression   +0.7530
Democracy: People choose their leaders in free elections   +0.7380
Democracy: Women have the same rights as men   +0.7040
Democracy: Governments tax the rich and subsidize the poor   +0.4930
Importance of democracy   +0.4930
Democracy: The state makes people's incomes equal   +0.4480

Following the APA study, 1993, a climate of personal nonviolence must be deemed as a further, important component of an Open Society. It implies the rejection of domestic violence against women and children and the rejection of the use of violence against other people, and the climate of personal nonviolence also implies the rejection of taking bribes and stealing property.

Climate of Personal Nonviolence

Justifiable: For a man to beat his wife	−0.8460
Justifiable: Parents beating children	−0.7950
Justifiable: Violence against other people	−0.7860
Justifiable: Someone accepting a bribe	−0.6040
Justifiable: Stealing property	−0.5870

Trust in institutions (Alesina and Ferrara 2000; Fukuyama 1995) plays a further, vital role in the support of an Open Society. The climate of trust, vital for an Open Society, is characterized according to the empirics of the *World Values Survey* data and by trust in the government, the police, and the press and also by trust in the international order, ruling the world since 1945, symbolized by the United Nations.

Trust in Institutions

No confidence: The Government	−0.7760
No confidence: The Police	−0.7170
No confidence: The Press	−0.7150
No confidence: The United Nations	−0.6370

Also, happiness and good health (Post 2005) must be a part of the picture of the underlying factors, supporting an Open Society. A climate of trust, important for an Open Society, also implies that the population in a country shares a feeling of care for the state of health, a feeling of happiness, and commitment to global citizenship. Security in the neighborhood is guaranteed, and all generations participate in that Open Society.

Happiness, Good Health

State of health (bad) (subjective)	−0.7710
Feeling of unhappiness	−0.7160
Age	−0.4400
I don't see myself as a world citizen	−0.4050
Insecurity in neighborhood	−0.3640

Religious fundamentalism (Huntington 2000) is one of the great dangers facing the future of the Open Society around the globe. The factor "no redistributive religious fundamentalism" as a basic tenet of an Open Society also neatly rejects some of the basic assumptions of "liberation theologies" of various denominations. This factor and acceptancy of the market economy (Elzinga 1999; Glahe and Vorhies 1989; von Hayek 2012; Novak 1991a, b) might be considered perhaps to be the most controversial element in our index construction. But neoliberal critics of "liberation theologies" are correct in maintaining that basic tenets of such a theology are not very well compatible with a long-run stable democracy and a long-run stable market economy. What does the evidence of the *World Values Survey* tell us? According to the empirics of global surveys, the belief in the importance of religion is combined with the understanding of democracy as a redistributive state, making people's income equal, and the taxation of the rich and the subsidy of the poor. So far, so good: but at the same time, such "religious socialism" is combined with a call for religious authorities to interpret the laws, which contradicts the very essence of a secular, liberal, Western democracy.

No Redistributive Religious Fundamentalism

Democracy: Religious authorities interpret the laws	−0.6870
Not important in life: Religion	+0.5960
Democracy: The state makes people's incomes equal	−0.4600
Democracy: Governments tax the rich and subsidize the poor	−0.3890

We already said that accepting the market economy (Elzinga 1999; Glahe and Vorhies 1989; von Hayek 2012; Novak 1991a, b) is another important element in the patterns of supporting opinions, vital for an Open Society. This factor combines the belief that competition is good, that hard work brings success, and that private ownership and not state ownership is necessary.

Accepting the Market Economy

Competition [good or] harmful	−0.7600
Hard work does not bring success	−0.7330
[Private vs] state ownership of business	−0.3530

Feminism (Ferber and Nelson 2009) is another important element in the structures making up the landscape of a free and open society. Important indicators of feminism in the *World Values Survey* data base are the belief that men and women can be equally good political leaders and that today a university education is equally important for a young man and a young woman.

Feminism

Reject: Men make better political leaders than women do	+0.7170
University is not more important for a boy than for a girl	+0.6820
Gender (female)	+0.5550

Ever since the writings of Seymour Martin Lipset (Lipset 1959), involvement in politics has been thought to be an important element in the support structure of the Open Society. According to the *World Values Survey* data base, involvement in politics above all means that people are interested in politics and that politics is important in life.

Involvement in Politics

No interest in politics	−0.8490
Not important in life: Politics	−0.8370

Optimism and engagement (Oishi et al. 1999) and the rejection of nihilism are additional further and important inputs in the general framework of support for an Open Society. According to the *World Values Survey* data base, optimism and engagement consists, above all, in the shared belief that friends, leisure time, work, and the family are all important elements in life.

Optimism and Engagement

Not important in life: Friends	−0.6900
Not important in life: Leisure time	−0.6690
Not important in life: Work	−0.4950
Not important in life: Family	−0.4780

No welfare mentality, acceptancy of the Calvinist work ethics (Giorgi and Marsh 1990) is the last component in our index construction for an Open Society Index. In a nutshell, the empirics of the factor loadings of this factor neatly go back to the sociology of Max Weber (Weber 1922/1964) and are to be found today among leading political proponents of the neoliberal agenda—from Republicanism in the United States to the Conservative Party in the United Kingdom or, for that matter, Likud in Israel: accepting larger income differences, importance of work and religion, and the rejection of the redistributive state.

No Welfare Mentality, Acceptancy of the Calvinist Work Ethics

Supporting larger income differences	+0.6770
Not important in life: Work	−0.4670
Not important in life: Religion	−0.4000
Democracy: The state makes people's incomes equal	−0.3950

Combining these components by the weight of their *Eigenvalues* in factor analysis, this yielded the following summarizing maps (Maps 4.1, 4.2 and 4.3):

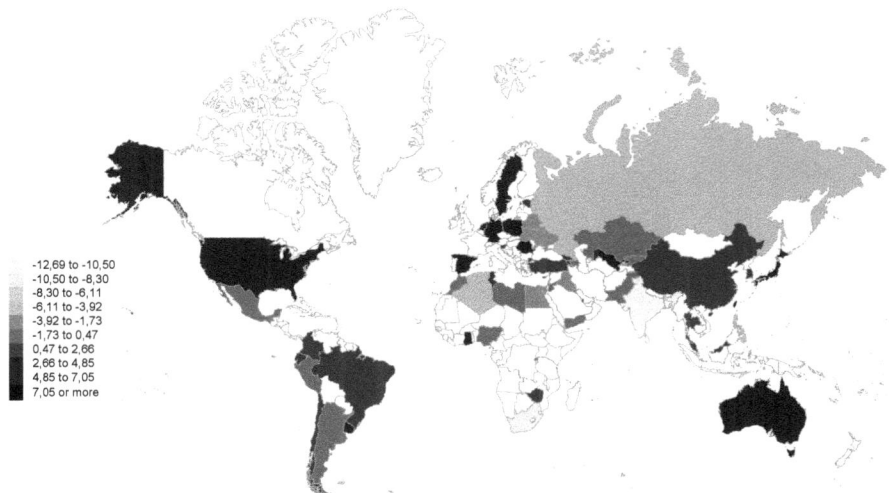

-12,69 to -10,50
-10,50 to -8,30
-8,30 to -6,11
-6,11 to -3,92
-3,92 to -1,73
-1,73 to 0,47
0,47 to 2,66
2,66 to 4,85
4,85 to 7,05
7,05 or more

Map 4.1 Overall Civil Society Index. Best: Sweden, Trinidad and Tobago, Australia, Japan, and the Netherlands. Worst: India, South Africa, Philippines, Lebanon, and Russia

Map 4.2 Overall Catholic Civil Society Index. Best: Trinidad and Tobago, Ghana, Australia, Germany, and the United States. Worst: South Africa, Philippines, Lebanon, Belarus, and Peru

Map 4.3 Catholicism—lighthouse of the world or democratic deficits? (data from Maps 4.1 and 4.2 compared). Best: Ukraine, Ghana, Trinidad and Tobago, Chile, and Lebanon. Worst: South Africa, Spain, Peru, Belarus, and Slovenia

Table 4.5 The successful and less Open Society-oriented Catholic civil societies on a global scale

Country/ region	Overall Civil Society Index— *Dominicantes*	Overall Civil Society Index	Catholicism—lighthouse of civil society?
Ukraine	−1.005	−3.060	2.055
Ghana	6.808	4.760	2.048
Trinidad and Tobago	7.783	5.751	2.032
Chile	2.596	1.312	1.284
Lebanon	−4.381	−5.183	0.801
Germany	5.004	4.274	0.730
Colombia	1.327	0.631	0.696
Brazil	2.419	1.752	0.667
Mexico	−0.728	−0.947	0.220
Ecuador	1.061	0.945	0.116
Rwanda	0.511	0.402	0.109
The United States	3.294	3.197	0.097
Poland	2.89	2.802	0.088
Philippines	−5.763	−5.774	0.011
Singapore	−1.621	−1.482	−0.139
Australia	5.325	5.487	−0.162
Argentina	0.006	0.342	−0.336
Nigeria	−0.334	0.042	−0.375
Zimbabwe	1.402	1.789	−0.387
South Korea	1.421	1.906	−0.485
Slovenia	0.067	0.730	−0.663
Belarus	−3.460	−2.711	−0.749
Peru	−1.829	−0.931	−0.898
Spain	2.159	3.197	−1.039
South Africa	−10.733	−9.691	−1.042

In Table 4.5, we also mention the vital difference ratios between the active Catholic communities and overall society. Only the active Catholic publics in Ukraine, Ghana, Trinidad and Tobago, Chile, Lebanon, Germany, Colombia, Brazil, Mexico, Ecuador, Rwanda, the United States, Poland, and the Philippines were more committed to the goals of an overall democratic civil society than the respective overall country population, while in several countries, most dramatically in South Africa, Spain, and Peru, active Catholic publics had to be considered as less supportive of a democratic civil society than the general publics of their countries.

Conclusion and Policy Perspectives from This Chapter

Our overall assessment produces not only pessimistic results. One of our hypotheses in Chap. 3 was that the Roman Catholic Second Vatican Council and its commitment to interreligious tolerance (see Bea 1966; Connelly 2012; D'Costa 2014; Heschel 1966; Kimelman 2004; Valkenberg and Cirelli 2016) in many ways paved the way for the high degree of societal tolerance in of predominantly Catholic Western countries over many decades, irrespective of the fact whether Catholics in those countries live a secular or a more religious life. Let us recall here the declaration *Nostra Aetate* of the Second Vatican Council, which has become the main pillar of the evolving Catholic global interreligious dialogue, honored, among others, by the US Conference of Catholic Bishops (see Chap. 3).[18]

At this point of our reflections, it is important to recall what adherents of other faiths sometimes feel they have to tell Catholics about the achievements of the Second Vatican Council. In no other global denomination, the call for something like the Second Vatican Council is as strong as it is sometimes heard in the Muslim world. The Second Vatican Council as a best-practice model shows how to adapt to the modern world. Considering the evidence which emerges from the data, Egyptian President Abdel-Fattah el-Sisi[19] was right to say at the World Economic Forum in Davos, 2015, that:

> [...] Muslims need to adapt their religious discourse to the present and eliminate elements of their rhetoric that could foster violence. "Islam is a tolerant religion, but this wasn't always clear to the rest of the world during the last 20 or 30 years," Sisi said during a speech at the World Economic Forum in Davos, Switzerland. "The terrible terrorist attacks and this terrible image of Muslims led us to think that we must stop and think and change the religious discourse and remove from it things that have led to violence and extremism."

> "There can be no religious discourse which is in conflict with its environment and with the world," Sisi continued. "And therefore, we Muslims need to modify this religious discourse. And this has nothing to do with conviction and with religious beliefs, because those are immutable. But we need a new discourse that will be adapted to a new world and which will remove some of the misconceptions."

> [...] Speaking to a group of Muslim clerics at Al-Azhar University in Cairo earlier this month, Sisi struck a similar tone, saying **Islam needed a "religious revolution"** and calling on clerics to take the lead. "We are in need of a religious revolution. You imams are responsible before Allah," he said. "The entire world is waiting for your word ... because the Islamic world is being torn, it is being destroyed, it is being lost ... by our own hands."

---

[18]http://www.usccb.org/beliefs-and-teachings/ecumenical-and-interreligious/index.cfm (Download April 10, 2019).

[19]http://www.aljazeera.com/news/2016/06/sisi-calls-religious-reforms-extremists-160629181523576.html   and   http://www.huffingtonpost.com/2015/01/22/sisi-muslims-adapt_n_6508808.html (Download April 10, 2019).

In response to these comments, rare for a Muslim head of state, some have speculated that Sisi may be aiming to reform Islam as a sort of "Muslim Martin Luther."[20]

Precisely, the Second Vatican Council provided the Roman Catholic Church with the theoretical tools to leave behind the centuries of Antisemitism and intolerance which are too well known in history (Jikeli and Allouche-Benayoun 2012; Kertzer 2007; Michael 2008; Rosenfeld 2013; von Bieberstein 1977; Wistrich 2010; see also Bauer 1993; Wistrich 2004, 2007, 2010).

Reasons of space do not permit us to debate here some more results about the trajectories of tolerance of different world religious cultures and their presumed correlates, presented in this work's Appendix tables. But these brief comments should be allowed: electronic Appendix Table 4.10 compares the population-unweighted tolerance indicators (factor scores) for the different global numerically major denominations according to the levels of religious service attendance rates. Electronic Appendix Tables 11–14 highlight the correlations between the indicators, presented in this work, with overall social and political country indicators and highlight the close correlations between them in the direction of confirming the relationship between value development and an Open Society. The graph series in electronic Appendix Graph 4.9 underlines the trajectories of "modernization" and human security, measured by the GDP per capita (natural logarithm) and the factor scores achieved in our research endeavor. We show that most often, value development is a curve linear function of development. In each graph, it is clearly visible whether at different stages of socioeconomic development, practicing Roman Catholics achieve higher or lower country factor scores in their value development curves than general populations and Muslim populations.

We emphasize that the American sociologist Ronald Inglehart is right in underlining the close connection between the religious factor and the level of a country's socioeconomic development. Based on *European Social Survey*-based criteria, we think it is fair to suggest that in not a single European country, practicing Catholics were more liberal in their attitudes toward immigration than the overall societies surrounding them.

The global country-based evidence based on the *World Values Survey* also indicates that *only in a limited number of countries, Catholic Dominicantes are at the forefront of a democratic, Open Society*, based on 11-factor analytical criteria, well compatible with the theoretical literature. The best-performing Roman Catholic *Dominicantes* communities were to be found in Trinidad and Tobago, Ghana, Australia, Germany, and the United States, while the worst performances were recorded in South Africa, Philippines, Lebanon, Belarus, and Peru. We also document the vital difference ratios between the active Catholics and overall society. Only the active Catholic publics in Ukraine, Ghana, Trinidad and Tobago, Chile, Lebanon, Germany, Colombia, Brazil, Mexico, Ecuador, Rwanda, the United States, Poland, and the Philippines were more committed to the goals of an overall

---

[20]http://www.huffingtonpost.com/2015/01/22/sisi-muslims-adapt_n_6508808.html   (Download April 10, 2019).

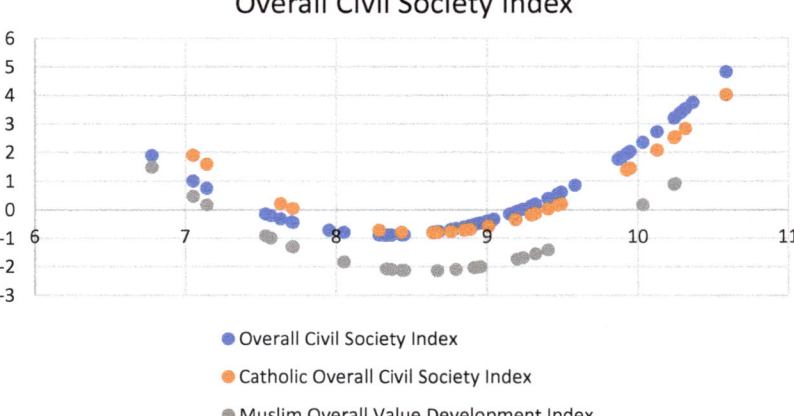

Graph 4.1 Value development in global society, as predicted by our data and GDP per capita (for the GDP per capita data, see Tausch and Heshmati 2013)

democratic civil society than the general populations of these countries, while in several countries, most dramatically in South Africa, Spain, and Peru, active Catholic publics had to be considered as less supportive of a democratic civil society than the general publics.

In Graph 4.1, we now summarize the trajectories of global value development, as they emerge from our data: at lower levels of socioeconomic development, active Roman Catholicism indeed is a countervailing force of humanizing societies, but it fails to influence developments at higher "stages of development":

In Table 4.6, we also show the different indicators for the major denominational groups in the United States. By far, Judaism is at the forefront of the positive value developments, which our work and our indicators attempted to capture.

Roman Catholicism in the United States still lags behind Judaism and Protestantism concerning its value development of its rank and file, but still, the overall value development indicator is higher than that of the average of the US society.

At the end of this chapter, we would like to emphasize as well that progressive Catholicism—both in the Vatican and in the general secretariat of the United Nations—would be well advised to come to terms with the real challenge which Islamist terrorism poses for humanity. Let us document this with a lengthier quotation from Pope Francis and what we feel is his very deficient explanation of terrorism which in no way considers the ideological trajectory of Islamism from the days of Sayyid Qutb onward (Qutb and David 2006; Qutb 1990, 2000; Qutb et al. 1979):

Pope Francis surprised reporters on a flight from Krakow to the Vatican late Sunday when he blamed the "god of money" for extremist violence in Europe and the Middle East, saying that a ruthless global economy leads disenfranchised people to violence. "Terrorism grows when there is no other option, and as long as the world economy has at its center the god of money and not the person," the Pope told reporters, according to the Wall Street Journal. "This is fundamental terrorism, against all humanity." The Pope was responding to a

Table 4.6 Values in the United States by denomination

	Jewish	Protestant	Roman Catholic	Total	Other	No religious denomination
The law-abiding society	1.032	2.393	0.487	0.880	0.995	−0.058
Democracy movement	1.056	0.019	−0.162	−0.089	−0.713	0.091
Climate of personal nonviolence	0.430	0.378	0.441	0.310	0.491	0.100
Trust in institutions	−0.152	−0.593	−0.182	−0.492	−0.682	−0.580
Happiness, good health	0.605	0.069	0.168	0.117	0.065	0.102
No redistributive religious fundamentalism	1.933	1.325	1.103	1.304	0.546	1.771
Accepting the market economy	0.450	0.902	0.480	0.421	0.515	−0.005
Feminism	0.978	0.589	0.763	0.669	0.680	0.633
Involvement in politics	0.895	0.674	0.392	0.345	0.273	0.095
Optimism and engagement	0.083	0.081	0.051	0.005	0.123	−0.158
No welfare mentality, acceptancy of the Calvinist work ethics	−0.038	−0.094	−0.059	−0.173	−0.062	−0.384
Overall Value Development Index	7.273	5.741	3.481	3.294	2.231	1.608

journalist's question about whether there is a link between Islam and terrorism, particularly focusing on the fatal attack on a priest by Muslim extremists in France last week.[21]

Naiveté will not be sufficient to confront the situation of the two trains of extremism in the West now about to collide, about which Rabbi Pinchas Goldschmidt was speaking recently to the European Parliament. Islamist Antisemitism and extremism are a new form and a continuation of the hatred and radicalism, which culminated in the *Shoah*, and Roman Catholics should be aware of it and should defend democracy against the new radicalisms, threatening the West.

Literature

Abdi, H. (2003). *Factor rotations in factor analyses. Encyclopedia for research methods for the social sciences* (pp. 792–795). Thousand Oaks, CA: Sage.

Albertson, B., & Gadarian, S. K. (2016). Anxiety over terrorism advantages Hillary Clinton. *Political Communication*, 1–5.

Alemán, J., & Woods, D. (2015). Value orientations from the world values survey how comparable are they cross-nationally? *Comparative Political Studies*, p. 0010414015600458.

---

[21] https://canadiandimension.com/articles/view/pope-francis-capitalism-is-terrorism-against-all-of-humanity (Download April 10, 2019).

Alesina, A., & Ferrara, E. L. (2000). *The determinants of trust* (No. w7621). National Bureau of Economic Research.

Alesina, A., & Guiliano, P. (2013). *Culture and institutions* (NBER Working Paper Series, Working Paper 19750). Download April 10, 2019, from http://scholar.harvard.edu/alesina/publications

Alesina, A., Algan, Y., Cahuc, P., & Giuliano, P. (2015). Family values and the regulation of labor. *Journal of the European Economic Association, 13*(4), 599–630.

Alexander, A. C., & Welzel, C. (2011). Islam and patriarchy: How robust is Muslim support for patriarchal values? *International Review of Sociology, 21*(2), 249–276.

Alexander, A. C., Inglehart, R. F., & Welzel, C. (2012). Measuring effective democracy: A defense. *International Political Science Review, 33*(1), 41–62.

Almond, G. A. (1948). The political ideas of Christian democracy. *The Journal of Politics, 10*(04), 734–763

Almond, G. A. (1996). *The civic culture: Prehistory, retrospect, and prospect* (CSD Working Papers). Center for the Study of Democracy, University of California at Irvine. Available at https://escholarship.org/uc/item/4mm1285j

Almond, G. A. (2002). *Ventures in political science: Narratives and reflections*. Boulder, CO: Lynne Rienner.

Almond, G. A., & Verba, S. (1963). *The civic culture: Political attitudes and democracy in five nations*. Princeton, NJ: Princeton University.

American Psychological Association Commission on Violence, & Youth. (1993). *Violence & youth: Psychology's response* (Vol. 1). Washington, DC: American Psychological Association.

Barro, R. J (1991). Economic growth in a cross-section of countries. *Quarterly Journal of Economics, 106*(2), 407–443.

Barro, R. J. (1996). Democracy and growth. *Journal of Economic Growth, 1*(1), 1–27.

Barro, R. J. (1998). *Determinants of economic growth: A cross-country empirical study*. Lionel Robbins Lectures (1st ed.). Cambridge, MA: MIT Press.

Barro, R. J. (2003a). Economic growth in a cross section of countries. *International Library of Critical Writings in Economics, 159*(1), 350–386.

Barro, R. J. (2003b). *Religion adherence data*. Harvard University, Department of Economics. Retrieved from https://scholar.harvard.edu/Barro/publications/religion-adherence-data

Barro, R. J. (2004). Spirit of capitalism religion and economic development. *Harvard International Review, 25*(4), 64–67.

Barro, R. J. (2012). *Convergence and modernization revisited*. Department of Economics, Harvard University.

Barro, R. J., & McCleary, R. M. (2003). Religion and economic growth across countries. *American Sociological Review, 68*(5), 760–781.

Barro, R. J., & Sala-i-Martin, X. (1992). Convergence. *Journal of Political Economy, 100*(2), 223–251.

Barro, R. J., & Sala-i-Martin, X. (2003). *Economic growth* (2nd ed.). Cambridge, MA: MIT Press.

Barro, R. J., & Ursúa, J. F. (2008). *Macroeconomic crises since 1870* (pp. 255–335). Brookings Papers on Economic Activity, Spring. Download April 10, 2019, from http://www.people.fas.harvard.edu/~jfursua/papers/bpea.pdf

Barro, R. J., Sala-i-Martin, X., et al. (1991). Convergence across states and regions. *Brookings Papers on Economic Activity, 1991*(1), 107–182.

Basáñez, M., & Inglehart, R. F. (2016). *A world of three cultures: Honor, achievement and joy*. New York: Oxford University Press.

Basáñez, T, Dennis, J. M., Crano, W. D., Stacy, A. W., & Unger, J. B. (2014). Measuring acculturation gap conflicts among Hispanics implications for psychosocial and academic adjustment. *Journal of Family Issues, 35*(13), 1727–1753.

Basilevsky, A. T. (2009). *Statistical factor analysis and related methods: Theory and applications* (Vol. 418). Hoboken, NJ: Wiley.

Bauer, Y. (1993). Antisemitism as a European and world problem. *Patterns of Prejudice, 27*(1), 15–24.

Bea, A. (1966). *The church and the Jewish people; a commentary on the Second Vatican Council's Declaration on the relation of the Church to non-Christian religions.* New York: Harper & Row.

Bergson, H. L. (1935). *The two sources of religion and morality* (R. Ashley Andrà, & C. Brereton with the assistance of W. Horsefall Carter, Trans.). New York: Henry Holt.

Bernstein, C., & Politi, M. (1996). *His Holiness: John Paul II and the hidden history of our time.* New York: Doubleday.

Berryman, P. (2016). The Argentine and Latin American background of Pope Francis. *American Catholic Studies, 127*(2), 55–70.

Brackley, D. (2004). *Divine revolution: Salvation and liberation in catholic thought.* Eugene, OR: Wipf and Stock.

Braithwaite, V. A., & Law, H. G. (1985). Structure of human values: Testing the adequacy of the Rokeach Value Survey. *Journal of Personality and Social Psychology, 49*(1), 250.

Brenner, P. S. (2016). Cross-national trends in religious service attendance. *Public Opinion Quarterly*, nfw016.

Browne, M. W. (2001). An overview of analytic rotation in exploratory factor analysis. *Multivariate Behavioral Research, 36*(1), 111–150.

Burns, G. (1990). The politics of ideology: The papal struggle with liberalism. *American Journal of Sociology, 95*, 1123–1152.

Carrera, S., Blockmans, S., Gros, D., & Guild, E. (2015). The EU's response to the refugee crisis: Taking stock and setting policy priorities. *CEPS Essay* (20/16).

Cattell, R. (Ed.). (2012). *The scientific use of factor analysis in behavioral and life sciences.* New York: Springer.

Ciftci, S. (2010). Modernization, Islam, or social capital: What explains attitudes toward democracy in the Muslim world. *Comparative Political Studies, 43*(11), 1442–1470.

Ciftci, S. (2012). Islamophobia and threat perceptions: Explaining anti-Muslim sentiment in the west. *Journal of Muslim Minority Affairs, 32*(3), 293–309. https://doi.org/10.1080/13602004.2012.727291.

Ciftci, S. (2013). Secular-Islamist cleavage, values, and support for democracy and Shari'a in the Arab World (December 26, 2012). *Political Research Quarterly, 66*(4), 781–793. Available at SSRN: https://ssrn.com/abstract=2920382

Ciftci, S., & Bernick, E. M. (2015). Utilitarian and modern: Clientelism, citizen empowerment, and civic engagement in the Arab World (August 8, 2014). *Democratization, 22*(7), 1161–1182. Available at SSRN: https://ssrn.com/abstract=2920373

Clauß, G., & Ebner, H. (1970). *Grundlagen der Statistik für Psychologen, Pädagogen und Soziologen.* Berlin: Volk und Wissen Volkseigener Verlag.

Connelly, J. (2012). *From enemy to brother: The revolution in Catholic teaching on the Jews, 1933–1965.* Cambridge, MA: Harvard University Press.

Corrin, J. P. (2002). *Catholic intellectuals and the challenge of democracy.* Notre Dame: University of Notre Dame Press.

Coughlin, J. J. (2003). Pope John Paul II and the dignity of the human being. *Harvard Journal of Law and Public Policy, 27*(65), 1–17.

Davidov, E., Schmidt, P., & Schwartz, S. H. (2008). Bringing values back in the adequacy of the European Social Survey to measure values in 20 countries. *Public Opinion Quarterly, 72*(3), 420–445.

Davidov, E., Schmidt, P., & Billiet, J. (2011). *Cross-cultural analysis: Methods and applications.* New York: Routledge.

D'Costa, G. (2014). *Vatican II: Catholic Doctrines on Jews and Muslims.* Oxford: Oxford University Press.

De Maio, M., Alkazemi, M., & Wanta, W. (2016). An examination of the Roman Catholic Church's agenda-setting function in Argentina. *Journal of Media and Religion, 15*(1), 15–28.

Dien, J., Beal, D. J., & Berg, P. (2005). Optimizing principal components analysis of event-related potentials: Matrix type, factor loading weighting, extraction, and rotations. *Clinical Neurophysiology, 16*, 1808–1825.

Dunlap, R. E., & York, R. (2008). The globalization of environmental concern and the limits of the postmaterialist values explanation: Evidence from four multinational surveys. *The Sociological Quarterly, 49*(3), 529–563.

Dziuban, C. D., & Shirkey, E. C. (1974). When is a correlation matrix appropriate for factor analysis? *Psychological Bulletin, 81*, 358–361.

Elzinga, K. G. (1999). Economics and religion. In *Religion and economics: Normative social theory* (pp. 131–139). Dordrecht: Springer.

Etzioni, A. (1998). *The active society: A theory of societal and political processes.* London/New York: Collier-Macmillan/Free Press.

Fabrigar, L. R., Wegener, D. T., MacCallum, R. C., & Strahan, E. J. (1999). Evaluating the use of exploratory factor analysis in psychological research. *Psychological Methods, 4*(3), 272.

Ferber, M. A., & Nelson, J. A. (Eds.). (2009). Beyond economic man: Feminist theory and economics. University of Chicago Press, Chicago, IL.

Finch, H. (2006). Comparison of the performance of Varimax and Promax rotations: Factor structure recovery for dichotomous items. *Journal of Educational Measurement, 43*(1), 39–52.

Francis, Pope. (2014). *The church of mercy: A vision for the church.* Chicago, IL: Loyola Press (Journal for the Sociological Integration of Religion and Society, 5 (1)).

Fry, D. (2016). Kāfir Pride: An examination of the recent apparent rise in Australian anti-Islamic activity and the challenges it presents for national security. *Journal for Deradicalization* (6), 105–131.

Fukuyama, F. (1995). *Trust.* New York: Free Press.

Fukuyama, F. (2006). *The end of history and the last man.* New York: Simon and Schuster.

Fukuyama, F. (2016, Summer). American political decay or renewal? The meaning of the 2016 election. *Foreign Affairs.* Available at: https://www.foreignaffairs.com/articles/united-states/2016-06-13/american-political-decay-or-renewal

Gillis, C. (2016). *Political Papacy: John Paul II, Benedict XVI, and their influence.* New York: Routledge.

Giorgi, L., & Marsh, C. (1990). The protestant work ethic as a cultural phenomenon. *European Journal of Social Psychology, 20*(6), 499–517.

Giroux, H. A. (2016). Donald Trump and neo-fascism in America. *Arena Magazine (Fitzroy, Vic)* (140), 31.

Glahe, F., & Vorhies, F. (1989). Religion, liberty and economic development: An empirical investigation. *Public Choice, 62*(3), 201–215.

Gorsuch, R. L. (1983). *Factor analysis.* Hillsdale, NJ: Erlbaum.

Guiso, L., Sapienza, P., & Zingales, L. (2003). People's opium? Religion and economic attitudes. *Journal of Monetary Economics, 50*(1), 225–282.

Hanson, E. O. (2014). *The Catholic Church in world politics.* Princeton, NJ: Princeton University Press.

Hedges, L. V., & Olkin, I. (2014). *Statistical methods for meta-analysis.* Orlando, FL: Academic.

Heschel, A. J. (1966). No religion is an island. *Union Theological Seminary Quarterly Review, 21* (2), 1.

Hofstede, G. (2001). *Culture's consequences: Comparing values, behaviors, institutions, and organizations across nations.* Thousand Oaks, CA: Sage.

Hofstede, G., & Minkov, M. (2010). Long- versus short-term orientation: New perspectives. *Asia Pacific Business Review, 16*(4), 493–504.

Hofstede, G., Hofstede, G. J., & Minkov, M. (2010). *Cultures and organizations: Software of the mind* (Rev. and expanded 3rd ed.). New York: McGraw-Hill.

Hogan, J., & Haltinner, K. (2015). Floods, invaders, and parasites: Immigration threat narratives and right-wing populism in the USA, UK and Australia. *Journal of Intercultural Studies, 36*(5), 520–543.

Hollifield, J., Martin, P., & Orrenius, P. (2014). *Controlling immigration: A global perspective*. Stanford, CA: Stanford University Press.

Hotelling, H. (1933). Analysis of a complex of statistical variables into principal components. *Journal of Educational Psychology, 24*, 417–441, 24, 498–520

Huntington, S. P. (1993). *The third wave: Democratization in the late twentieth century* (Vol. 4). Norman: University of Oklahoma Press.

Huntington, S. P. (2000). The clash of civilizations? In *Culture and politics* (pp. 99–118). New York: Palgrave Macmillan.

Inglehart, R. F. (1988). The renaissance of political culture. *American Political Science Review, 82*(04), 1203–1230.

Inglehart, R. F. (1990). *Culture shift in advanced industrial countries*. Princeton, NJ: Princeton University Press.

Inglehart, R. F. (2000). Globalization and postmodern values. *Washington Quarterly, 23*(1), 215–228.

Inglehart, R. F. (2006). Mapping global values. *Comparative Sociology, 5*(2), 115–136.

Inglehart, R. F. (2008). Changing values among western publics from 1970 to 2006. *West European Politics, 31*(1–2), 130–146.

Inglehart, R. F. (2015). *The silent revolution: Changing values and political styles among Western publics*. Princeton, NJ: Princeton University Press.

Inglehart, R. F. (2018). *Cultural evolution: People's motivations are changing, and reshaping the world*. Cambridge: Cambridge University Press.

Inglehart, R. F., & Baker, W. E. (2000). Modernization, cultural change, and the persistence of traditional values. *American Sociological Review, 65*(1), 19–51. Download April 10, 2019 http://my.fit.edu/~gabrenya/cultural/readings/Inglehart-Baker-2000.pdf

Inglehart, R. F., & Norris, P. (2003). *Rising tide: Gender equality and cultural change around the world*. New York: Cambridge University Press.

Inglehart, R. F., & Norris, P. (2009, November 4). The true clash of civilizations. *Foreign Policy*. Download April 10, 2019, from http://foreignpolicy.com/2009/11/04/the-true-clash-of-civilizations/

Inglehart, R. F., & Norris, P. (2012). The four horsemen of the apocalypse: Understanding human security. *Scandinavian Political Studies, 35*(1), 71–95.

Inglehart, R. F., & Norris, P. (2016). *Trump, Brexit, and the rise of populism: Economic have-nots and cultural backlash*. Download April 10, 2019, from SSRN: http://ssrn.com/abstract=2818659 HKS Working Paper No. RWP16-026.

Inglehart, R. F., & Welzel, C. (2003). Political culture and democracy: Analyzing cross-level linkages. *Comparative Politics, 36*(1), 61–79.

Inglehart, R. F., & Welzel C. (2009, March, April). How development leads to democracy. What we know about modernization. *Foreign Affairs*. Download April 10, 2019, from http://www.foreignaffairs.com/articles/64821/ronald-inglehart-and-christian-welzel/how-development-leads-to-democracy

Inglehart, R. F., & Welzel, C. (2010). Changing mass priorities: The link between modernization and democracy. *Perspectives on Politics, 8*(02), 551–567.

Inglehart, R. F., Ponarin, E., & Inglehart, R. C. (2017). Cultural change, slow and fast: The distinctive trajectory of norms governing gender equality and sexual orientation. *Social Forces, 95*(4), 1313–1340.

Jikeli, G., & Allouche-Benayoun, J. (Eds.). (2012). *Perceptions of the Holocaust in Europe and Muslim communities: Sources, comparisons and educational challenges* (Vol. 5). New York: Springer.

John Paul II. (1994). *Catechism of the Catholic church*. Rome: Urbi Et Orbi Communications. Download April 10, 2019, from http://www.vatican.va/archive/ENG0015/_INDEX.HTM

Jolliffe, J. (2002). *Principal component analysis*. London: Wiley.

Juergensmeyer, M. (2000). *Terror in the mind of G'd: The global rise of religious violence*. Berkeley: University of California Press.

Juergensmeyer, M. (2011). *The Oxford handbook of global religions (Oxford Handbooks)*. Oxford: Oxford University Press.

Kasper, W. (2015). *Pope Francis' revolution of tenderness and love*. New York: Paulist Press.

Kertzer, D. I. (2007). *The Popes against the Jews: The Vatican's role in the rise of modern Antisemitism*. New York: Vintage.

Kieffer, K. M. (1998). *Orthogonal versus oblique rotation: A review of the literature regarding the pros and cons*. Paper presented at the Annual Meeting of the Mid-South Educational Research Association, New Orleans, LA, November 1998.

Kim, S. Y. (2010). Do Asian values exist? Empirical tests of the four dimensions of Asian values. *Journal of East Asian Studies, 10*, 315–344.

Kimelman, R. (2004). Rabbis Joseph B. Soloveitchik and Abraham Joshua Heschel on Jewish-Christian relations. *Modern Judaism, 24*(3), 251–271.

Kline, P. (2014). *An easy guide to factor analysis*. New York: Routledge.

Knippenberg, H. (2015). Secularization and transformation of religion in post-War Europe. In *The changing world religion appendix map* (pp. 2101–2127). Dordrecht: Springer.

Küng, H. (1997). *A global ethic for global politics and economics* (J. Bowden from the German, Trans.). London: SCM Press.

Küng, H. (2002). *Tracing the way: Spiritual dimensions of the world religions*. New York: Continuum.

Kuznets, S. (1976). *Modern economic growth: Rate, structure and spread*. New Haven, CT: Yale University Press.

Lenoir, F. (2008). *Le Christ philosophe*. Paris: Plon.

Lenoir, F., & Etchegoin, M.-F. (2009). *La Saga des francs-maçons*. Paris: Robert Laffont.

Lenoir, F., & Tardan-Masquelier, Y. (1997). *Encyclopédie des religions*. Paris: Bayard.

Linz, J. J., & Stepan, A. (1996). *Problems of democratic transition and consolidation: Southern Europe, South America, and post-communist Europe*. Baltimore: Johns Hopkins University Press.

Lipset, S. M. (1959). Some social requisites of democracy: Economic development and political legitimacy. *American Political Science Review, 53*(01), 69–105.

Lipset, S. M. (1969, December). The socialism of fools—The left, the Jews and Israel. *Encounter*, 24.

Mainwaring, S. (2003). *Christian democracy in Latin America: Electoral competition and regime conflicts*. Stanford, CA: Stanford University Press.

Manuel, P. C., Reardon, L. C., & Wilcox, C. (2006). *The Catholic church and the nation-state: Comparative perspectives*. Washington, DC: Georgetown University Press.

Maritain, J. (1936). *Humanisme integral. Problemes temporels et spirituels d'une nouvelle chretiente*. Paris: Aubier. 334 S. 8°. Aubier.

Maritain, J. (2012). *Christianity and democracy, the rights of man and natural law*. San Francisco, CA: Ignatius Press.

McCleary, R. M., & Barro, R. J. (2006a). Religion and economy. *The Journal of Economic Perspectives, 20*(2), 49–72.

McCleary, R. M., & Barro, R. J. (2006b). Religion and political economy in an international panel. *Journal for the Scientific Study of Religion, 45*(2), 149–175.

McDonald, R. P. (1997). *Test theory: A unified treatment*. Mahwah, NJ: Erlbaum.

McDonald, R. P. (2014). *Factor analysis and related methods*. London: Psychology Press.

McLeod, L. D., Swygert, K. A., & Thissen, D. (2001). Factor analysis for items scored in two categories. In D. Thissen & H. Wainer (Eds.), *Test scoring* (pp. 189–216). Mahwah, NJ: Erlbaum.

Michael, R. (2008). *A history of Catholic antisemitism: The dark side of the church*. New York: Springer.

Minkov, M. (2014). The K factor, societal hypometropia, and national values: A study of 71 nations. *Personality and Individual Differences, 66*, 153–159.

Minkov, M., & Hofstede, G. (2011). *Cultural differences in a globalizing world*. Bingley: Emerald.

Minkov, M., & Hofstede, G. (2013). *Cross-cultural analysis: The science and art of comparing the world's modern societies and their cultures*. Los Angeles: Sage.

Minkov, M., & Hofstede, G. (2014). Nations versus religions: Which has a stronger effect on societal values? *Management International Review, 54*(6), 801–824.

Moaddel, M., & Karabenick, S. A. (2013). *Religious fundamentalism in the Middle East: A cross-national, inter-faith, and inter-ethnic analysis*. Amsterdam: Brill.

Morel, J. S. J. (1972). *Glaube und Säkularisierung: Religion im Christentum als Problem*. Innsbruck: Tyrolia.

Morel, J. S. J. (1977). *Enthüllung der Ordnung: Grundbegriffe und Funktionen der Soziologie*. Innsbruck: Tyrolia.

Morel, J. S. J. (1986). *Ordnung und Freiheit: die soziologische Perspektive*. Innsbruck: Tyrolia.

Morel, J. S. J. (1997). *Soziologische Theorie: Abriss der Ansätze ihrer Hauptvertreter*. München: Oldenbourg.

Morel, J. S. J. (1998). *Glauben hat Zukunft: persönliche Wege einer neuen Sinnfindung*. Innsbruck: Tyrolia.

Morel, J. S. J. (2003). *Radikale Kirchenreform. Für eine mutige Erneuerung*. Tyrolia: Innsbruck.

Moyser, G. (2005). European religion in comparative perspective. *Political Theology, 6*(3), 325–342.

Mulaik, S. A. (2009). *Foundations of factor analysis*. Boca Raton, FL: CRC Press.

Napolitano, V. (2015). *Migrant hearts and the Atlantic return: Transnationalism and the Roman Catholic Church*. Oxford: Oxford University Press.

Nelsen, B. F., & Guth, J. L. (2003). *Roman Catholicism and the founding of Europe: How Catholics shaped the European Communities* (pp. 28–31). In Prepared for delivery at the Annual Meeting of the American Political Science Association, Philadelphia, PA.

Norris, P., & Inglehart, R. F. (2002). Islamic culture and democracy: Testing the 'clash of civilizations' thesis. *Comparative Sociology, 1*(3), 235–263.

Norris, P., & Inglehart, R. F. (2011). *Sacred and secular: Religion and politics worldwide*. New York: Cambridge University Press.

Norris, P., & Inglehart, R. F. (2012). Muslim integration into Western cultures: Between origins and destinations. *Political Studies, 60*(2), 228–251.

Norris, P., & Inglehart, R. F. (2015). Are high levels of existential security conducive to secularization? A response to our critics. In *The changing world religion map* (pp. 3389–3408). Dordrecht: Springer.

Novak, M. (1984). *Catholic social thought and liberal institutions: Freedom with justice*. New Brunswick, NJ: Transaction Publishers.

Novak, M. (1991a). *The spirit of democratic capitalism*. Totowa, NJ: Rowman, & Littlefield.

Novak, M. (1991b). *Will it liberate? questions about liberation theology*. New York: Madison Books.

Oates, S., & Moe, W. W. (2016, August). *Donald Trump and the 'Oxygen of Publicity': Branding, social media, and mass media in the 2016 Presidential Primary Elections*. In American Political Science Association Annual Meeting.

Oishi, S., Diener, E. F., Lucas, R. E., & Suh, E. M. (1999). Cross-cultural variations in predictors of life satisfaction: Perspectives from needs and values. *Personality and Social Psychology Bulletin, 25*(8), 980–990.

Park, J. (2015). *Europe's migration crisis*. New York: Council of Foreign Relations. Download April 10, 2019, from http://www.cfr.org/refugees-and-the-displaced/europes-migration-crisis/p32874

Petrella, I. (2004). *The future of liberation theology: An argument and manifesto*. Aldershot: Gower.

PEW Research Center, Global Attitudes and Trends. (2015). Download April 10, 2019, from http://www.pewglobal.org/category/datasets/

Philpott, D. (2004). The Catholic wave. *Journal of Democracy, 15*(2), 32–46.

Popper, K. S. (2012). *The open society and its enemies*. Routledge.

Post, S. G. (2005). Altruism, happiness, and health: It's good to be good. *International Journal of Behavioral Medicine, 12*(2), 66–77.

Putnam, R. D. (1993). *Making democracy work: Civic traditions in modern Italy*. Princeton, NJ: Princeton University Press.

Qutb, S. (1990). *Milestones*. Indianapolis: American Trust.

Qutb, S. (2000). *Social justice in Islam*. Oneonta, NY: Islamic Publications International.

Qutb, S., & David, R. (2006). *Basic principles of the Islamic worldview*. North Haledon, NJ: Islamic Publications International.

Qutb, S., Salahi, M. A., & Shamis, A. A. (1979). *In the shade of the Qur'ān*. London: MWH.

Röhrich, W. (2004). *Die Macht der Religionen: Glaubenskonflikte in der Weltpolitik*. München: Beck.

Röhrich, W. (2010). *Rückkehr der Kulturen: die neuen Mächte in der Weltpolitik*. Baden-Baden: Nomos.

Rosenfeld, A. H. (2013). *Resurgent antisemitism: Global perspectives*. Bloomington, IN: Indiana University Press.

Rummel, R. J. (1970). *Applied factor analysis*. Evanston, IL: Northwestern University Press.

Sacks, J. (1998). Morals and markets: Seventh annual IEA Hayek Memorial Lecture given in London on Tuesday, 2 June 1998. London: Institute of Economic Affairs, 1999.

Sacks, J. (2003). *The dignity of difference: How to avoid the clash of civilizations*. New York: Continuum.

Sacks, J. (2005). *To heal a fractured world: The ethics of responsibility*. Montreal: McGill-Queens University Press.

Sacks, J. (2014). *The religious other: Hostility, hospitality, and the hope of human flourishing*. Lanham, MA: Lexington Books.

Scanone, J. C. (2016). Pope Francis and the theology of the people. *Theological Studies, 77*(1), 118–135.

Schwartz, S. H. (2006a). A theory of cultural value orientations: Explication and applications. *Comparative Sociology, 5*(2), 137–182.

Schwartz, S. H. (2006b). *Basic human values: An overview*. The Hebrew University of Jerusalem. Download April 10, 2019, from http://segr-did2.fmag.unict.it/Allegati/convegno%207-8-10-05/Schwartzpaper.pdf

Schwartz, S. H. (2007a). Universalism values and the inclusiveness of our moral universe. *Journal of Cross-Cultural Psychology, 38*(6), 711–728.

Schwartz, S. H. (2007b). Value orientations: Measurement, antecedents and consequences across nations. In *Measuring attitudes cross-nationally: Lessons from the European Social Survey* (pp. 161–193). London: Sage.

Schwartz, S. H. (2009). *Cultural value orientations: Nature, and implications of national differences*. The Hebrew University of Jerusalem, Israel Science Foundation Grant No. 921/02. Download April 10, 2019, from http://blogs.helsinki.fi/valuesandmorality/files/2009/09/Schwartz-Monograph-Cultural-Value-Orientations.pdf

Schwartz, S. H. (2014). Rethinking the concept and measurement of societal culture in light of empirical findings. *Journal of Cross-Cultural Psychology, 45*(1), 5–13.

Sengupta, S. (2015, September 30). Refugee crisis in Europe prompts Western engagement in Syria. *New York Times*.

Sigmund, P. E. (1987). The Catholic tradition and modern democracy. *The Review of Politics, 49* (04), 530–548.

Silver, B. D., & Dowley, K. M. (2000). Measuring political culture in multiethnic societies reaggregating the World Values Survey. *Comparative Political Studies, 33*(4), 517–550.

SPSS (IBM-SPSS). (2007). *Statistical package for the social sciences*. User Guide. Version 14, August 2007.

Stepan, A., Linz, J. J., & Yadav, Y. (2011). *Crafting state-nations: India and other multinational democracies*. Baltimore, MD: Johns Hopkins University Press.

Suhr, D. (2012). Exploratory factor analysis with the World Values Survey. In *Proceedings of the SAS Global Forum 2012 Conference*.

Tabachnick, B. G., & Fidell, L. S. (2001). *Using multivariate statistics*. Needham Heights, MA: Allyn, & Bacon.

Tausch, A. (2011). *El Papa ¿Cuántas Divisiones Tiene? Sondeo Global del Catolicismo Mundial Según el 'World Values Survey' y el 'European Social Survey'*. E-Book N° 49 Centro Argentino de Estudios Internacionales (in Spanish) [English Title: 'The Pope – How Many Divisions Does He Have?' a First Global Survey of World Catholicism Based on the 'World Values Survey' and the 'European Social Survey']. Download April 10, 2019, from http://www.caei.com.ar/es/irebooks.htm

Tausch, A. (2014, Fall). The new global Antisemitism: Implications from the recent Adl-100 data. *Middle East Review of International Affairs, 18*(3).

Tausch, A. (2015a). *Europe's refugee crisis. Zur aktuellen politischen Ökonomie von Migration, Asyl und Integration in Europa*. (Europe's Refugee Crisis. On the Current Political Economy of Migration, Asylum and Integration in Europe), October 22, 2015. Download April 10, 2019, from http://ssrn.com/abstract=2677645 or https://doi.org/10.2139/ssrn.2677645

Tausch, A. (2015b). Further insight into global and Arab Muslim opinion structures: Statistical reflections on the 2013 Pew report "The World's Muslims". *Middle East Review of International Affairs, 18*(1) (Spring 2014).

Tausch, A. (2016a). Islamism and Antisemitism. Preliminary evidence on their relationship from cross-national opinion data. *Social Evolution & History, 15*(2), 50–99 (Uchitel Publishing House, Moscow), and Journal of Globalization Studies, 7, 2, November 2016: 137 – 170 (Uchitel Publishing House, Moscow).

Tausch, A. (2016b, Summer). Muslim immigration continues to divide Europe: A quantitative analysis of European social survey data. *Middle East Review of International Affairs, 20*(2).

Tausch, A. (2016c). *The civic culture of the Arab World: A comparative analysis based on World Values Survey data*. Middle East Review of International Affairs, Rubin Center, Research in International Affairs, IDC Herzliya, Israel (April 2016). Download April 10, 2019, from https://papers.ssrn.com/sol3/papers.cfm?abstract_id=2827232

Tausch, A. (2017). Global Catholicism in the age of mass migration and the rise of populism: Comparative analyses, based on recent world values survey and European Social Survey Data (September 20, 2017). Available at SSRN: https://ssrn.com/abstract=2875289

Tausch, A., & Heshmati, A. (2013). *Globalization, the human condition, and sustainable development in the twenty-first century: Cross-national perspectives and European implications*. London: Anthem.

Tausch, A., & Moaddel, M. (2009). *What 1.3 billion Muslims really think. An answer to a recent Gallup study, based on the 'World Values Survey'*. Hauppauge, NY: Nova Science.

Tausch, A., Heshmati, A., & Karoui, H. (2014). *The political algebra of global value change: General models and implications for the Muslim World*. Hauppauge, NY: Nova Science.

Thompson, B. (2004). *Exploratory and confirmatory factor analysis: Understanding concepts and applications*. Washington, DC: American Psychological Association.

Tyler, T. R., & Darley, J. M. (1999). Building a law-abiding society Taking public views about morality and the legitimacy of legal authorities into account when formulating substantive law. *Hofstra Law Review, 28*, 707.

UNDP. (2014). *Human development report*. New York: Oxford University Press.

UNDP. (2017a). *Human development data (1990–2015)*. Download April 10, 2019, from http://hdr.undp.org/en/data

UNDP. (2017b). *Human development report*. New York: Oxford University Press.

Valkenberg, P., & Cirelli, A. (2016). *Nostra aetate: Celebrating 50 Years of the Catholic Church's dialogue with Jews and Muslims*. Washington, DC: Catholic University of America Press.

von Bieberstein, J. R. (1977). The story of the Jewish-Masonic conspiracy, 1776–1945. *Patterns of Prejudice, 11*(6), 1–21.

von Hayek, F. A. (1960). *The constitution of liberty*. Chicago, IL: University of Chicago Press.

von Hayek, F. A. (2012). *Law, legislation and liberty: A new statement of the liberal principles of justice and political economy*. Routledge.

von Hayek, F. A., & Bartley, W. W. (1988). *The fatal conceit: The errors of socialism*. Chicago, IL: University of Chicago Press.

Weber, M. (1964 [1922]). *The sociology of religion* (E. Fischoff, Trans.). Boston, MA: Beacon Press.

Weigel, G. (2001). *Witness to hope: The biography of Pope John Paul II*. New York: Harper Collins.

Weigel, G. (2010). *The end and the beginning: Pope John Paul II – The Victory of Freedom, the last years, the legacy*. New York: Image.

Whitehead, L. (1996). *The international dimensions of democratization: Europe and the Americas*. New York: Oxford University Press.

Wills, G. (2016). *The future of the Catholic Church with Pope Francis*. New York: Penguin Books.

Wistrich, R. S. (1991). *Antisemitism: The longest hatred*. New York: Pantheon Books.

Wistrich, R. S. (2004). Anti-Zionism and anti-Semitism. *Jewish Political Studies Review, 16*, 27–31.

Wistrich, R. S. (2007). *Anti-Semitism and multiculturalism: The uneasy connection*. Vidal Sassoon International Center for the Study of Anti-Semitism, The Hebrew University of Jerusalem.

Wistrich, R. S. (2010). *A lethal obsession: Antisemitism from antiquity to the global Jihad*. New York: Random House.

World Bank (2017). *World Bank open data*. Washington, DC: World Bank: data.worldbank.org

World Values Survey. (2017). Download April 10, 2019, from http://www.worldvaluessurvey.org/wvs.jsp

Wright, C. F. (2015). Why do states adopt liberal immigration policies? The policymaking dynamics of skilled visa reform in Australia. *Journal of Ethnic and Migration Studies, 41*(2), 306–328.

Yeşilada, B. A., & Noordijk, P. (2010). Changing values in Turkey: Religiosity and tolerance in comparative perspective. *Turkish Studies, 11*(1), 9–27.

Chapter 5
The Open Society and Catholic Religious Tolerance

Introduction

In this chapter, we would like to reflect in a detached and empirical way on global religious tolerance and on the role of the active, global Catholics in the formation of global tolerance values, using advanced methods of comparative social science research. We are interested in what the active Roman Catholics—in comparison with overall society—think about tolerance, and not in the theology of tolerance and ecumenism itself. In terms of the methodology and the data, we refer our readers to what we have already established in Chaps. 3 and 4, i.e., the systematic social scientific study of global values and opinions (Davidov et al. 2011) and the use of systematic and comparative opinion surveys over time, like the *World Values Survey* (*WVS*).[1]

The globalization of goods, capital, services, and labor implied that international social sciences are analyzing not only these "four freedoms" but also the structures of values in an increasingly interconnected international society (Tausch et al. 2014). In the following brief analysis, based on the latest survey wave of the *World Values Survey* (2015), we will show how much religious tolerance or intolerance shapes public opinion in the individual countries of the world. On the basis of the five relevant questions about religious tolerance from the *World Values Survey* (2015), an attempt will be made to formulate a global index of religious tolerance. We then ask ourselves whether or not active, practicing Roman Catholics who attend Church services each Sunday (in Catholic jargon the *Dominicantes*) are more or less tolerant than overall society concerning our chosen tolerance indicators.

We thus compare the performance of the practicing Roman Catholics with overall society. The present chapter again is well within a large and growing tradition to

---

[1] http://www.worldvaluessurvey.org/wvs.jsp

© Springer Nature Switzerland AG 2020
A. Tausch, S. Obirek, *Global Catholicism, Tolerance and the Open Society*,
https://doi.org/10.1007/978-3-030-23239-9_5

study "real existing" Catholicism in an empirical social scientific framework (see Chaps. 3 and 4; Fox et al. 2004; Philpott 2004; Shelledy 2004).

In a final section, we will deal with some of the conclusions to be drawn.

Background: Studying Catholic Tolerance

One of our hypotheses was already mentioned in the chapters above—that the Roman Catholic Second Vatican Council and its commitment to interreligious tolerance (see Bea 1966; Connelly 2012; Valkenberg and Cirelli 2016) in many ways paved the way for the high degree of societal tolerance in predominantly Catholic Western countries over many decades, irrespective of the fact whether Catholics in those countries live a secular or a more religious life. Our second hypothesis is that the Second Vatican Council and its message of international ecumenical understanding have become the social reality in the lives of the Catholic faithful only to a different degree and that not everywhere Roman Catholics are at the vanguard of ecumenical tolerance. The process of secularization, especially in countries where the Roman Catholic Church once was a very powerful institution, often implied that the remaining "hard core" of practicing Roman Catholics is less tolerant than the society surrounding the faithful. By contrast, the Roman Catholic faithful are often at the vanguard of tolerance in countries where Roman Catholics are in a minority position.

In the field of Christian theology, a solid scholarly tradition of a theology of tolerance has developed (D'Costa 2000, 2009, 2011, 2014; D'Costa and Harris 2013; D'Costa et al. 2011; Dupuis 2001; Dupuis et al. 2012; Hebblethwaite and Hebblethwaite 2000; Hick 1994, 1995, 2010; Hick and Hebblethwaite 2001; Hick and Knitter 1987; Knitter 2002, 2005). Let us recall here again the pivotal central role of the declaration "Nostra Aetate" of the Second Vatican Council, honored, among others, by the US Conference of Catholic Bishops.[2]

Data and Methods in Studying Global Tolerance

So, this chapter again firmly shares the established methodology of *World Values Survey*-based comparative opinion research, already mentioned above (Davidov et al. 2008; Inglehart 2006; Tausch et al. 2014). Our present chapter again relies on the statistical analysis of open survey data and is based on the commonly used statistical software IBM-SPSS XXIV, utilized at many universities and research

---

[2]http://www.usccb.org/beliefs-and-teachings/ecumenical-and-interreligious/index.cfm (Download April 10, 2019).

centers around the world.[3] Our simple statistical calculations relied this time only on cross tables and comparisons of means. The chosen IBM-SPSS data files from the *WVS* database again were the database named "WVS_Longitudinal_1981_ 2014_spss_v2015_04_18.sav." For all analyzed groups and subgroups, again a minimum sample of at least 30 respondents per country had to be available in the original data sets to be able to attempt reasonable predictions for the general or sectoral publics to be analyzed (for a survey of the vast methodological literature on this subject, see Tausch et al. 2014).

For the calculation of the indicator of global religious tolerance, we again relied on the well-established methodology of the United Nations Human Development Program and its UNDP Human Development Index (UNDP 2014; Chap. 3). The *World Values Survey* offers fairly encompassing and comparable data on tolerance items. The chosen *World Values Survey* tolerance indicators were as follows:

1. Disagree or strongly disagree: The only acceptable religion is my religion (mean) F203.
2. Agree or strongly agree: All religions should be taught in public schools (mean) F204.
3. Agree or strongly agree: People who belong to different religions are probably just as moral as those who belong to mine (mean) F205.
4. Trust completely or somewhat: People of another religion (mean) G007_35B.
5. Meaning of religion: Do good to other people (%, percentages) F200.

In Chap. 3, we already highlighted that since the 1990s, the United Nations Human Development Program (UNDP 2014) calculates the internationally recognized "Human Development Index," which equally weights life expectancy, education, and real income. Life expectancy, education, and real incomes are projected on a scale from 0 (worst value) to 1 (best value). Although UNDP calculation methods have become somewhat more complicated in recent years, the simple rationale remains—our index of religious tolerance is the average of the five components: other religions are acceptable; all religions should be taught in public schools; people who belong to different religions are probably just as moral as those who belong to mine; trust people of another religion; and the meaning of religion is to do good to other people.

---

[3]IBM-SPSS Statistics, http://www-03.ibm.com/software/products/en/spss-statistics (Download April 10, 2019).

Results: The Global Tolerance Index

We have made available our full results in our electronic Appendix. There are complete data for the 59 states in the world. While, e.g., in Sweden and the United States 30% or less of the population have no confidence in people with a religious denomination other than their own, these percentages in Algeria, Armenia, Yemen, Kyrgyzstan, Libya, Morocco, Mexico, Palestinian territories, Peru, Romania, Tunisia, and Uzbekistan are over 70% each. Unfortunately, the clear North-South divide of religious tolerance on our globe also corresponds to a clear denominational gap. Among the ten states with the lowest general religious tolerance, based on our five indicators, there are nine predominantly Muslim states.

Only public opinion in predominantly Christian Armenia is among this laggard group. Our surveys also show the large relative deficit of religious tolerance in Germany, the worst-ranked member of the European Union. Germany occupies only rank 40 of 59 ranked states. Unfortunately, after all the pogroms of German history, the Thirty Years' War, the *Shoah*, and the two world wars of the twentieth century, flexibility and tolerance in religious thought in Germany still seem to be rare, compared to the best-practice countries like Sweden, Trinidad and Tobago, Brazil, New Zealand, and Australia.

Some food for thought is also provided by our statistical data for the decision-makers of the Catholic Church. The Church celebrated recently the 55th anniversary of the beginning of the Second Vatican Council (October 11, 1962) as well as the 54th anniversary of the proclamation of the Declaration of the Council *Nostra Aetate* (December 8, 1965). But do the nearly 500 million of the 1.3 billion Catholics who still celebrate Holy Mass on Sundays, as *Nostra Aetate* suggests, really believe in religious tolerance?

According to our data, the religiously most liberal Catholic community in the world is found in the Caribbean state of Trinidad and Tobago, followed by the practicing Catholics in Australia, Brazil, the Netherlands, and the United States. The worst results were reported from Peru, Lebanon, Mexico, Germany, and Nigeria. Our data also provide an answer to the question of where practicing Catholics represent a more tolerant attitude toward members of other religions than the respective total populations. The Catholic communities in the Netherlands, Australia, and Uruguay, in particular, are to be mentioned positively, while the lamentable practice of Catholicism in Ukraine, Spain, and Lebanon falls far short of the development of tolerance in these societies as a whole.

It is also being mentioned that there are equally substantial ranges of examples of best and worst practice within the Muslim communities of the world. According to our data, flagship models of a liberal and tolerant Islam can be encountered in Trinidad and Tobago and also in Georgia, India, Ghana, and South Africa.

Religious tolerance is also a matter of urgent consideration by the global South, and not just for the global North and the global migration recipient countries. In some countries of the Muslim world, there are sometimes to be encountered extreme

Table 5.1 Index of Religious Tolerance—total populations

Country/region	Not only my religion is acceptable	All religions should be taught in public schools	People who belong to different religions are probably just as moral as those who belong to mine	Trust: People of another religion (B)	Do good to other people	Index of Religious Tolerance
Sweden	1.000	0.846	0.810	0.973	0.958	0.917
Trinidad and Tobago	0.828	0.920	0.825	0.711	0.913	0.840
Brazil	0.791	0.612	0.701	0.617	0.872	0.719
New Zealand	0.906	0.176	0.730	1.000	0.772	0.717
Australia	0.943	0.282	0.766	0.785	0.732	0.702
Chile	0.820	0.612	0.708	0.537	0.774	0.690
Poland	0.627	0.612	0.832	0.631	0.719	0.684
United States	0.820	0.271	0.693	0.819	0.770	0.675
Taiwan	0.803	0.431	0.613	0.638	0.875	0.672
Argentina	0.844	0.255	0.540	0.718	0.844	0.640
South Africa	0.484	0.771	0.745	0.732	0.452	0.636
Spain	0.791	0.271	0.584	0.597	0.907	0.630
Belarus	0.754	0.351	0.723	0.523	0.749	0.620
Estonia	0.783	0.436	0.723	0.537	0.598	0.615
Ukraine	0.660	0.314	0.730	0.537	0.830	0.614
Uruguay	0.836	0.176	0.526	0.584	0.907	0.606
Russia	0.697	0.426	0.650	0.463	0.790	0.605
Ecuador	0.701	0.489	0.577	0.416	0.825	0.602
Ghana	0.598	0.755	0.511	0.611	0.537	0.602
India	0.602	0.697	0.620	0.651	0.438	0.602
Slovenia	0.742	0.420	0.701	0.389	0.759	0.602
Netherlands	0.914	0.293	0.577	0.577	0.616	0.595
Colombia	0.615	0.543	0.540	0.376	0.879	0.590
Kazakhstan	0.693	0.266	0.569	0.544	0.827	0.580
Lebanon	0.566	0.559	0.591	0.604	0.548	0.574
Romania	0.590	0.516	0.672	0.349	0.736	0.573
Singapore	0.783	0.362	0.555	0.718	0.446	0.573
Nigeria	0.381	0.766	0.584	0.557	0.551	0.568
Philippines	0.414	0.617	0.584	0.433	0.741	0.568
Rwanda	0.787	0.340	0.496	0.658	0.533	0.563
Zimbabwe	0.791	0.314	0.482	0.470	0.625	0.536
Hong Kong	0.652	0.314	0.380	0.617	0.698	0.532
Thailand	0.594	0.500	0.657	0.369	0.533	0.531
Bahrain	0.307	0.665	0.569	0.570	0.457	0.514
Cyprus	0.549	0.170	0.723	0.336	0.781	0.512
Mexico	0.623	0.282	0.474	0.302	0.849	0.506

(continued)

Table 5.1 (continued)

Country/region	Not only my religion is acceptable	All religions should be taught in public schools	People who belong to different religions are probably just as moral as those who belong to mine	Trust: People of another religion (B)	Do good to other people	Index of Religious Tolerance
Peru	0.619	0.383	0.474	0.188	0.813	0.495
South Korea	0.820	0.170	0.401	0.537	0.444	0.474
Georgia	0.234	0.117	0.686	0.523	0.795	0.471
Germany	0.742	0.266	0.387	0.597	0.315	0.461
Malaysia	0.377	0.638	0.606	0.463	0.219	0.461
Uzbekistan	0.270	0.271	0.803	0.141	0.622	0.422
Azerbaijan	0.406	0.186	0.496	0.342	0.666	0.419
China	0.922	0.048	0.000	0.275	0.786	0.406
Kyrgyzstan	0.365	0.319	0.496	0.255	0.570	0.401
Turkey	0.283	0.489	0.635	0.383	0.196	0.397
Japan	0.766	0.261	0.066	0.201	0.651	0.389
Iraq	0.262	0.383	0.380	0.403	0.392	0.364
Jordan	0.078	0.261	0.409	0.403	0.460	0.322
Kuwait	0.201	0.223	0.204	0.530	0.346	0.301
Pakistan	0.139	0.606	0.314	0.275	0.128	0.292
Armenia	0.279	0.048	0.263	0.094	0.658	0.268
Tunisia	0.152	0.277	0.401	0.034	0.380	0.249
Libya	0.045	0.000	0.401	0.141	0.616	0.241
Qatar	0.000	0.069	0.321	0.584	0.219	0.239
Palestinian Terr.	0.164	0.191	0.095	0.134	0.413	0.200
Morocco	0.180	0.037	0.117	0.242	0.140	0.143
Yemen	0.127	0.011	0.117	0.000	0.432	0.137
Algeria	0.082	0.011	0.051	0.101	0.254	0.100

forms of aversion against the religions of the "others," while there are also outstanding examples of religiously tolerant Muslim communities.

However, it is also worrying that the performance of Germany, the main destination of European inward immigration from summer 2015 onward, is relatively poor in terms of religious tolerance: not only the Catholic community but also other religious groups in Germany and also German Muslims are among the worse-ranked communities of their fellow believers in the world.

Tables 5.1 and 5.2 and Maps 5.1, 5.2 and 5.3 now inform readers about our UNDP-type index and its components. The original data and many more international comparisons are available in the electronic Appendix of this work.

Table 5.2 Index of Religious Tolerance—*Dominicantes*

Country/ region	Not only my religion is acceptable	All religions should be taught in public schools	People who belong to different religions are probably just as moral as those who belong to mine	Trust: People of another religion (B)	Do good to other people	Index of Religious Tolerance
Trinidad and Tobago	0.807	0.973	0.978	0.691	0.903	0.871
Australia	0.811	0.463	0.927	0.913	0.897	0.802
Brazil	0.717	0.676	0.737	0.685	0.876	0.738
Netherlands	0.738	0.548	0.818	0.792	0.741	0.727
United States	0.775	0.394	0.759	0.919	0.788	0.727
Chile	0.795	0.644	0.766	0.584	0.651	0.688
Argentina	0.824	0.436	0.569	0.772	0.807	0.682
Uruguay	0.709	0.399	0.591	0.711	1.000	0.682
Poland	0.541	0.628	0.810	0.631	0.782	0.678
Ghana	0.648	0.782	0.613	0.671	0.501	0.643
South Africa	0.398	0.798	0.796	0.799	0.362	0.630
Singapore	0.758	0.426	0.642	0.785	0.473	0.617
Ecuador	0.672	0.473	0.672	0.430	0.793	0.608
Slovenia	0.607	0.548	0.752	0.349	0.765	0.604
Belarus	0.631	0.096	0.781	0.550	0.852	0.582
Colombia	0.561	0.495	0.511	0.383	0.865	0.563
Philippines	0.414	0.596	0.599	0.490	0.714	0.562
Rwanda	0.852	0.319	0.489	0.678	0.452	0.558
Spain	0.615	0.314	0.518	0.497	0.741	0.537
South Korea	0.721	0.319	0.599	0.571	0.329	0.528
Zimbabwe	0.795	0.351	0.496	0.423	0.528	0.519
Ukraine	0.627	0.154	0.460	0.517	0.820	0.516
Nigeria	0.426	0.601	0.474	0.362	0.689	0.511
Germany	0.578	0.457	0.474	0.617	0.401	0.506
Mexico	0.541	0.319	0.504	0.282	0.855	0.500
Lebanon	0.455	0.585	0.606	0.389	0.427	0.492
Peru	0.561	0.410	0.496	0.208	0.770	0.489

Conclusion and Prospects from This Chapter

So, this chapter developed a new indicator of global religious tolerance and analyzed the performance of the practicing Roman Catholics in comparison with the national performances. This chapter has shown that there are astonishing vast differences in the sharing of religious tolerance values around the globe.

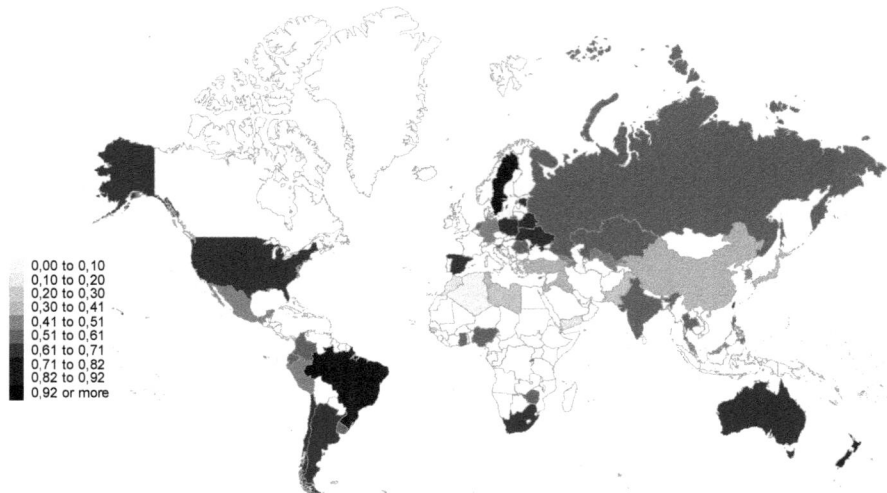

Map 5.1 Index of Religious Tolerance. Best: Sweden, Trinidad and Tobago, Brazil, New Zealand, Australia. Worst: Algeria, Yemen, Morocco, Palestinian territories, Qatar

Map 5.2 *Dominicantes*: Index of Religious Tolerance. Best: Trinidad and Tobago, Australia, Brazil, the Netherlands, the United States. Worst: Peru, Lebanon, Mexico, Germany, Nigeria

Map 5.3 *Dominicantes* Global leaders or laggards: Index of Religious Tolerance. Best: the Netherlands, Australia, Uruguay, South Korea, the United States. Worst: Ukraine, Spain, Lebanon, Nigeria, Belarus

Literature

Bea, A. (1966). *The church and the Jewish people; a commentary on the Second Vatican Council's Declaration on the relation of the Church to non-Christian religions.* New York: Harper & Row.

Connelly, J. (2012). *From enemy to brother: The revolution in Catholic teaching on the Jews, 1933–1965.* Cambridge, MA: Harvard University Press.

D'Costa, G. (2009). *Christianity and world religions: Disputed questions in the theology of religions.* Chichester: Wiley-Blackwell.

Davidov, E., Schmidt, P., & Schwartz, S. H. (2008). Bringing values back in the adequacy of the *European Social Survey* to measure values in 20 countries. *Public Opinion Quarterly, 72*(3), 420–445.

Davidov, E., Schmidt, P., & Billiet, J. (2011). *Cross-cultural analysis: Methods and applications.* New York: Routledge.

D'Costa, G. (2000). *The meeting of religions and the trinity (Faith meets faith).* Maryknoll, NY: Orbis Books.

D'Costa, G. (2011). *The catholic church and the world religions: A theological and phenomenological account.* London: T & T Clark.

D'Costa, G. (2014). *Vatican II: Catholic doctrines on Jews and Muslims.* Oxford: Oxford University Press.

D'Costa, G., & Harris, E. (Eds.). (2013). *The second Vatican council: Celebrating its achievements and the future.* London: Bloomsbury.

D'Costa, G., Knitter, P., & Strange, D. (2011). *Only one way? Three Christian responses to the uniqueness of Christ in a religiously pluralist world.* London: SCM.

Dupuis, J. (2001). *Toward a Christian theology of religious pluralism.* Maryknoll, NY: Orbis Books.

Dupuis, J., Burrows, W., & Catholic Church Congregatio pro Doctrina Fidei. (2012). *Jacques Dupuis faces the inquisition: Two essays by Jacques Dupuis on Dominus Iesus and the roman investigation of his work*. Eugene, OR: Pickwick.

Fox, J. (2000). *A world survey of religion and the state*. Cambridge, MA: Cambridge University Press.

Fox, J., Sandler, S., & Sandier, S. (2004). *Bringing religion into international relations* (pp. 9–10). New York: Palgrave Macmillan.

Hebblethwaite, P., & Hebblethwaite, M. (2000). *John XXIII: Pope of the century*. London: Continuum.

Hick, J. (1994). *The second Christianity*. London: Xpress Reprints.

Hick, J. (1995). *A Christian theology of religions: The rainbow of faiths* (1st American ed.). Louisville, KY: Westminster John Knox Press.

Hick, J. (2010). *Dialogues in the philosophy of religion*. New York: Palgrave Macmillan.

Hick, J., & Hebblethwaite, B. (2001). *Christianity and other religions: Selected readings* (Rev. ed.). Oxford: Oneworld.

Hick, J., & Knitter, P. (1987). *The myth of Christian uniqueness: Toward a pluralistic theology of religions (Faith meets faith series)*. Maryknoll, NY: Orbis Books.

Inglehart, R. F. (2006). Mapping global values. *Comparative Sociology, 5*(2), 115–136.

Inglehart, R. F., & Baker, W. E. (2000). Modernization, cultural change, and the persistence of traditional values. *American Sociological Review, 65*(1), 19–51. Download April 10, 2019, from http://my.fit.edu/~gabrenya/cultural/readings/Inglehart-Baker-2000.pdf

Knitter, P. (2002). *Introducing theologies of religions*. Maryknoll, NY: Orbis Books.

Knitter, P. (2005). *The myth of religious superiority: Multifaith explorations of religious pluralism (Faith meets faith)*. Maryknoll, NY: Orbis Books.

Philpott, D. (2004). The Catholic wave. *Journal of Democracy, 15*(2), 32–46.

Shelledy, R. B. (2004). The Vatican's role in global politics. *SAIS Review of International Affairs, 24*(2), 149–162.

Tausch, A. (2011). El Papa ¿Cuántas Divisiones Tiene? Sondeo Global del Catolicismo Mundial Según el '*World Values Survey*' y el '*European Social Survey*'. E-Book N° 49 Centro Argentino de Estudios Internacionales (in Spanish) [English Title: 'The Pope – How Many Divisions Does He Have?' a First Global Survey of World Catholicism Based on the '*World Values Survey*' and the '*European Social Survey*']. Download April 10, 2019, from http://www.caei.com.ar/es/irebooks.htm

Tausch, A., & Heshmati, A. (2013). *Globalization, the human condition, and sustainable development in the twenty-first century: Cross-national perspectives and European implications*. London: Anthem.

Tausch, A., Heshmati, A., & Karoui, H. (2014). *The political algebra of global value change: General models and implications for the Muslim world*. Hauppauge, NY: Nova Science.

UNDP. (2014). *Human development report*. New York: Oxford University Press.

UNDP. (2017a). *Human development data (1990–2015)*. Download April 10, 2019, from http://hdr.undp.org/en/data

UNDP. (2017b). *Human development report*. New York: Oxford University Press.

Valkenberg, P., & Cirelli, A. (2016). *Nostra Aetate: Celebrating 50 Years of the Catholic Church's dialogue with Jews and Muslims*. CUA.

Chapter 6
Catholics, the Open Society, and Tolerance of Homosexuals

Introduction

With the publication of Reverend Krzysztof Charamsa's book[1] (Charamsa 2016), written by a Polish former official at the Congregation for the Doctrine of the Faith in the Vatican, accusing the Roman Catholic Church of making the lives of gay and transgender people *a hell*, the entire issue of homosexuality and Roman Catholicism has moved again into the focus of international media attention. While Pope Francis went on the record to say "Who am I to condemn the homosexuals,"[2] the influential Cardinal Robert Sarah of Guinea said[3]: "What Nazi-Fascism and Communism were in the 20th Century, Western homosexual and abortion ideologies and Islamic fanaticism are today."[4] But the opposition to homosexuality and gay marriages is not restricted to Roman Catholicism. The former British Chief Rabbi, Lord Jonathan Sacks, for example, has been among the most prominent Orthodox Jewish theologians to voice his opposition.[5] In several Muslim countries around the world, the death penalty for homosexuality is still being in force, among others in Iran (Adamczyk 2017).

---

[1]*New York Times*, October 28, 2015, available at https://www.nytimes.com/2015/10/29/world/europe/gay-priest-who-lost-vatican-job-assails-the-church-in-letter-to-pope-francis.html (Download April 10, 2019).

[2]National Catholic Reporter, January 10, 2016, available at https://www.ncronline.org/news/vatican/francis-explains-who-am-i-judge (Download April 10, 2019).

[3]Catholic Hierarchy Org, available at http://www.catholic-hierarchy.org/bishop/bsarahr.html (Download April 10, 2019).

[4]*New York Times*, October 28, 2015, available at https://www.nytimes.com/2015/10/29/world/europe/gay-priest-who-lost-vatican-job-assails-the-church-in-letter-to-pope-francis.html (Download April 10, 2019).

[5]*Daily Telegraph*, June 25, 2012, available at http://www.telegraph.co.uk/news/religion/9352603/Chief-Rabbi-voices-opposition-to-gay-marriage.html (Download April 10, 2019).

© Springer Nature Switzerland AG 2020   143
A. Tausch, S. Obirek, *Global Catholicism, Tolerance and the Open Society*,
https://doi.org/10.1007/978-3-030-23239-9_6

Charamsa (2016) offers a far-reaching and often very personal insider view of the issues involved. But while Charamsa's account was debated controversially in the international press and while the Catholic doctrine of marriage and the family in the context of homosexuality and same-sex marriages has also been amply debated recently by social science and the legal profession (Case 2016; Reid 2016), growing international sociological evidence seems to suggest that more and more Roman Catholic faithful do not follow anymore the condemnation of the homosexual act as a "deadly sin," voiced by the official current *Catechism* of the Roman Catholic Church, which is binding for Catholics, worldwide (Adamczyk 2017; John Paul II 1994a, b). Precisely these sociological facts and not the theological debates about homosexuality are of interest in this chapter. In simple, for theologians perhaps even vulgar terms, the question here is only whether the rejection of homosexuality still enjoys the support of the rank and file of the global Catholic faithful.

We again especially want to know more about the hitherto undocumented opinions of those Roman Catholics around the globe who attend Church services on Sundays, usually described in the Catholic tradition as the *Dominicantes*. They are the still existing *divisions of the Pope*. Current social science research as yet does not offer any data on this aspect (Adamczyk 2017). Do the *Dominicantes* follow the Church leaders and the Catholic official teaching, called the *magisterium*, on this issue? Such analyses are now possible with data from the *World Values Survey* (see also Chaps. 3 and 4 and Norris and Inglehart 2011; Davidov et al. 2011; Inglehart and Norris 2009).

Catholic opposition to gender theories and mainstream feminism continues to be very sharp (Case 2016; Reid 2016). In this chapter, we would like to reflect then in a detached and empirical way on the role of the active, global Catholics in the formation of global tolerance values vis-à-vis the homosexuals, using advanced methods of comparative social science research. We are only interested in what the active Roman Catholics—in comparison with overall society—think about homosexuality and the homosexuals, and we do say much less on what the Catholic doctrine on homosexuality *should* be.

Background: Studying Homosexuality and Catholicism

The Roman Catholic's official teaching on homosexuality, to be found in its binding form in its so-called Catechism (John Paul II 1994a), is stated briefly as follows:

> 2357 Basing itself on Sacred Scripture, which presents homosexual acts as acts of grave depravity, tradition has always declared that "homosexual acts are intrinsically disordered." They are contrary to the natural law. (. . .) Under no circumstances can they be approved.
>
> 2358 The number of men and women who have deep-seated homosexual tendencies is not negligible. This inclination, which is objectively disordered, constitutes for most of them a trial. They must be accepted with respect, compassion, and sensitivity. Every sign of unjust discrimination in their regard should be avoided.

> 2359 Homosexual persons are called to chastity. (. . .) By prayer and sacramental grace, they can and should gradually and resolutely approach Christian perfection.[6]

It is evident however that a large and growing number of Roman Catholics, including the faithful, do not follow or do not follow entirely this particular teaching of the Church.

Among recent research publications comparing global values, Adamczyk (2017) established that by international comparison, acceptance of homosexuality has risen especially in countries whose majority populations belong to the Roman Catholic Church. According to this empirical study, the level of development and the level of democracy in a country are important drivers of the growing global acceptance of homosexuality. In one of the most comprehensive series of surveys on the subject so far, McGee (2016a, b, c) also found that tolerance toward homosexuality is least likely to be found in Muslim societies and that in 47 countries with complete data, attitudes toward homosexuality shifted toward more tolerance over time since the 1980s, especially in Western countries, while in 6 countries, attitudes remained fairly stable (Bosnia, Cyprus, Nigeria, Romania, Rwanda, and Turkey) and in 11 countries, attitudes have become more restrictive (Albania, Armenia, Azerbaijan, Georgia, Germany, Ghana, Malaysia, Montenegro, Serbia, Thailand, Trinidad, and Tobago). In the study (2016a), McGee also analyzes the attitudes toward homosexuality by different denominational groups in different countries around the world, where we can reasonably assess attitudes according to the national denominational subgroups for which sufficiently large representative subsamples of respondents, usually 30 or more persons, are available from the surveys. Colombia, Cyprus, Germany, Ghana, India, Kazakhstan, Lebanon, Malaysia, the Netherlands, Nigeria, Pakistan, Philippines, Russia, Singapore, South Korea, and the United States were entered by McGee into these comparisons. Interestingly enough, people without denomination and Roman Catholics and Orthodox believers came out as the denominational groupings most tolerant of homosexuality, while Taoists, Hindus, and Evangelical Christians were the groups least tolerant of homosexuality.

It must be emphasized that from the viewpoint of a liberal and open society (Popper 2012), Pope Francis' widely circulated comments on homosexuality[7] often quoted as saying "Who am I to condemn gay people" on his flight with journalists on July 28, 2013, from Rio de Janeiro to Rome, were combined with the following statement by the Pontiff, using an old Catholic anti-Masonic stereotype, which seems to be a constant feature of Catholic thinking since the days of the Enlightenment in the middle of the eighteenth century and which culminated sadly enough in the European authoritarian states of the 1930s and 1940s, especially in Nazi

---

[6]http://www.vatican.va/archive/ccc_css/archive/catechism/p3s2c2a6.htm   (Download   April 10, 2019).

[7]https://www.cnsnews.com/news/article/pope-francis-masonic-lobbies-most-serious-problem-me and http://www.bbc.com/news/world-europe-23489702 (Download April 10, 2019).

Germany, and which, it seems, the Roman Catholic Church has still in common with those ideologies[8]:

> The problem is not having this [homosexual] orientation. No, we must be brothers and sisters. The problem is lobbying for this orientation, or lobbies of greed, political lobbies, Masonic lobbies, so many lobbies. This is the most serious problem for me. And thank you so much for this question. Thank you very much!

With such a statement raising the specter of a "masonic lobby" to "push" homosexual orientation, the current Pontiff overlooked the fact that apart from Jews and Sintis and Romas, homosexuals and Freemasons were the main target of *National Socialism* (Doney 1993; Lewy 2009; Plant 2011).

Data and Methods in Studying Catholicism and Homosexuality

The *World Values Survey* offers fairly encompassing and comparable data on two homosexuality research items, i.e., the rejection of homosexuality and the rejection of homosexual neighbors.

The question wording was[9]:

Rejection of homosexuality *Please tell me for each of the following actions whether you think it can always be justified, never be justified, or something in between: Homosexuality (scale ranges from never justifiable—0 to always justifiable—10).*

Homosexual neighbors *On this list are various groups of people. Could you please mention any that you would not like to have as neighbors: Homosexuals?*

Our research design first of all aims to establish the data about acceptancy of homosexuality and the rejection of homosexual neighbors on the level of the nation states with complete data. Then, we aim to establish the data for the practicing Catholics, the *Dominicantes*.

The present chapter again relies on the statistical analysis of open survey data and is based on the commonly used statistical software IBM-SPSS XXIV.[10] The use of this program is especially relevant in our context to assess the opinions of the *Dominicantes* subsamples from the wider survey results, also freely available from

---

[8]It should be emphasized that authoritarian movements in Europe of the 1930s, especially the Nazis, combined Jews, Freemasons, and homosexuals as object of their hatred; see http://www.jewishvirtuallibrary.org/homosexuals-and-the-third-reich. This tendency is evident as well for a long period of time of Roman Catholic history. Especially, Burleigh (2000) highlights the close connection between the anti-Masonic and Antisemitic agenda in Nazi ideology.

[9]http://www.worldvaluessurvey.org/WVSOnline.jsp (Download April 10, 2019).

[10]IBM-SPSS Statistics, http://www-03.ibm.com/software/products/en/spss-statistics (Download April 10, 2019).

the official website of the *World Values Survey* via its routine: online data analysis.[11] The chosen IBM-SPSS data files from the *WVS* data base again were the database named "WVS_Longitudinal_1981_2014_spss_v2015_04_18.sav."

For the calculation of error margins, readers are again, as in the preceding chapters, referred to the easily readable introduction to opinion survey error margins, prepared by Cornell University Roper Center's https://ropercenter.cornell.edu/sup port/polling-fundamentals-total-survey-error/. Readers more interested in the details again, as in the preceding chapters, are also being referred to the site: http://www. langerresearch.com/moe/ (Download April 10, 2019).

Our main statistical calculations relied on cross tables and comparisons of means (see Tausch et al. 2014). For all analyzed groups and subgroups, again, a minimum sample of at least 30 respondents per country had to be available in the original data sets to attempt reasonable predictions for the general or sectoral publics to be analyzed, thus keeping in line with standard traditions of empirical opinion survey research (for a survey of the vast methodological literature on the subject, again see Tausch et al. 2014).

Results: Estimating Catholic (In)Tolerance of Homosexuality

The attitudes of the global populations on homosexuality can be summarized in Map 6.1 and Table 6.1. There is a clear tendency that homosexuality is tolerated much more in developed than in developing countries. The former Communist countries of Eastern Europe are somewhat in a middle position.

The absolute "electoral" majority of the population[12] in Andorra, Sweden, the Netherlands, France, Czech Republic, Germany, Norway, Spain, Great Britain, Canada, Switzerland, New Zealand, Australia, Slovakia, Uruguay, Philippines, Thailand, the United States, Hong Kong, Finland, Japan, Serbia and Montenegro, Slovenia, Cyprus, Croatia, Singapore, Taiwan, Argentina, Bahrain, Bulgaria, Chile, Guatemala, Peru, Brazil, Lebanon, and Ecuador already does not share anymore the view that homosexuality can never be justified and thus reject the basic teaching of the Church on the subject. The list of these countries contains, notably enough, also the Muslim majority countries Bahrain and Lebanon and several predominantly Catholic countries around the world.

The official Catechism position that homosexuality can never be justified[13] is still an "electoral" majority position in Egypt, Bangladesh, Tunisia, Jordan, Tanzania, Qatar, Indonesia, Uganda, Azerbaijan, Morocco, Iran, Pakistan, Yemen, Georgia, Zimbabwe, Armenia, El Salvador, Palestinian territories, Algeria, China, Burkina

---

[11]Website *World Values Survey*: http://www.worldvaluessurvey.org/wvs.jsp (Download April 10, 2019).

[12]In descending order.

[13]In descending order.

Map 6.1 Homosexuality never justifiably. Highest: Egypt, Bangladesh, Tunisia, Jordan, and Tanzania. Lowest: Andorra, Sweden, the Netherlands, France, and Germany

Faso, Ghana, Libya, Macedonia, Turkey, Uzbekistan, Ethiopia, Trinidad and Tobago, Vietnam, Albania, Lithuania, Kyrgyzstan, Nigeria, Iraq, Montenegro, Russia, Bosnia, Romania, Rwanda, Serbia, India, Belarus, Kazakhstan, Moldova, Bosnia, Venezuela, Mali, Ukraine, Hungary, South Korea, Poland, Zambia, Puerto Rico, Colombia, Latvia, Estonia, Dominican Republic, Malaysia, South Africa, Italy, and Mexico.

A majority in an impressive number of countries, including Iran, where the regime still castigates homosexuality by the death penalty, and in the Muslim majority countries Bahrain, Pakistan, and Bangladesh, also would already accept a homosexual neighbor[14]: these countries of majority tolerance are Andorra, the Netherlands, Sweden, Norway, Spain, Switzerland, Canada, Guatemala, Germany, Bahrain, Great Britain, New Zealand, Uruguay, Australia, Brazil, Italy, Pakistan, Argentina, the United States, Finland, Philippines, Puerto Rico, France, Colombia, Vietnam, Thailand, Czech Republic, Mexico, Singapore, Ecuador, Chile, Cyprus, Hong Kong, Slovenia, Bangladesh, Bulgaria, Hungary, South Africa, Croatia, Peru, Iran, and the Dominican Republic.

The rejection of homosexual neighbors[15] is still the majority position in Egypt, Azerbaijan, Morocco, Turkey, Armenia, Jordan, Georgia, Qatar, Ethiopia, Burkina Faso, Zimbabwe, Iraq, Montenegro, Ghana, El Salvador, Nigeria, Lithuania, Albania, Libya, Rwanda, Uganda, Moldova, Kazakhstan, Tanzania, Kyrgyzstan, Zambia, Russia, Algeria, Belarus, Japan, Serbia and Montenegro, Tunisia, Yemen, Mali,

---

[14]In descending order.
[15]In descending order.

Table 6.1 Tolerance of homosexuals and of homosexuality: overall population

	Rejecting homosexual neighbors (%)	Homosexuality never justifiable (%)
Albania	76	75
Algeria	70	80
Andorra	6	8
Argentina	23	42
Armenia	87	81
Australia	20	27
Azerbaijan	92	90
Bahrain	18	42
Bangladesh	45	99
Belarus	70	67
Bosnia Sample 1	64	72
Bosnia Sample 2	61	66
Brazil	22	48
Bulgaria	45	42
Burkina Faso	81	79
Canada	16	24
Chile	40	44
China	64	80
Colombia	31	55
Croatia	46	40
Cyprus	41	38
Czech Republic	37	17
Dominican Republic	49	53
Ecuador	39	49
Egypt	100	100
El Salvador	78	81
Estonia	54	54
Ethiopia	82	76
Finland	26	35
France	29	15
Georgia	84	86
Germany	17	17
Ghana	79	79
Great Britain	19	20
Guatemala	16	46
Hong Kong	43	34
Hungary	45	61
India	55	69
Indonesia	62	91
Iran	48	88
Iraq	80	73
Italy	22	51

(continued)

Table 6.1 (continued)

	Rejecting homosexual neighbors (%)	Homosexuality never justifiable (%)
Japan	69	36
Jordan	85	95
Kazakhstan	74	67
Kyrgyzstan	73	74
Latvia	59	55
Lebanon	59	48
Libya	76	79
Lithuania	77	75
Macedonia	60	78
Malaysia	64	52
Mali	66	63
Mexico	38	51
Moldova	75	67
Montenegro	80	73
Morocco	89	90
The Netherlands	6	14
New Zealand	19	26
Nigeria	78	74
Norway	10	17
Pakistan	22	88
Palestinian Territories	65	81
Peru	47	46
Philippines	28	30
Poland	53	60
Puerto Rico	28	56
Qatar	83	92
Romania	57	71
Russia	71	73
Rwanda	76	70
Serbia	62	70
Serbia and Montenegro	69	36
Singapore	38	41
Slovakia	53	27
Slovenia	44	37
South Africa	45	52
South Korea	63	61
Spain	15	19
Sweden	6	8
Switzerland	15	24
Taiwan	54	41
Tanzania	74	94
Thailand	36	33

(continued)

Table 6.1 (continued)

	Rejecting homosexual neighbors (%)	Homosexuality never justifiable (%)
Trinidad and Tobago	57	76
Tunisia	69	97
Turkey	89	78
Uganda	76	91
Ukraine	63	63
The United States	24	33
Uruguay	19	28
Uzbekistan	65	77
Venezuela	63	66
Vietnam	33	76
Yemen	69	88
Zambia	73	59
Zimbabwe	81	82

Palestinian territories, Uzbekistan, Bosnia, China, Malaysia, South Korea, Ukraine, Venezuela, Indonesia, Serbia, Bosnia, Macedonia, Latvia, Lebanon, Romania, Trinidad and Tobago, India, Estonia, Taiwan, Poland, and Slovakia. Map 6.1 and Table 6.1 further summarize the results.

The majority of practicing Roman Catholics (i.e., more than 50%, in descending order of acceptancy) in Andorra, the Netherlands, Guatemala, New Zealand, Brazil, Canada, Germany, Italy, the United States, Australia, Singapore, Spain, Philippines, Puerto Rico, Argentina, Uruguay, Great Britain, Colombia, Switzerland, Vietnam, Czech Republic, Ecuador, Mexico, South Africa, France, Chile, Dominican Republic, and Trinidad and Tobago now would accept a homosexual neighbor, and a majority (i.e., more than 50%, in descending order) of practicing Roman Catholics in the Netherlands, Andorra, Germany, Canada, Czech Republic, France, Philippines, the United States, Great Britain, Singapore, Australia, Slovakia, New Zealand, South Africa, Spain, Guatemala, Lebanon, Bosnia, Switzerland, Uruguay, Brazil, Malaysia, Chile, and the Dominican Republic also reject the opinion that homosexuality can never be justified.

The countries with a high rejection of homosexual neighbors by the practicing Roman Catholics (more than 50% each, in descending order) are as follows: Lithuania, Ghana, Zimbabwe, Albania, Burkina Faso, Nigeria, Rwanda, El Salvador, Uganda, Tanzania, Zambia, South Korea, Indonesia, Belarus, Ukraine, Romania, Hungary, Venezuela, Bosnia, Malaysia, Slovakia, Slovenia, Croatia, Poland, India, Lebanon, and Peru.

The rejection of homosexuality as such (homosexuality never justified) is shared by more than 50% of the practicing Roman Catholics (in descending order) in Tanzania, Uganda, Lithuania, Indonesia, Hungary, Burkina Faso, El Salvador, Zimbabwe, Trinidad and Tobago, Vietnam, Ghana, Albania, Belarus, India,

Ukraine, Bosnia, Italy, Romania, Venezuela, Rwanda, Nigeria, Poland, South Korea, Zambia, Croatia, Puerto Rico, Colombia, Mexico, Argentina, Ecuador, Slovenia, and Peru.

Limited as our knowledge may be, we can now offer at least the following Table 6.2 on the tolerance of homosexuality among the global Catholic *Dominicantes*.

Maps 6.2 and 6.3 summarize our results in geographical form:

Are practicing Roman Catholics less "liberal" than overall societies regarding attitudes on homosexuality and homosexuals? Table 6.3 offers a comparison between the attitudes of Catholic *Dominicantes* and overall society on homosexuality:

Our analysis on the basis of *World Values Survey* data concludes that in a number of countries, the rejection of homosexuality among practicing Roman Catholics is already weaker than in the overall society surrounding the practicing Roman Catholics, such as (in descending order) in Bosnia, South Africa, Singapore, Indonesia, Nigeria, Guatemala, Lebanon, Dominican Republic, Malaysia, the United States, Philippines, Ghana, Romania, Rwanda, Zimbabwe, El Salvador, South Korea, and Zambia.

Practicing Roman Catholics (in descending order) in Singapore, Trinidad and Tobago, Lebanon, Malaysia, Bosnia, South Africa, Guatemala, Dominican Republic, Philippines, El Salvador, India, Nigeria, Zambia, Brazil, Puerto Rico, Vietnam were also more tolerant of homosexual neighbors than overall society.

The closer look at the data seems to suggest that especially in the old, traditional Catholic cultures of Europe, practicing Roman Catholics seem to hold a more excluding opinion on homosexuals and homosexuality than the (already very secularized) societies surrounding the Catholic communities. But the same tendency also holds in some non-European societies.

In the following countries, the Catholic *Dominicantes* rejection of homosexuality was stronger than in overall society (in descending order): Switzerland, Spain, Hungary, Italy, Uruguay, Croatia, Slovenia, France, Andorra, New Zealand, Ukraine, Czech Republic, Argentina, Lithuania, Great Britain, Belarus, Slovakia, India, Mexico, Peru, Chile, Australia, Venezuela, Ecuador, Trinidad and Tobago, Vietnam, Tanzania, the Netherlands, Germany, Canada, Puerto Rico, Colombia, Uganda, Bosnia, Burkina Faso, and Albania.

In the following countries, practicing Catholic *Dominicantes* were also less tolerant of homosexual neighbors than overall society (in descending order): Hungary, Switzerland, France, Slovenia, Croatia, Spain, Indonesia, Romania, Great Britain, South Korea, Lithuania, Uruguay, Canada, Australia, Ukraine, Poland, Albania, Germany, Chile, Slovakia, Argentina, Ghana, the Netherlands, Mexico, Peru, Ecuador, Zimbabwe, Venezuela, Italy, the United States, Rwanda, Bosnia, Burkina Faso, Belarus, Czech Republic, and New Zealand. Maps 6.4 and 6.5 highlight these tendencies:

To wind up our results, we present a comparison of the country population-unweighted means of the acceptability of homosexuality among the major global denominations and their regular monthly religious service attenders, ranging from

Table 6.2 Tolerance of homosexuality among the *Dominicantes*

	% *Dominicantes* rejecting homosexual neighbors	*n Dominicantes*	% *Dominicantes* saying homosexuality never justifiable	*n Dominicantes*
Albania	82	130	76	127
Andorra	6	53	19	53
Argentina	28	888	52	962
Australia	26	279	32	272
Belarus	71	97	76	93
Bosnia Sample 1	65	94	73	92
Bosnia Sample 2	60	84	45	83
Brazil	21	1153	48	1109
Burkina Faso	82	385	80	360
Canada	22	444	26	415
Chile	45	983	49	939
Colombia	31	2759	56	3914
Croatia	58	263	57	247
Czech Republic	38	150	27	130
Dominican Republic	47	121	49	117
Ecuador	42	371	52	371
El Salvador	76	340	80	328
France	44	50	27	49
Germany	22	297	19	289
Ghana	83	443	77	436
Great Britain	29	45	30	37
Guatemala	14	397	41	395
Hungary	66	105	81	207
India	53	131	74	122
Indonesia	72	50	82	50
Italy	24	312	69	295
Lebanon	52	148	43	148
Lithuania	86	131	85	123
Malaysia	59	63	48	63
Mexico	42	3336	56	4101
The Netherlands	10	60	16	57
New Zealand	20	92	37	78
Nigeria	78	963	66	960
Peru	51	1749	51	1290
Philippines	27	1676	27	1669
Poland	58	1668	60	1528

(continued)

Table 6.2 (continued)

	% Dominicantes rejecting homosexual neighbors	n Dominicantes	% Dominicantes saying homosexuality never justifiable	n Dominicantes
Puerto Rico	27	601	57	588
Romania	67	132	69	121
Rwanda	77	1380	68	1371
Singapore	26	146	31	147
Slovakia	58	488	34	457
Slovenia	58	541	52	506
South Africa	43	955	39	990
South Korea	72	376	60	461
Spain	26	1281	40	1157
Switzerland	32	170	46	351
Tanzania	74	292	96	292
Trinidad and Tobago	48	172	78	166
Uganda	76	283	92	281
Ukraine	69	139	74	118
The United States	25	627	29	601
Uruguay	28	164	46	156
Venezuela	65	597	69	588
Vietnam	32	97	78	89
Zambia	72	361	58	351
Zimbabwe	83	401	80	402

the high rejection among the regular service attenders among[16] the global adherents of the Jain religion, the global members of the Armenian Apostolic Church, and the global Muslims to lowest[17] among global Anglicans, Presbyterians, and global adherents of Confucianism. Among global adherents of the Anglican and Confucian denomination, acceptability of homosexuality among monthly religious service attenders was even greater than among the respective entire Anglican and Confucian global population, showing how the practice of tolerance is already part of the beliefs of the denominational active rank and file.

---

[16]In descending order.
[17]In descending order.

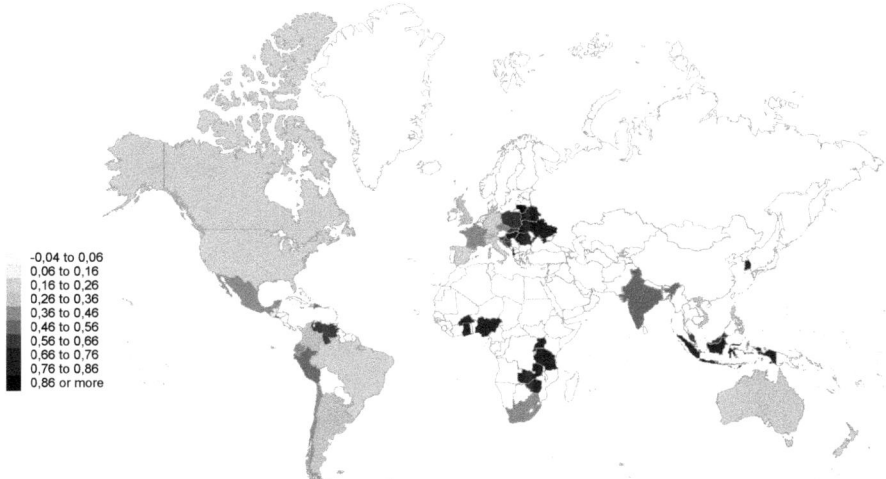

Map 6.2 % of the *Dominicantes* saying they reject to have a homosexual neighbor (scale ranging from 0.0 = 0% to 1.0 = 100%). Highest: Lithuania, Ghana, Zimbabwe, Albania, and Burkina Faso. Lowest: Andorra, the Netherlands, Guatemala, New Zealand, and Brazil

Map 6.3 % of the *Dominicantes* saying homosexuality can never be justified (scale ranging from 0.0 = 0% to 1.0 = 100%). Highest: Tanzania, Uganda, Lithuania, Indonesia, and Hungary. Lowest: The Netherlands, Andorra, Germany, Canada, and Czech Republic

Table 6.3 The tolerance of homosexual neighbors and of homosexuality as such by Catholic communities around the globe by international comparison

	Overall population rejecting homosexual neighbors (%)	Overall population: homosexuality never justifiable (%)	*Dominicantes:* rejecting homosexual neighbors (%)	*Dominicantes:* homosexuality never justifiable (%)	Relative rejection of homosexual neighbors by the *Dominicantes* (%)	Relative rejection of homosexuality by the *Dominicantes* (%)
Albania	76	75	82	76	5	1
Andorra	6	8	6	19	0	11
Argentina	23	42	28	52	5	10
Australia	20	27	26	32	6	5
Belarus	70	67	71	76	1	9
Bosnia Sample 1	64	72	65	73	1	1
Bosnia Sample 2	61	66	60	45	−2	−21
Brazil	22	48	21	48	−1	0
Burkina Faso	81	79	82	80	1	1
Canada	16	24	22	26	6	2
Chile	40	44	45	49	5	5
Colombia	31	55	31	56	0	1
Croatia	46	40	58	57	12	17
Czech Republic	37	17	38	27	1	10
Dominican Republic	49	53	47	49	−2	−4
Ecuador	39	49	42	52	3	3
El Salvador	78	81	76	80	−2	−1
France	29	15	44	27	15	12
Germany	17	17	22	19	5	2
Ghana	79	79	83	77	4	−2

Great Britain	19	20	29	30	10	10
Guatemala	16	46	14	41	−2	−5
Hungary	45	61	66	81	21	20
India	55	69	53	74	−2	5
Indonesia	62	91	72	82	10	−9
Italy	22	51	24	69	2	18
Lebanon	59	48	52	43	−7	−5
Lithuania	77	75	86	85	9	10
Malaysia	64	52	59	48	−5	−4
Mexico	38	51	42	56	4	5
The Netherlands	6	14	10	16	4	2
New Zealand	19	26	20	37	1	11
Nigeria	78	74	78	66	−1	−8
Peru	47	46	51	51	4	5
Philippines	28	30	27	27	−2	−3
Poland	53	60	58	60	5	0
Puerto Rico	28	56	27	57	−1	1
Romania	57	71	67	69	10	−2
Rwanda	76	70	77	68	1	−2
Singapore	38	41	26	31	−12	−10
Slovakia	53	27	58	34	5	7
Slovenia	44	37	58	52	14	15
South Africa	45	52	43	39	−2	−13
South Korea	63	61	72	60	9	−1
Spain	15	19	26	40	11	21
Switzerland	15	24	32	46	17	22

(continued)

Table 6.3 (continued)

	Overall population rejecting homosexual neighbors (%)	Overall population: homosexuality never justifiable (%)	*Dominicantes:* rejecting homosexual neighbors (%)	*Dominicantes:* homosexuality never justifiable (%)	Relative rejection of homosexual neighbors by the *Dominicantes* (%)	Relative rejection of homosexuality by the *Dominicantes* (%)
Tanzania	74	94	74	96	0	2
Trinidad and Tobago	57	76	48	78	−9	2
Uganda	76	91	76	92	0	1
Ukraine	63	63	69	74	6	11
The United States	24	33	25	29	1	−4
Uruguay	19	28	28	46	9	18
Venezuela	63	66	65	69	2	3
Vietnam	33	76	32	78	−1	2
Zambia	73	59	72	58	−1	−1
Zimbabwe	81	82	83	80	2	−2

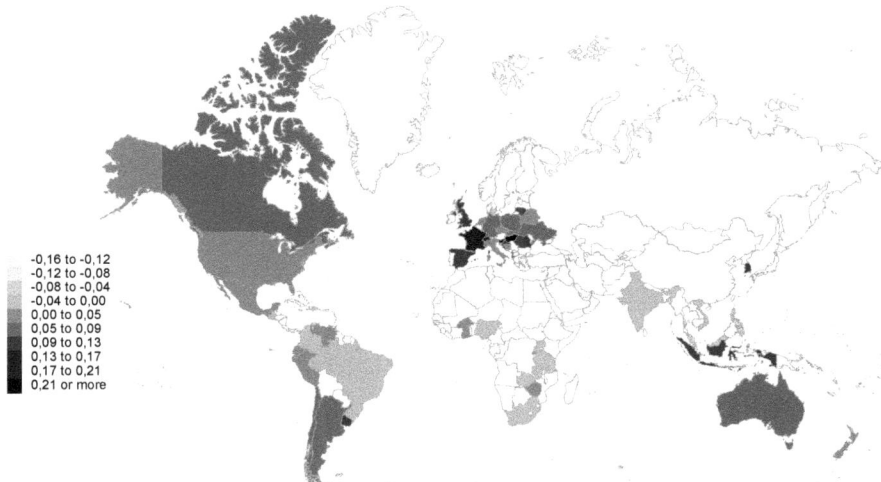

Map 6.4 *Dominicantes*—are they more or less restrictive than overall society in rejecting to have a homosexual neighbor (scale ranging theoretically from $-1.0 = -100\%$ to $1.0 = 100\%$; see Table 6.3)? Highest: Hungary, Switzerland, France, Slovenia, and Croatia. Lowest: Singapore, Trinidad and Tobago, Lebanon, Malaysia, and Dominican Republic

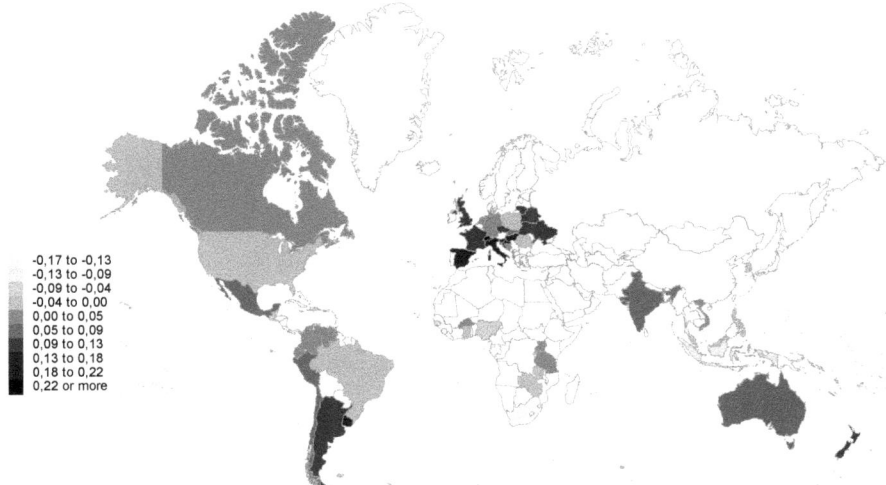

Map 6.5 *Dominicantes*—are they more or less following the official Church position than the overall society in saying that homosexuality can never be justified (scale ranging theoretically from $-1.0 = -100\%$ to $1.0 = 100\%$; see Table 6.3)? Highest: Switzerland, Spain, Hungary, Italy, and Uruguay. Lowest: South Africa, Singapore, Indonesia, Nigeria, and Guatemala

Table 6.4 Acceptability of homosexuality among the different global major denominations (ranked by the justifiability of homosexuality)

Religious denomination	Justifiable: homosexuality	N	Justifiable: homosexuality	N	Monthly religious service attendance rate (%)	% difference in saying homosexuality justifiable
Jain	1760	73	1550	55	75	−12
Armenian Apostolic Church	1640	2580	1590	881	34	−3
Muslim	1640	45,554	1640	21,687	48	0
Pentecostal	1850	804	1770	732	91	−4
Orthodox	2300	30,162	2040	9359	31	−11
Jehovah Witnesses	2300	433	2250	342	79	−2
Hindu	2410	8173	2370	4695	57	−2
Sikh	2730	102	2450	75	74	−10
Protestant	3210	28,874	2470	16,687	58	−23
Baptist	2740	117	2540	89	76	−7
Buddhist	3040	10,453	2790	3950	38	−8
Taoist	3170	428	2810	107	25	−11
Greek Catholic	3010	85	2820	44	52	−6
Mormon	3400	46	2880	40	87	−15
No religious denomination	4230	54,062	3160	4131	8	−25
Roman Catholic	3650	74,358	3170	43,539	59	−13
Confucianism	2900	71	3390	28	39	17
Presbyterian	5080	243	4510	41	17	−11
Anglican	4490	630	4870	53	8	8

Conclusion and Policy Perspectives from This Chapter

According to our figures, less than 50% of the Roman Catholic faithful regular Church attenders[18] in the Netherlands, Andorra, Germany, and a host of other countries nowadays think that homosexuality is never justifiable. Practicing Roman Catholics in the multicultural environment of Singapore, Trinidad and Tobago, Lebanon, and Malaysia were especially tolerant to homosexual neighbors in comparison with the society surrounding them.

Muslims, Evangelical Christians, and other denominations often take a still much tougher stance on homosexuality than the Roman Catholic Church (see Table 6.4 of this study). Table 6.4 shows that monthly religious service attenders among the adherents of the Jain, Armenian Apostolic Church, Muslim, Pentecostal, Orthodox, Jehovah Witnesses, Hindu, Sikh, Protestant, Baptist, Buddhist, Taoist, Greek Catholic, and Mormon, as well as adherents of no religious denomination, share a higher rejection rate of homosexuality than the monthly religious service attenders among the Roman Catholics.

But seen in the light of our data, decision-makers of the Roman Catholic Church might perhaps start to look for better-practice models among the ecumenical Presbyterian and Anglican fellow Christian Churches as well as among the Confucians—after all, the Ethics of *Love and Responsibility* (Pope John Paul II 1994a, b) were written for humankind.

Our analysis cannot claim to tell the decision-makers of the Roman Catholic Church which path to follow, but it is sufficiently clear that the Church's teaching on this point has less and less followers and that in the name of the relationships with indicators of an *Open Society*, a rethinking of the entire issue would be very necessary. To speak about *Masonic lobbies* in such a context is highly out of place and reminds us, by contrast, that the Roman Catholic Church throughout its history from around 300 A.D. to the end of the Second World War had so many problems in adapting to the trends toward democracy.

Literature

Adamczyk, A. (2017). *Cross-national public opinion about homosexuality. Examining attitudes across the globe.* Berkeley, CA: University of California Press.

Adamczyk, A., & Pitt, C. (2009). Shaping attitudes about homosexuality: The role of religion and cultural context. *Social Science Research, 38*(2), 338–351.

Burleigh, M. (2000). *The Third Reich: A new history.* Basingstoke: Pan Macmillan.

Case, M. A. (2016). *The role of the Popes in the Invention of Complementarity and the Vatican's Anathematization of Gender* (February 25, 2016). Forthcoming Religion and Gender Habemus Gender Special Issue 2016; U of Chicago, Public Law Working Paper No. 565. Available at SSRN: https://ssrn.com/abstract=2740008

---

[18]In descending order.

Charamsa, K. (2016). *La Prima Pietra. Io, prete gay a la mia ribellione all'ipocrisia della Chiesa*. Milano: Rizzoli.

Davidov, E., Schmidt, P., & Schwartz, S. H. (2008). Bringing values back in the adequacy of the *European Social Survey* to measure values in 20 countries. *Public Opinion Quarterly, 72*(3), 420–445.

Davidov, E., Schmidt, P., & Billiet, J. (2011). *Cross-cultural analysis: Methods and applications*. New York: Routledge.

Doney, K. (1993). *Freemasonry in France during the Nazi occupation and it's rehabilitation after the end of the Second World War*. Ph.D. thesis, University of Aston, Birmingham.

Inglehart, R. F. (1988). The renaissance of political culture. *American political science review, 82* (04), 1203–1230.

Inglehart, R. F. (1990). *Culture shift in advanced industrial countries*. Princeton, NJ: Princeton University Press.

Inglehart, R. F. (2000). Globalization and postmodern values. *Washington Quarterly, 23*(1), 215–228.

Inglehart, R. F. (2006). Mapping global values. *Comparative Sociology, 5*(2), 115–136.

Inglehart, R. F. (2008). Changing values among western publics from 1970 to 2006. *West European Politics, 31*(1–2), 130–146.

Inglehart, R. F. (2015). *The silent revolution: Changing values and political styles among Western publics*. Princeton, NJ: Princeton University Press.

Inglehart, R. F., & Baker, W. E. (2000). Modernization, cultural change, and the persistence of traditional values. *American Sociological Review, 65*(1), 19–51. Download April 10, 2019, from http://my.fit.edu/~gabrenya/cultural/readings/Inglehart-Baker-2000.pdf

Inglehart, R. F., & Norris, P. (2003). *Rising tide: Gender equality and cultural change around the world*. Cambridge, MA: Cambridge University Press.

Inglehart, R. F., & Norris, P. (2009, November 4). The true clash of civilizations. *Foreign Policy*. Download April 10, 2019, from http://foreignpolicy.com/2009/11/04/the-true-clash-of-civilizations/

Inglehart, R. F., & Norris, P. (2012). The four horsemen of the apocalypse: Understanding human security. *Scandinavian Political Studies, 35*(1), 71–95.

Inglehart, R F., & Norris, P. (2016). *Trump, Brexit, and the rise of populism: Economic have-nots and cultural backlash* (HKS Working Paper No. RWP16-026). Available at SSRN. Download April 10, 2019, from http://ssrn.com/abstract=2818659

Inglehart, R. F., & Welzel, C. (2003). Political culture and democracy: Analyzing cross-level linkages. *Comparative Politics, 36*(1), 61–79.

Inglehart, R F., & Welzel C. (2009, March, April). How development leads to democracy. What we know about modernization. *Foreign Affairs*. Download April 10, 2019, from http://www.foreignaffairs.com/articles/64821/ronald-inglehart-and-christian-welzel/how-development-leads-to-democracy

Inglehart, R. F., & Welzel, C. (2010). Changing mass priorities: The link between modernization and democracy. *Perspectives on Politics, 8*(02), 551–567.

Inglehart, R. F., Ponarin, E., & Inglehart, R. C. (2017). Cultural change, slow and fast: The distinctive trajectory of norms governing gender equality and sexual orientation. *Social Forces, 95*(4), 1313–1340.

John Paul, II. (1994a). *Catechism of the Catholic church*. Rome: Urbi Et Orbi Communications. Download April 10, 2019, from http://www.vatican.va/archive/ENG0015/_INDEX.HTM

John Paul, II. (1994b). *Love and responsibility*. San Francisco, CA: Ignatius Press.

Lewy, G. (2009). *The Catholic church and Nazi Germany*. Boston: Da Capo Press.

McGee, R. W. (2016a). *Does religion influence views toward homosexuality: An empirical study of 16 countries*. Available at SSRN: https://ssrn.com/abstract=2799871

McGee, R. W. (2016b). *Has homosexuality become more accepted over time? A longitudinal study of 98 countries*. Available at SSRN: https://ssrn.com/abstract=2799843

McGee, R. W. (2016c). *The relationship between religion and views toward homosexuality: An empirical study of 98 countries*. Available at SSRN: https://ssrn.com/abstract=2799870

Norris, P., & Inglehart, R. F. (2002). Islamic culture and democracy: Testing the 'clash of civilizations' thesis. *Comparative Sociology, 1*(3), 235–263.

Norris, P., & Inglehart, R. F. (2011). *Sacred and secular: Religion and politics worldwide*. Cambridge, MA: Cambridge University Press.

Norris, P., & Inglehart, R. F. (2012). Muslim integration into Western cultures: Between origins and destinations. *Political Studies, 60*(2), 228–251.

Norris, P., & Inglehart, R. F. (2015). Are high levels of existential security conducive to secularization? A response to our critics. In S. D. Brunn (Ed.), *The changing world religion map* (pp. 3389–3408). Dordrecht: Springer.

Plant, R. (2011). *The pink triangle: The Nazi war against homosexuals*. New York: Holt Paperbacks.

Popper, K. S. (2012). *The open society and its enemies*. New York: Routledge.

Reid, C. J. (2016). *Same sex unions and the Catholic Church: How law and doctrine evolve*. University of St. Thomas (Minnesota) Legal Studies Research Paper No. 16-27. Available at SSRN. Download April 10, 2019, from https://ssrn.com/abstract=2868201 or https://doi.org/10.2139/ssrn.2868201

Tausch, A., Heshmati, A., & Karoui, H. (2014). *The political algebra of global value change: General models and implications for the Muslim world*. Hauppauge, NY: Nova Science.

Chapter 7
Global Catholicism and the Open Society: A Final Statistical Synopsis

Final Global Rankings of Open Society Catholicism

Summarizing our results and putting them into perspective with new and especially designed statistical analyses developed for the aims of this chapter, we first of all have to emphasize that among all denominations around the globe, there is a wide range of country-level achievement scores according to the Open Society Index, developed in Chap. 4. Hofstede (2001), Hofstede and Minkov (2010), and Hofstede et al. (2010) were thus correct in emphasizing that differences between cultures are far less decisive than differences between countries in determining value development. There is a breathtaking variety of Catholicism around the world. Graph 7.1 highlights the best and worst country performances per denominational group in world society.

In the light of the main indicators of this work, Table 7.1 offers a synoptic glance at the different types of Catholicism we are faced with in the world today. In terms of the combined performance on our *Nostra Aetate* Index (Chap. 3), our new Civil Society Index (Chap. 4), overall religious tolerance (Chap. 5), and tolerance of homosexuality (Chap. 6), the US Catholic community leads the international comparison of countries with complete data, followed by the *Dominicantes* in Germany, Chile, Argentina, and Poland, while the *Dominicantes* in Spain, Slovenia, and Mexico are in the lower ranks in our comparison of Catholic tolerance.

From a Culture Inspired by a Theology of Liberation to a Culture Inspired by a Theology of Global Tolerance?

The good rankings of the enlightened Catholicism of Argentina and Chile on the one hand and the poor rankings of the most numerous Catholic practicing community of the world in Mexico on the other hand, which in many ways resembles the values of

© Springer Nature Switzerland AG 2020
A. Tausch, S. Obirek, *Global Catholicism, Tolerance and the Open Society*,
https://doi.org/10.1007/978-3-030-23239-9_7

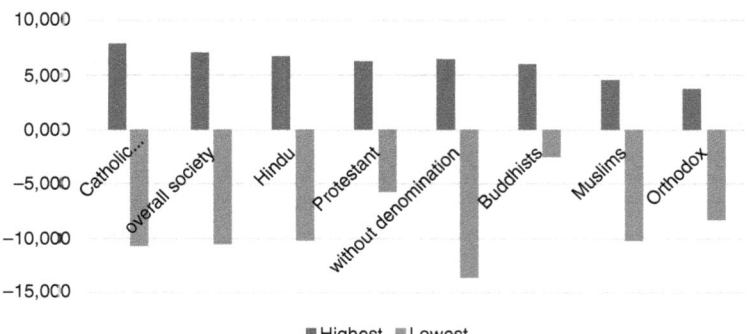

■ Highest ■ Lowest

Graph 7.1 Open Society Index among the different denominations around the globe

Table 7.1 A synoptic glance at the different types of Global Catholicism—rankings of this study at one glance

	The United States	Germany	Chile	Argentina	Poland	Spain	Slovenia	Mexico
Nostra Aetate Index	0.711	0.588	0.586	0.622	0.361	0.122	0.383	0.409
Rank *Nostra Aetate* Index	1	3	4	2	7	8	6	5
Overall Civil Society Index—*Dominicantes*	3.294	5.004	2.596	0.006	2.890	2.159	0.067	−0.728
Rank Overall Civil Society Index—*Dominicantes*	2	1	4	7	3	5	6	8
% *Dominicantes* saying homosexuality never justifiable	0.290	0.190	0.490	0.520	0.600	0.400	0.520	0.560
Rank % *Dominicantes* saying homosexuality never justifiable	2	1	4	5	8	3	6	7
Index of Religious Tolerance	0.727	0.506	0.688	0.682	0.678	0.537	0.604	0.500
Rank Religious Tolerance Index	1	7	2	3	4	6	5	8
Average rank	1.500	3.000	3.500	4.250	5.500	5.500	5.750	7.000

the *Dominicantes* in the other poorer Latin American countries, also offer several suggestions for the differentiated way we should now view liberation theology in the future in the light of our results. Liberation theology (Müller et al. 2000) as the theology of the churches of the poor global South must become a theology of global tolerance. It now must address the problems of Antisemitism, religious intolerance, and homophobia among its millions of adherents. It cannot be blind to the issues of gender. Our factor analytical results from Chap. 4, which wielded among others the factor *no redistributive religious fundamentalism*, raise another important problem for the way in which liberation theology interpreted the world and as yet did not confront the issues of societal violence, including domestic violence in Roman Catholic households. Liberation theology must care about how its values and aims became the values and aims of its millions and millions of adherents in Latin America, Africa, and Asia. The belief in the importance of religion and the belief that in democracies the state has to make people's incomes equal and the government has to tax the rich and subsidize the poor strongly coincide with the belief that religious authorities should interpret the laws. The separation of church and state is thus a point liberation theology and the social practice inspired by it must tackle in the future, suggesting that Maritain (1936, 2012) in many ways offered already credible alternatives for a theology of the twenty-first century to follow, also among the churches of the global South.

At this point, we should also mention the neoliberal critique of liberation theology. Hayek, in his often overlooked and really scathing neoliberal critique of liberation theology (von Hayek and Bartley 1988), asked—liberation, but from what?—and suggested that liberation theology is leading a society into an absolutely false direction when basic tenets of property rights and the work ethics are dismissed. Although we initially tended to discard such arguments, our factor analysis in Chap. 4 revealed that the belief that competition is harmful is shared by millions of *Dominicantes* around the world, combined with the call for state ownership of the means of production and the disbelief in hard work as the basis of societal success.

In Graph 7.2, we now show how the rejection of the basic tenet of a liberal Hayekian market economy—the rejection of free competition—is associated with clear negative effects among the Catholic *Dominicantes* of the world.

Only the very hard core of people, rejecting the basic precondition of a free market economy—competition—again are characterized by also holding more pronounced values of societal and personal nonviolence, but else there is a clear and linear effect of attitudes on competition policy and religious fundamentalism: the more people reject competition and thus the free market, the more they are religious fundamentalists.

In Chap. 4, we also could show that today, holding no welfare mentality and the acceptancy of the Calvinist work ethics (Giorgi and Marsh 1990) go back to the sociology of Max Weber (Weber 1922/1964) and are to be found among leading political proponents of the neoliberal agenda: accepting larger income differences, importance of work and religion, and the rejection of the redistributive state. We leave it up to our readers to draw their conclusions in the framework of such a clear neoliberal agenda in debating liberation theology. Others have done so, while our own empirical results at least suggest that there are enough *Dominicantes*

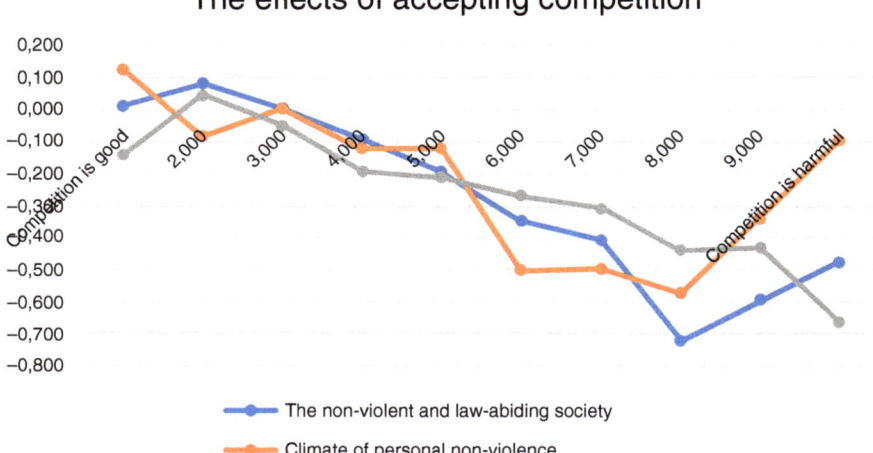

Graph 7.2 Was Hayek right in criticizing liberation theology? The effects of attitudes on competition policy on three essential dimensions of values among global Catholic *Dominicantes*

communities of the global South, serving as an alternative role model for the global Catholic Church to follow, indicating that there are best-practice examples in the global South:

The law-abiding society: Trinidad and Tobago, Ghana, Rwanda
Democracy movement: Chile
Climate of personal nonviolence: Chile, Ecuador
Trust in institutions: Chile, Singapore, Philippines, Ghana
Happiness, good health: Ghana, Nigeria, Rwanda, Trinidad and Tobago, Mexico
No redistributive religious fundamentalism: Trinidad and Tobago
Accepting the market economy: Ghana, Trinidad and Tobago, Zimbabwe, Brazil
Feminism: Trinidad and Tobago, Peru, Brazil, Mexico, Colombia
Involvement in politics: Philippines, Trinidad and Tobago
Optimism and engagement: Ghana, Trinidad and Tobago, Nigeria, Rwanda, Mexico
No welfare mentality, acceptancy of the Calvinist work ethics: Ghana, Trinidad and Tobago, Zimbabwe, Peru, Mexico

On the other hand, our analysis has shown that it would be absolutely wrong to portray the Catholic Church communities of the global South as general role models for the global Church to follow in general terms. The following *Dominicantes* communities in the countries of the global South recorded the bottom performances of global Catholicism:

The law-abiding society: South Africa, Philippines, Mexico, Peru, LebanonSpain
Democracy movement: Singapore, Ecuador, South Africa, Colombia, Lebanon

Climate of personal nonviolence: South Africa, Rwanda, Zimbabwe, Nigeria, Philippines
Trust in institutions: Lebanon, Peru, Mexico
Happiness, good health: Chile
No redistributive religious fundamentalism: Philippines, South Africa, Nigeria, Ecuador
Accepting the market economy: South Africa, Argentina, Singapore
Feminism: Nigeria, Lebanon, Philippines, Ghana, Singapore
Involvement in politics: Colombia, Chile, Peru
Optimism and engagement: Philippines, Peru
No welfare mentality, acceptancy of the Calvinist work ethics: Rwanda

A Concluding Factor Analysis Including Catholic Antisemitism

In the following brief synoptical promax factor analysis, we analyze the opinions of *all baptized Catholics* in Albania, Argentina, Belarus, Bosnia, Canada, Chile, Czech Republic, India, Mexico, Nigeria, Slovakia, South Africa, South Korea, Spain, Uganda, the United States, Uruguay, Venezuela, and Zimbabwe, where there were complete available data with the necessary variables (Table 7.2) to study Catholic Antisemitism in a very broad global value studies framework (see also Chaps. 2 and 3). For the first time in the literature, the following dimensions from the *World Values Survey* data base were studied in conjunction with Catholic Antisemitism:

- Acceptancy of homosexuality versus homophobia
- Age
- Attitudes on family and work
- Attitudes on labor and labor rights
- Attitudes on the sociopolitical and economic
- Position in the economic and social hierarchy
- Strength of the adherence to the church in fundamental religious questions
- Values in education
- Xenophobia versus a culture of welcome

Thus, the dimensions analyzed in the four chapters earlier were combined again in a last empirical synthesis.

A 55.55% of the overall variance were explained, and the following factors resulted after the appropriate promax rotation of the factors:

- Secularism
- Xenophobia
- Distance to sociopolitical and economic order
- Poverty
- Acceptancy of homosexuality

Table 7.2 The variables of our summarizing factor analytical model of global Catholicism including Antisemitism

	% of total variance explained (0 = 0%, 1.0 = 100%)
Not important in life: family	0.622
Not important in life: politics	0.464
Not important in life: work	0.577
Not important in life: religion	0.652
Feeling of happiness (unhappy)	0.595
State of health (subjective) (bad)	0.578
Important child qualities: hard work	0.554
Important child qualities: tolerance and respect for other people	0.766
Important child qualities: religious faith	0.463
Important child qualities: obedience	0.505
Rejecting neighbors: people of a different race	0.658
Rejecting neighbors: immigrants/foreign workers	0.671
Rejecting neighbors: homosexuals	0.579
Rejecting neighbors: Jews	0.606
Satisfaction with financial situation of household	0.499
Important in a job: good pay	0.569
Important in a job: good job security	0.562
Self-positioning in political scale (right)	0.351
Competition good or harmful (harmful)	0.344
No confidence: churches	0.608
No confidence: armed forces	0.523
No confidence: the press	0.566
No confidence: major companies	0.566
How often do you attend religious services (never)	0.567
Justifiable: homosexuality	0.560
Sex	0.370
Age	0.625

- Trade-unionism
- Unimportance of family and work (Nihilism)
- Age
- Obedience (value in education)
- Education: tolerance and respect for other people

Our electronic statistical Appendix lists among the results for this chapter the factor loadings after factor rotation as well as the country-level factor scores. Table 7.3 is devoted to the analysis of the correlations between the different factors characterizing the analyzed opinions of the baptized global Catholics with complete data.

Table 7.3 Correlations between the factors of the model

Component	Secularism	Xenophobia	Distance to sociopolitical and economic order	Poverty	Acceptancy of homosexuality	Trade-unionism	Unimportance of family and work (Nihilism)	Age	Obedience (value in education)	Education: tolerance and respect for other people
Secularism	1.000	−0.071	0.234	0.065	0.165	0.037	0.052	−0.112	−0.159	−0.005
Xenophobia	−0.071	1.000	−0.044	0.087	−0.093	0.112	0.051	0.049	0.026	−0.070
Distance to sociopolitical and economic order	0.234	−0.044	1.000	0.125	0.176	−0.022	0.021	−0.031	0.034	0.105
Poverty	0.065	0.087	0.125	1.000	0.058	0.069	0.010	0.024	0.075	0.012
Acceptancy of homosexuality	0.165	−0.093	0.176	0.058	1.000	−0.063	0.063	−0.038	0.011	0.183
Trade-unionism	0.037	0.112	−0.022	0.069	−0.063	1.000	−0.136	0.098	−0.088	−0.090
Unimportance of family and work (Nihilism)	0.052	0.051	0.021	0.010	0.063	−0.136	1.000	0.100	0.094	−0.009
Age	−0.112	0.049	−0.031	0.024	−0.038	0.098	0.100	1.000	−0.074	−0.073
Obedience (value in education)	−0.159	0.026	0.034	0.075	0.011	−0.088	0.094	−0.074	1.000	0.177
Education: tolerance and respect for other people	−0.005	−0.070	0.105	0.012	0.183	−0.090	−0.009	−0.073	0.177	1.000

The Country Results for the Biggest Catholic Communities with Complete Data

Tables 7.4, 7.5, 7.6, 7.7, 7.8 and 7.9 summarize the factor analytical main characteristics of the opinions of Roman Catholics in the most important countries of global Catholicism, defined by the population size of active *Dominicantes*. The countries are listed alphabetically, starting with Argentina and ending with the United States. *In each case, the analysis is based on all baptized Roman Catholics.*

Table 7.4 The factor scores for the Catholicism of Argentina

	Argentina
Distance to sociopolitical and economic order	0.500
Acceptancy of homosexuality	0.249
Secularism	0.134
Age	0.127
Education: tolerance and respect for other people	0.068
Poverty	0.029
Obedience (value in education)	−0.157
Unimportance of family and work (Nihilism)	−0.171
Trade-unionism	−0.178
Xenophobia	−0.370

Table 7.5 The factor scores for the Catholicism of Canada

	Canada
Acceptancy of homosexuality	0.657
Age	0.362
Secularism	0.256
Education: tolerance and respect for other people	0.208
Unimportance of family and work (Nihilism)	0.117
Distance to sociopolitical and economic order	−0.090
Trade-unionism	−0.142
Obedience (value in education)	−0.293
Xenophobia	−0.399
Poverty	−0.676

Table 7.6 The factor scores for the Catholicism of India

	India
Unimportance of family and work (Nihilism)	0.503
Age	0.269
Trade-unionism	0.061
Xenophobia	−0.188
Obedience (value in education)	−0.217
Poverty	−0.259
Education: tolerance and respect for other people	−0.382
Secularism	−0.483
Distance to sociopolitical and economic order	−0.718
Acceptancy of homosexuality	−1.074

Table 7.7 The factor scores for the Catholicism of Mexico

	Mexico
Unimportance of family and work (Nihilism) (Nihilism)	0.429
Xenophobia	0.216
Obedience (value in education)	0.048
Poverty	−0.080
Distance to sociopolitical and economic order	−0.088
Education: tolerance and respect for other people	−0.150
Acceptancy of homosexuality	−0.186
Secularism	−0.263
Trade-unionism	−0.275
Age	−0.286

Table 7.8 The factor scores for the Catholicism of Spain

	Spain
Secularism	0.682
Acceptancy of homosexuality	0.676
Distance to sociopolitical and economic order	0.166
Age	0.125
Education: tolerance and respect for other people	0.098
Unimportance of family and work (Nihilism)	0.069
Obedience (value in education)	0.059
Trade-unionism	0.032
Poverty	0.013
Xenophobia	−0.004

Table 7.9 The factor scores for the Catholicism of the United States

	The United States
Age	0.455
Acceptancy of homosexuality	0.447
Trade-unionism	0.170
Unimportance of family and work (Nihilism)	0.137
Education: tolerance and respect for other people	0.121
Distance to sociopolitical and economic order	−0.163
Xenophobia	−0.218
Secularism	−0.326
Obedience (value in education)	−0.549
Poverty	−0.651

A Final Glance at Catholic Antisemitism

The factor "xenophobia" of the practicing Roman Catholics, which is evident from our Appendix Table 7.5, clearly locates Catholic Antisemitism within the larger framework of general xenophobia. The factor loadings of xenophobia are as follows:

Rejecting neighbors: immigrants/foreign workers	0.817
Rejecting neighbors: people of a different race	0.810
Rejecting neighbors: Jews	0.775
Rejecting neighbors: homosexuals	0.205
Important child qualities: hard work	0.107
Feeling of (un)happiness	0.075
Important in a job: good job security	0.072
Competition good or harmful	0.072
Important in a job: good pay	0.071
State of health (subjective) (not good)	0.064
Gender—female	0.059
Unimportant in life: family	0.052
Important child qualities: religious faith	0.045
Important child qualities: obedience	0.033
Unimportant in life: work	0.028
Age	0.016
Self-positioning in political scale (right)	0.011
No confidence: major companies	−0.002
Satisfaction with financial situation of household	−0.008
Unimportant in life: politics	−0.012
Unimportant in life: religion	−0.015
No confidence: churches	−0.026
No confidence: armed forces	−0.033
Important child qualities: tolerance and respect for other people	−0.048
No confidence: the Press	−0.069
Justifiable: homosexuality	−0.087
How often do you attend religious services? (never)	−0.099

However, it must be noted that the loadings with the variables other than from the xenophobia dimension are rather small. Table 7.10 lists the factor loadings for global Catholic Antisemitism with the other factors of the model, ranging from the positive loadings of Catholic to working class trade-unionism to the negative loadings of the acceptancy of homosexuality, *again emphasizing the importance of the findings of Inglehart about the close connection between tolerance for homosexuality and overall tolerance in a society* (Inglehart 2008; Inglehart and Baker 2000; Inglehart and Welzel 2010):

Graph 7.3 summarizes the results of Table 7.10 in graphical form.

Table 7.11 is devoted to the analysis of the salient, main product–moment correlations between Catholic Antisemitism with the other indicators of the present

Table 7.10 The factor loadings for Catholic Antisemitism

	Rejecting neighbors: Jews
Trade-unionism	0.093
Age	0.045
Poverty	0.037
Unimportance of family and work (Nihilism)	0.017
Obedience (value in education)	0.012
Education: tolerance and respect for other people	−0.032
Secularism	−0.050
Distance to sociopolitical and economic order	−0.055
Acceptancy of homosexuality	−0.118

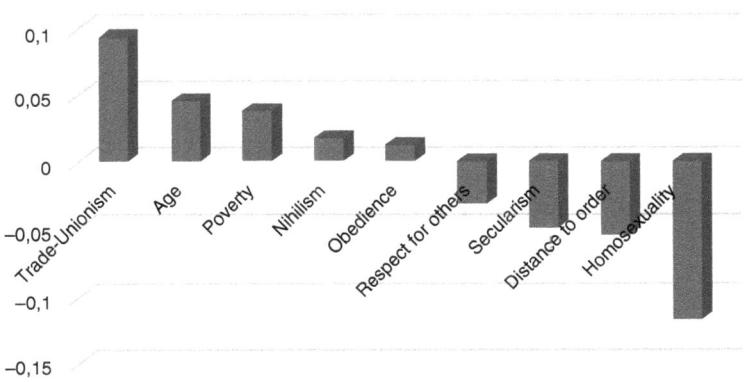

Graph 7.3 The drivers and blockades against Catholic Antisemitism

work on a country level, again showing the importance of the factor: no redistributive religious fundamentalism.

The Correlates of the Tolerance of Homosexuality

We now look into the country-level correlates of the rejection of homosexuality, and we also analyze some multivariate relationships between the country-level rejection of homosexuality/homosexual neighbors and Antisemitism and other country-level tolerance indicators. The "Catholic" component in the factors, shaping global attitudes on homosexuality, has received due attention in published research already (Adamczyk and Pitt 2009; Kappler et al. 2013).

Table 7.11 The main correlation between the indicators from this work on a country to country level

Predicted variable	Correlation coefficient	R^2	With factor from global value analysis
% practicing Catholics—rejecting Jewish neighbors	−0.532	28.321	Catholic: no redistributive religious fundamentalism
% practicing Catholics—rejecting Jewish neighbors	−0.514	26.401	Catholic: feminism
% practicing Catholics—rejecting Jewish neighbors	−0.484	23.388	Catholic: the law-abiding society
% practicing Catholics—rejecting Jewish neighbors	−0.438	19.222	Catholic: Overall Civil Society Index
% practicing Catholics—rejecting Jewish neighbors	−0.346	11.968	Catholic: climate of personal nonviolence
% practicing Catholics—rejecting Jewish neighbors	−0.317	10.063	Catholic: democracy movement

Following a vast literature tradition, we are inclined to view in our multivariate analysis a connection between the rejection of homosexuals/homosexuality and authoritarian ideologies, which victimized Jews, homosexuals, Freemasons, and other groups (Bytwerk 2015; Hastings 2009; Phayer 2000; Plant 2011; Rittner and Roth 2016).

It emerges from our research that tolerance of homosexuality indeed coincides with basic patterns of a liberal and democratic society. Briefly stated, the correlates of the acceptancy of homosexuality reveal interesting patterns. Following Alexander et al. (2012), the *Index of Effective Democracy* combines civil rights and the freedom from corruption. The global geographical distribution of the Index is shown in Map 7.1, with its predictable "North/South" and "West/East" gaps, reflecting well the current structure of the world system.

Graph 7.4 shows the interesting bivariate correlation between the rejection of homosexuality and *effective democracy*. The correlation, which explains more than 65% of the variance of the rejection of homosexuality, cannot be dismissed simply out of hand. Tolerance of homosexuality indeed even can be considered as one of the hallmarks of the existence of an overall climate of societal tolerance.

Table 7.12 summarizes other bivariate correlations of the rejection of homosexuality with a series of economic, social, and political indicators, presented at great length in Tausch and Heshmati (2013) and Tausch (2019).[1] It emerges that practically all indicators of a positive overall social and political development of a society are highly and negatively correlated with the rejection of homosexuality. In addition, we can say that Muslim countries and societies are at the forefront of the rejection of homosexuality.

---

[1] As to the variable definitions and their sources, see Tausch and Heshmati (2013) and Tausch (2019).

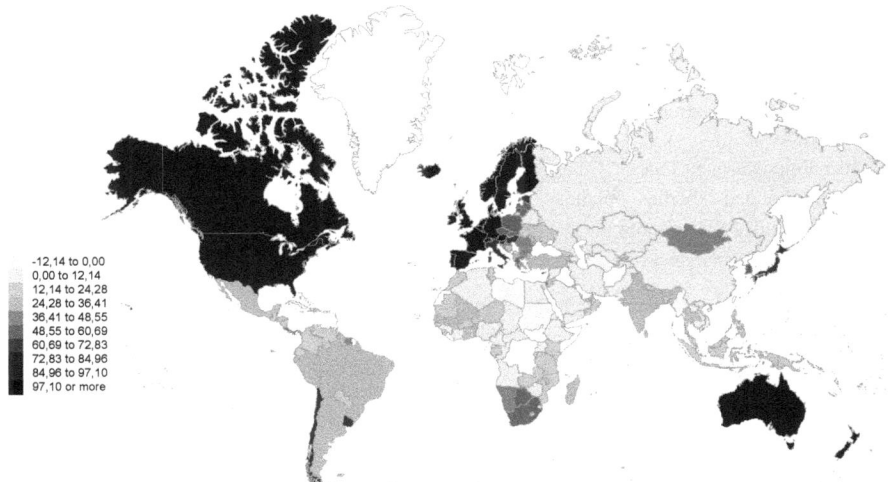

Map 7.1 Effective democracy combining civil rights and the freedom from corruption. Highest: Finland, Iceland, Denmark, New Zealand, and Switzerland. Lowest: Burma, Cuba, Libya, Sudan, and Turkmenistan

homosexuality never justifiable

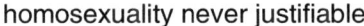

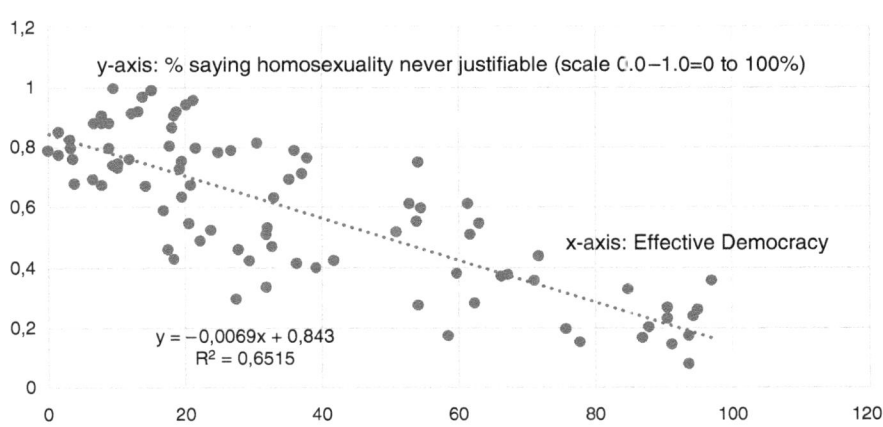

Graph 7.4 Rejection of homosexuality and *effective democracy*

Table 7.12   The correlates of the rejection of homosexuality

Indicators of development according to Tausch and Heshmati (2013)	Pearson Correlation with rejection of homosexuality	R^2 in %
Overall social development index, based on 35 indicators	−0.811	65.81
Gender Empowerment Index	−0.770	59.29
Civil and Political Liberties violations	0.736	54.18
Combined Failed States Index	0.730	53.26
Corruption avoidance measure	−0.720	51.82
Rule of law	−0.709	50.24
Democracy measure	−0.684	46.77
Happy Life Years	−0.655	42.89
Human Development Index (HDI)	−0.633	40.07
Tertiary enrollment	−0.630	39.63
Closing of the global gender gap overall score 2009	−0.629	39.58
Life satisfaction (0–10)	−0.623	38.76
Muslim population share per total population	0.617	38.03
Per capita world class universities	−0.613	37.54
Environmental Performance Index (EPI)	−0.580	33.67
Membership in the Islamic Conference	0.568	32.26
Life expectancy (years)	−0.537	28.81
UNDP education index	−0.536	28.70
2000 Economic Freedom Score	−0.528	27.83
Closing political gender gap	−0.510	26.00
Female survival probability of surviving to age 65 female	−0.481	23.12
% women in government, all levels	−0.479	22.99
Annual population growth rate, 1975–2005 (%)	0.473	22.33
Closing economic gender gap	−0.459	21.04
Closing educational gender gap	−0.417	17.40
Closing health and survival gender gap	−0.405	16.44

In Table 7.13, we look at the interesting relationships between our homosexuality variables for the *Dominicantes* and some indicators of tolerance and value development. Only the most salient results are reported here.

The religious tolerance indicators from the *World Values Survey* were explained already in Chaps. 3 and 5. Our indicators of the Antisemitism of the *Dominicantes* were derived as follows:

- Are practicing Catholics more or less Antisemitic than overall society in rejecting to have a Jewish neighbor?
- % practicing Catholics—rejecting Jewish neighbors
- Rate of change of Antisemitism among *Dominicantes* (rejecting Jewish neighbors) in % per decade

Table 7.13 Selected correlates of opinions of *Dominicantes* on homosexuality with other *World Values Survey*-related indicators of value development ($R^2 > 10\%$)

	r with rejecting homosexual neighbor	R^2	r with homosexuality never justifiable	R^2
Dominicantes: trust—people of another religion	−0.3582	12.8343	−0.3333	11.1081
Dominicantes: religion is all about to do good to other people	−0.3233	10.4550	0.0812	0.6596
Dominicantes: Index of Religious Tolerance	−0.3914	15.3176	−0.1296	1.6789
% of *Dominicantes*—rejecting Jewish neighbors	0.5454	29.7502	0.3212	10.3154

Again, the relatively stable relationship between *effective democracy* and acceptancy of homosexuality cannot be dismissed out of hand, since also leading other benchmarks of a tolerant society are highly negatively correlated with the rejection of homosexual neighbors and/or the rejection of homosexuality.

The Multivariate Relationship Between Our Indicators

In this paragraph, we would like to look at the societal drivers of Antisemitism, intolerance, and the failure of the *Nostra Aetate* process on the basis of the ADL, 2014, and other data, already presented in this work.

We are interested in the relationships between development levels, our combined indicator of tolerance, and the acceptancy of homosexuality (see also Chaps. 5 and 6) as an especially strong predictor of global value change toward more tolerance (Inglehart et al. 2017) and Antisemitism (see also Chap. 3).

In our regression analysis, presented in Table 7.14, it emerges that apart from the Kuznets curve of Antisemitism already presented in Table 3.3 (i.e., Antisemitism rises and then falls with rising per capita incomes), religious tolerance and the acceptancy of homosexuality wield an especially strong negative effect on the country rates of Antisemitism. Our equation explains three-fifth of Antisemitism in the 47 countries with complete data.

Two-thirds of religious tolerance are explained by a Kuznets curve of first rising and then falling per capita incomes, by the share of Protestants per total population and—negatively—by the share of Muslims per total population (Table 7.15).

Finally, we also test the drivers and bottlenecks of the *Nostra Aetate* process in Table 7.16.

Table 7.14 The predictors of global Antisemitism (ADL 100 rates of Antisemitism)[a]

Antisemitism	Unstandardized regression coefficient B	Standard error	Beta	T	Error p
Constant	19.721	26.409		0.747	0.459
Income 2013 (nat. logarithm of EU = 100) (World Bank 2017)[b]	28.519	13.215	1.165	2.158	0.037
Income 2013 (nat. logarithm of EU = 100)^2 (World Bank 2017)[c]	−3.634	1.905	−1.023	−1.907	0.063
Homosexuality never acceptable[d]	31.416	14.499	0.293	2.167	0.036
Index of Religious Tolerance[e]	−94.869	17.330	−0.650	−5.474	0.000
Adj. R^2	0.605				
F	18.579				
Error p	0.000				
N	47				

[a]As to the variable definitions and their sources, see Tausch and Heshmati (2013) and Tausch (2019)
[b]https://data.worldbank.org/indicator (Download April 10, 2019)
[c]https://data.worldbank.org/indicator (Download April 10, 2019)
[d]See the data reported in this essay
[e]UNDP *Human Development Index* type of indicator; see text above

Table 7.15 The predictors of religious tolerance

Index of Religious Tolerance	Unstandardized regression coefficient B	Standard error	Beta	T	Error p
Constant	0.405	0.090		4.475	0.000
Income 2013 (nat. logarithm of EU = 100) (World Bank 2017)	0.101	0.058	0.721	1.740	0.088
Income 2013 (nat. logarithm of EU = 100)^2 (World Bank 2017)	−0.015	0.009	−0.669	−1.576	0.121
Share of Protestants per total population, 2000 (Barro 2003)	0.441	0.127	0.350	3.465	0.001
Share of Muslims per total population, 2000 (Barro 2003)	−0.275	0.041	−0.607	−6.744	0.000
Adj. R^2	0.643				
F	25.365				
Error p	0.000				
N	55				

As to the variable definitions and their sources, again see Tausch and Heshmati (2013) and Tausch (2019)

Table 7.16 Drivers and bottlenecks of the *Nostra Aetate* Index among global *Dominicantes*

Nostra Aetate Index	Unstandardized regression coefficient B	Standard error	Beta	T	Error p
Constant	0.829	1.791		0.463	0.650
Income 2013 (nat. logarithm of EU = 100) (World Bank 2017)	0.165	0.872	0.585	0.189	0.853
Income 2013 (nat. logarithm of EU = 100)^2 (World Bank 2017)	−0.009	0.103	−0.269	−0.087	0.932
Share of Roman Catholics per total population	−0.398	0.098	−0.709	−4.071	0.001
Gallup poll about satisfaction: safety	−0.008	0.003	−0.616	−2.926	0.010
Adj. R^2	0.586				
F	7.712				
Error p	0.001				
N	20				

As to the variable definitions and their sources, again see Tausch and Heshmati (2013) and Tausch (2019)

Almost three-fifth of the success or failure of *Nostra Aetate* in the 20 countries with complete data can be explained by the following processes:

- A Kuznets type of function of a rising and then falling implementation of *Nostra Aetate* along per capita income levels.
- *Nostra Aetate* could best be implemented where Roman Catholicism is not the dominant culture.
- Satisfaction of the country's population with the overall safety situation had a considerable effect on the prevalence or absence of Antisemitism of practicing Roman Catholics.

Catholic Best Practice and Catholic Worst Practice

We conclude this chapter by a summary of the best- and worst-practice models of global Catholicism.

- **The law-abiding society—worst-practice model compared to all baptized Catholics (in descending order)**: Lebanon, Peru, the United States, Philippines, Rwanda, Slovenia, South Korea, Zimbabwe
- **The law-abiding society—best-practice model compared to all baptized Catholics (in descending order)**: Chile, Germany, Ukraine, Spain, Poland,

(continued)

Colombia, Ghana, Australia, Brazil, Singapore, Ecuador, Mexico, Argentina, Trinidad and Tobago, South Africa, Nigeria, Belarus

- **Democracy movement—worst-practice model compared to all baptized Catholics (in descending order)**: Belarus, Spain, Germany, Rwanda, Australia, the United States, Brazil, Peru, South Korea, Philippines, Colombia, Ecuador, Slovenia, Singapore, Poland, Ghana, Zimbabwe, Mexico, Argentina, Trinidad and Tobago
- **Democracy movement—best-practice model compared to all baptized Catholics (in descending order)**: Ukraine, Chile, Nigeria, South Africa, Lebanon
- **Climate of personal nonviolence—worst-practice model compared to all baptized Catholics (in descending order)**: The United States, Philippines, Peru, Chile, South Korea, Belarus, Australia, Lebanon, Zimbabwe, Rwanda, Mexico
- **Climate of personal nonviolence—best-practice model compared to all baptized Catholics (in descending order)**: Ukraine, Trinidad and Tobago, Argentina, Brazil, South Africa, Singapore, Slovenia, Ecuador, Nigeria, Colombia, Germany, Poland, Spain, Ghana
- **Trust in institutions—worst-practice model compared to all baptized Catholics (in descending order)**: Ukraine, Australia, Slovenia
- **Trust in institutions—best-practice model compared to all baptized Catholics (in descending order)**: Chile, Belarus, Germany, South Korea, Trinidad and Tobago, Brazil, Spain, Lebanon, Argentina, South Africa, Ecuador, Ghana, Peru, the United States, Mexico, Poland, Singapore, Rwanda, Philippines, Colombia, Nigeria, Zimbabwe
- **Happiness, good health—worst-practice model compared to all baptized Catholics (in descending order)**: Germany, Chile, Belarus, Spain, Lebanon, Ecuador, Poland, Slovenia, Singapore, Brazil, South Africa, South Korea, Peru, Colombia, Trinidad and Tobago, Ukraine, Mexico, Nigeria, Philippines
- **Happiness, good health—best-practice model compared to all baptized Catholics (in descending order)**: The United States, Rwanda, Ghana, Argentina, Australia, Zimbabwe
- **No redistributive religious fundamentalism—worst-practice model compared to all baptized Catholics (in descending order)**: Spain, Belarus, Slovenia, Australia, Germany, Argentina, Chile, Poland, Brazil, Trinidad and Tobago, South Korea, the United States, Lebanon, Mexico, Peru, South Africa, Philippines, Colombia, Ecuador, Zimbabwe, Nigeria
- **No redistributive religious fundamentalism—best-practice model compared to all baptized Catholics (in descending order)**: Ukraine, Rwanda, Singapore, Ghana

(continued)

- **Accepting the market economy—worst-practice model compared to all baptized Catholics (in descending order)**: Lebanon, Trinidad and Tobago, Argentina, Peru, Belarus, Philippines, Chile, Poland, Rwanda, Germany
- **Accepting the market economy—best-practice model compared to all baptized Catholics (in descending order)**: Spain, Australia, Slovenia, South Korea, the United States, South Africa, Singapore, Zimbabwe, Brazil, Nigeria, Mexico, Ukraine, Colombia, Ghana, Ecuador
- **Feminism—worst-practice model compared to all baptized Catholics (in descending order)**: Ukraine, South Korea, Germany, Chile, Singapore, Australia, the United States, Nigeria
- **Feminism—best-practice model compared to all baptized Catholics (in descending order)**: Belarus, Trinidad and Tobago, Slovenia, South Africa, Brazil, Peru, Ecuador, Mexico, Colombia, Philippines, Rwanda, Poland, Zimbabwe, Lebanon, Argentina, Spain, Ghana
- **Involvement in politics—worst-practice model compared to all baptized Catholics (in descending order)**: Zimbabwe, Lebanon, South Africa, Nigeria, Philippines
- **Involvement in politics—best-practice model compared to all baptized Catholics (in descending order)**: Spain, Trinidad and Tobago, Australia, Germany, Belarus, the United States, Singapore, Slovenia, Ukraine, Poland, Chile, Brazil, Argentina, Ecuador, Ghana, Colombia, Mexico, South Korea, Rwanda, Peru
- **Optimism and engagement—worst-practice model compared to all baptized Catholics (in descending order)**: Lebanon, Australia, Argentina, Chile, Germany, Ukraine, Spain, Brazil, Singapore, Nigeria, Belarus, Ecuador, Rwanda, Zimbabwe, Mexico, Poland, Philippines
- **Optimism and engagement—best-practice model compared to all baptized Catholics (in descending order)**: Trinidad and Tobago, Slovenia, Ghana, Colombia, South Korea, South Africa, Peru, the United States
- **No welfare mentality, acceptancy of the Calvinist work ethics—worst-practice model compared to all baptized Catholics (in descending order)**: Trinidad and Tobago, Argentina, Belarus, Singapore, Lebanon, Germany, Nigeria, Ecuador
- **No welfare mentality, acceptancy of the Calvinist work ethics—best-practice model compared to all baptized Catholics (in descending order)**: Slovenia, Australia, the United States, Spain, Poland, Mexico, Ghana, Colombia, Rwanda, Peru, South Korea, Chile, Ukraine, Brazil, Zimbabwe, South Africa, Philippines
- **Open Society Index—worst-practice model compared to all baptized Catholics (in descending order)**: Lebanon, Belarus, Peru, Philippines,

(continued)

Germany, Australia, Spain, South Korea, the United States, Zimbabwe, Slovenia, Argentina, Rwanda

- **Open Society Index—best-practice model compared to all baptized Catholics (in descending order)**: Ukraine, Chile, Trinidad and Tobago, Ghana, Colombia, South Africa, Mexico, Singapore, Brazil, Ecuador, Poland, Nigeria

The Open Society and the Dominicantes: The Country Evidence

Worst-practice performance list on a country to country basis: to-do-list for the bishops (Dominicantes compared to all locally baptized Roman Catholics; index performance in terms of the overall Open Society Index—see Chap. 4 in descending order)

- **Argentina**: No redistributive religious fundamentalism; Optimism and engagement; Accepting the market economy; Open Society Index; No welfare mentality, acceptancy of the Calvinist work ethics; Democracy movement
- **Australia**: No redistributive religious fundamentalism; Open Society Index; Democracy movement; Trust in institutions; Optimism and engagement; Climate of personal nonviolence; Feminism
- **Belarus**: Open Society Index; No redistributive religious fundamentalism; Democracy movement; Happiness, good health; Accepting the market economy; No welfare mentality, acceptancy of the Calvinist work ethics; Climate of personal nonviolence; Optimism and engagement
- **Brazil**: No redistributive religious fundamentalism; Democracy movement; Happiness, good health; Optimism and engagement
- **Chile**: Happiness, good health; No redistributive religious fundamentalism; Optimism and engagement; Climate of personal nonviolence; Feminism; Accepting the market economy
- **Colombia**: Democracy movement; No redistributive religious fundamentalism; Happiness, good health
- **Ecuador**: Happiness, good health; Democracy movement; No redistributive religious fundamentalism; No welfare mentality, acceptancy of the Calvinist work ethics; Optimism and engagement

(continued)

- **Germany**: Happiness, good health; No redistributive religious fundamentalism; Open Society Index; Democracy movement; Feminism; Optimism and engagement; No welfare mentality, acceptancy of the Calvinist work ethics; Accepting the market economy
- **Ghana**: Democracy movement
- **Lebanon**: Open Society Index; The law-abiding society; No redistributive religious fundamentalism; Accepting the market economy; Happiness, good health; Optimism and engagement; Involvement in politics; No welfare mentality, acceptancy of the Calvinist work ethics; Climate of personal nonviolence
- **Mexico**: No redistributive religious fundamentalism; Democracy movement; Happiness, good health; Climate of personal nonviolence; Optimism and engagement
- **Nigeria**: No redistributive religious fundamentalism; No welfare mentality, acceptancy of the Calvinist work ethics; Optimism and engagement; Involvement in politics; Happiness, good health; Feminism
- **Peru**: Open Society Index; The law-abiding society; Democracy movement; Climate of personal nonviolence; No redistributive religious fundamentalism; Accepting the market economy; Happiness, good health
- **Philippines**: Open Society Index; Climate of personal nonviolence; Democracy movement; The law-abiding society; No redistributive religious fundamentalism; Accepting the market economy; Happiness, good health; Involvement in politics; Optimism and engagement
- **Poland**: No redistributive religious fundamentalism; Happiness, good health; Democracy movement; Accepting the market economy; Optimism and engagement
- **Rwanda**: Democracy movement; The law-abiding society; Open Society Index; Optimism and engagement; Climate of personal nonviolence; Accepting the market economy
- **Singapore**: Happiness, good health; Democracy movement; No welfare mentality, acceptancy of the Calvinist work ethics; Feminism; Optimism and engagement
- **Slovenia**: No redistributive religious fundamentalism; Trust in institutions; Happiness, good health; Open Society Index; Democracy movement; The law-abiding society
- **South Africa**: No redistributive religious fundamentalism; Happiness, good health; Involvement in politics
- **South Korea**: Open Society Index; No redistributive religious fundamentalism; Democracy movement; Feminism; Happiness, good health; Climate of personal nonviolence; The law-abiding society
- **Spain**: No redistributive religious fundamentalism; Democracy movement; Open Society Index; Happiness, good health; Optimism and engagement

(continued)

- **Trinidad and Tobago**: No redistributive religious fundamentalism; No welfare mentality, acceptancy of the Calvinist work ethics; Accepting the market economy; Happiness, good health; Democracy movement
- **Ukraine**: Trust in institutions; Feminism; Optimism and engagement; Happiness, good health
- **The United States**: Climate of personal nonviolence; Democracy movement; No redistributive religious fundamentalism; The law-abiding society; Open Society Index; Feminism
- **Zimbabwe**: Open Society Index; Involvement in politics; No redistributive religious fundamentalism; Democracy movement; Climate of personal nonviolence; Optimism and engagement; The law-abiding society

---

Best-practice performance list on a country to country basis (*Dominicantes* compared to all locally baptized Roman Catholics; index performance in terms of the overall Open Society Index—see Chap. 2 in descending order)

- **Argentina**: Climate of personal nonviolence; The law-abiding society; Trust in institutions; Involvement in politics; Feminism; Happiness, good health
- **Australia**: The law-abiding society; Accepting the market economy; No welfare mentality, acceptancy of the Calvinist work ethics; Involvement in politics; Happiness, good health
- **Belarus**: Trust in institutions; Feminism; Involvement in politics; The law-abiding society
- **Brazil**: The law-abiding society; Trust in institutions; Open Society Index; Climate of personal nonviolence; Feminism; Involvement in politics; Accepting the market economy; No welfare mentality, acceptancy of the Calvinist work ethics
- **Chile**: The law-abiding society; Open Society Index; Trust in institutions; Democracy movement; Involvement in politics; No welfare mentality, acceptancy of the Calvinist work ethics
- **Colombia**: Open Society Index; The law-abiding society; Feminism; Climate of personal nonviolence; Optimism and engagement; Involvement in politics; No welfare mentality, acceptancy of the Calvinist work ethics; Trust in institutions; Accepting the market economy
- **Ecuador**: The law-abiding society; Open Society Index; Trust in institutions; Climate of personal nonviolence; Feminism; Involvement in politics; Accepting the market economy
- **Germany**: The law-abiding society; Trust in institutions; Involvement in politics; Climate of personal nonviolence

(continued)

- **Ghana**: Open Society Index; The law-abiding society; Trust in institutions; Optimism and engagement; Happiness, good health; Involvement in politics; No welfare mentality, acceptancy of the Calvinist work ethics; Feminism; Climate of personal nonviolence; Accepting the market economy; No redistributive religious fundamentalism
- **Lebanon**: Trust in institutions; Democracy movement; Feminism
- **Mexico**: Open Society Index; The law-abiding society; Feminism; Trust in institutions; No welfare mentality, acceptancy of the Calvinist work ethics; Involvement in politics; Accepting the market economy
- **Nigeria**: Open Society Index; Democracy movement; Climate of personal nonviolence; The law-abiding society; Accepting the market economy; Trust in institutions
- **Peru**: Trust in institutions; Feminism; No welfare mentality, acceptancy of the Calvinist work ethics; Optimism and engagement; Involvement in politics
- **Philippines**: Feminism; Trust in institutions; No welfare mentality, acceptancy of the Calvinist work ethics
- **Poland**: The law-abiding society; Open Society Index; Involvement in politics; Feminism; Trust in institutions; No welfare mentality, acceptancy of the Calvinist work ethics; Climate of personal nonviolence
- **Rwanda**: Happiness, good health; No redistributive religious fundamentalism; Feminism; Trust in institutions; No welfare mentality, acceptancy of the Calvinist work ethics; Involvement in politics
- **Singapore**: Open Society Index; The law-abiding society; Involvement in politics; Climate of personal nonviolence; Trust in institutions; Accepting the market economy; No redistributive religious fundamentalism
- **Slovenia**: No welfare mentality, acceptancy of the Calvinist work ethics; Feminism; Involvement in politics; Accepting the market economy; Climate of personal nonviolence; Optimism and engagement
- **South Africa**: Open Society Index; Climate of personal nonviolence; Feminism; Trust in institutions; The law-abiding society; Democracy movement; Accepting the market economy; Optimism and engagement; No welfare mentality, acceptancy of the Calvinist work ethics
- **South Korea**: Trust in institutions; Accepting the market economy; Optimism and engagement; Involvement in politics; No welfare mentality, acceptancy of the Calvinist work ethics
- **Spain**: The law-abiding society; Accepting the market economy; Involvement in politics; Trust in institutions; No welfare mentality, acceptancy of the Calvinist work ethics; Feminism; Climate of personal nonviolence
- **Trinidad and Tobago**: Open Society Index; Climate of personal nonviolence; Optimism and engagement; Trust in institutions; Involvement in politics; Feminism; The law-abiding society

(continued)

- **Ukraine**: Open Society Index; The law-abiding society; Democracy movement; Climate of personal nonviolence; No redistributive religious fundamentalism; Involvement in politics; No welfare mentality, acceptance of the Calvinist work ethics; Accepting the market economy
- **The United States**: Happiness, good health; Involvement in politics; No welfare mentality, acceptance of the Calvinist work ethics; Trust in institutions; Accepting the market economy; Optimism and engagement
- **Zimbabwe**: Feminism; Accepting the market economy; No welfare mentality, acceptancy of the Calvinist work ethics; Trust in institutions; Happiness, good health

Literature

Adamczyk, A. (2017). *Cross-national public opinion about homosexuality. Examining attitudes across the globe*. Berkeley, CA: University of California Press.

Adamczyk, A., & Pitt, C. (2009). Shaping attitudes about homosexuality: The role of religion and cultural context. *Social Science Research, 38*(2), 338–351.

Alexander, A. C., & Welzel, C. (2011). Islam and patriarchy: How robust is Muslim support for patriarchal values? *International Review of Sociology, 21*(2), 249–276.

Alexander, A. C., Inglehart, R. F., & Welzel, C. (2012). Measuring effective democracy: A defense. *International Political Science Review, 33*(1), 41–62.

Barro, R. J. (2003). *Religion adherence data*. Harvard University, Department of Economics. https://scholar.harvard.edu/Barro/publications/religion-adherence-data

Barro, R. J. (2004). Spirit of capitalism religion and economic development. *Harvard International Review, 25*(4), 64–67.

Barro, R. J., & McCleary, R. M. (2003). Religion and economic growth across countries. *American Sociological Review, 68*(5), 760–781.

Bytwerk, R. L. (2015). Believing in "Inner Truth": The protocols of the elders of Zion in Nazi Propaganda, 1933–1945. *Holocaust and Genocide Studies, 29*(2), 212–229.

Giorgi, L., & Marsh, C. (1990). The Protestant work ethic as a cultural phenomenon. *European Journal of Social Psychology, 20*(6), 499–517.

Hastings, A. (1991). *Modern Catholicism: Vatican II and after*. New York: Oxford University Press.

Hastings, D. (2009). *Catholicism and the roots of Nazism: Religious identity and national socialism*. Oxford: Oxford University Press.

Hofstede, G. (2001). *Culture's consequences: Comparing values, behaviors, institutions, and organizations across nations*. Thousand Oaks, CA: Sage.

Hofstede, G., & Minkov, M. (2010). Long- versus short-term orientation: New perspectives. *Asia Pacific Business Review, 16*(4), 493–504.

Hofstede, G., Hofstede, G. J., & Minkov, M. (2010). *Cultures and organizations: Software of the mind* (Rev. and Expanded 3rd ed.). New York: McGraw-Hill.

Inglehart, R. F. (1988). The renaissance of political culture. *American Political Science Review, 82*(04), 1203–1230.

Inglehart, R. F. (1990). *Culture shift in advanced industrial countries*. Princeton, NJ: Princeton University Press.

Inglehart, R. F. (2000). Globalization and postmodern values. *Washington Quarterly, 23*(1), 215–228.

Inglehart, R. F. (2006). Mapping global values. *Comparative Sociology, 5*(2), 115–136.

Inglehart, R. F. (2008). Changing values among western publics from 1970 to 2006. *West European Politics, 31*(1–2), 130–146.

Inglehart, R. F. (2015). *The silent revolution: Changing values and political styles among Western publics*. Princeton, NJ: Princeton University Press.

Inglehart, R. F., & Baker, W. E. (2000). Modernization, cultural change, and the persistence of traditional values. *American Sociological Review, 65(1)*, 19–51. Download April 10, 2019, from http://my.fit.edu/~gabrenya/cultural/readings/Inglehart-Baker-2000.pdf

Inglehart, R. F., & Norris, P. (2003). *Rising tide: Gender equality and cultural change around the world*. New York: Cambridge University Press.

Inglehart, R. F., & Norris, P. (2009, November 4). The true clash of civilizations. *Foreign Policy*. Download April 10, 2019, from http://foreignpolicy.com/2009/11/04/the-true-clash-of-civilizations/

Inglehart, R. F., & Norris, P. (2012). The four horsemen of the apocalypse: Understanding human security. *Scandinavian Political Studies, 35*(1), 71–95.

Inglehart, R. F., & Norris, P. (2016). *Trump, Brexit, and the rise of populism: Economic have-nots and cultural backlash*. Download April 10, 2019, from SSRN: http://ssrn.com/abstract=2818659 HKS Working Paper No. RWP16-026.

Inglehart, R. F., & Welzel, C. (2003). Political culture and democracy: Analyzing cross-level linkages. *Comparative Politics, 36*(1), 61–79.

Inglehart, R. F., & Welzel C. (2009, March, April). How Development leads to democracy. What we know about modernization. *Foreign Affairs*. Download April 10, 2019, from http://www.foreignaffairs.com/articles/64821/ronald-inglehart-and-christian-welzel/how-development-leads-to-democracy

Inglehart, R. F., & Welzel, C. (2010). Changing mass priorities: The link between modernization and democracy. *Perspectives on Politics, 8*(02), 551–567.

Inglehart, R. F., Ponarin, E., & Inglehart, R. C. (2017). Cultural change, slow and fast: The distinctive trajectory of norms governing gender equality and sexual orientation. *Social Forces, 95*(4), 1313–1340.

Kappler, S., Hancock, K., & Plante, T. G. (2013). Roman Catholic gay priests: Internalized homophobia, sexual identity, and psychological well-being. *Pastoral Psychology, 62*(6), 805–826.

Kuznets, S. (1976). *Modern economic growth: Rate, structure and spread*. New Haven, CT: Yale University Press.

Maritain, J. (1936). *Humanisme integral. Problemes temporels et spirituels d'une nouvelle chretiente*. Paris: Aubier. 334 S. 8°. Aubier

Maritain, J. (2012). *Christianity and democracy, the rights of man and natural law*. San Francisco, CA: Ignatius Press.

Müller, A., Tausch, A., Zulehner, P. M., & Wickens, H. (Eds.). (2000). *Global capitalism, liberation theology, and the social sciences: An analysis of the contradictions of modernity at the turn of the millennium*. Hauppauge, NY: Nova Science.

Phayer, M. (2000). *The Catholic Church and the Holocaust* (pp. 1930–1965). Bloomington, IN: Indiana University Press.

Phayer, M. (2001). Totalitarianism: Questions about Catholic Resistance. *Church History: Studies in Christianity and Culture, 70*(02), 328–344.

Plant, R. (2011). *The pink triangle: The Nazi war against homosexuals*. New York: Holt Paperbacks.

Rittner, C., & Roth, J. K. (Eds.). (2016). *Pope Pius XII and the Holocaust*. New: London.

Tausch, A. (2011). El Papa ¿Cuántas Divisiones Tiene? Sondeo Global del Catolicismo Mundial Según el '*World Values Survey*' y el '*European Social Survey*'. E-Book N° 49 Centro Argentino de Estudios Internacionales (in Spanish) [English Title: 'The Pope – How Many Divisions Does

He Have?' a First Global Survey of World Catholicism Based on the 'World Values Survey' and the 'European Social Survey']. Download April 10, 2019, from http://www.caei.com.ar/es/irebooks.htm

Tausch, A. (2014, Fall). The new global antisemitism: Implications from the recent Adl-100 data. *Middle East Review of International Affairs, 18*(3).

Tausch, A. (2017). Global Catholicism in the age of mass migration and the rise of populism: Comparative analyses, based on recent *World Values Survey* and *European Social Survey* Data (September 20, 2017). Available at SSRN: https://ssrn.com/abstract=2875289

Tausch, A. (2019). Migration from the Muslim World to the West: Its most recent trends and effects. *Jewish Political Studies Review (Jerusalem), 30*. Download June 15, 2019, from http://jcpa.org/jewish-political-studies-review-home/

Tausch, A., & Heshmati, A. (2013). *Globalization, the human condition, and sustainable development in the twenty-first century: Cross-national perspectives and European implications.* London: Anthem.

Tausch, A., Heshmati, A., & Karoui, H. (2014). *The political algebra of global value change: General models and implications for the Muslim world.* Hauppauge, NY: Nova Science.

von Hayek, F. A. (1960). *The constitution of liberty.* Chicago, IL: University of Chicago Press.

von Hayek, F. A. (2012). *Law, legislation and liberty: A new statement of the liberal principles of justice and political economy.* London: Routledge.

von Hayek, F. A., & Bartley, W. W. (1988). *The fatal conceit: The errors of socialism.* Chicago, IL: University of Chicago Press.

Weber, M. (1964 [1922]). *The sociology of religion* (E. Fischoff, Trans.) Boston: Beacon Press.

World Bank. (2017). *World Bank open data.* Washington, DC: World Bank: data.worldbank.org

Chapter 8
Executive Summary

"Good Catholics" and Yet Antisemitic?

From Roman Catholicism's early days, Antisemitism was its *Original Sin*. With its Second Vatican Council Declaration *Nostra Aetate*, many would have hoped that the Church buried the demons of Catholic Antisemitism for good. But just how thick is the ice that now separates global contemporary Catholic publics from the temptations of a reemergence of Catholic Antisemitism?

While the study of global Antisemitism received important new and global empirical insights from the ADL (Anti-Defamation League) 100 study (ADL 2014) covering more than 100 countries, comparative studies on Antisemitism among *practicing* global Roman Catholics are rather lacking. But Antisemitism is around in the world again, and it does so in staggering proportions. It is thus extremely important in view of Catholicism's still existing role in Western society to find out whether or not practicing Roman Catholics are an exemption from these trends.

Our *World Values Survey*-based study focuses on indicators of Antisemitism of the entire countries in comparison with their practicing Roman Catholic communities, i.e., those Catholics who attend Sunday Mass regularly, the so-called *Dominicantes*, which still make up some 45% of the global 1.3 billion Roman Catholics according to our population-weighted data. Our study is based on the rigorous statistical analysis of freely available cross-national opinion data sets, using the IBM-SPSS XXIV statistical software. Since our freely available global data base, the *World Values Survey*, does not offer better, alternative Antisemitism indicators, we had to rely on our work on the rates of rejection of Jewish neighbors, which explain 56.16% of the variance of the far superior ADL (2014) data series, for which the original interviews and the background variables are unfortunately not freely available to global publics.

A. Tausch, S. Obirek, *Global Catholicism, Tolerance and the Open Society*,
https://doi.org/10.1007/978-3-030-23239-9_8

Our proxy results about the anchoring of *Nostra Aetate* in the hearts and minds of active global Catholics, based on *World Values Survey* and other global opinion data, are not optimistic and suggest the following tendencies:

- On a global scale, about one in five practicing Roman Catholics still rejects to have a Jewish neighbor, irrespective of all the Church's teaching on Judaism since the Second Vatican Council.
- *Ceteris paribus*, adherence to Catholicism, Orthodox Christianity, and Islam all are still to be considered as significant drivers of the rate of societal Antisemitism (ADL data) in standard OLS multiple regression analyses.
- A combined *Nostra Aetate* Index, developed for this publication on the basis of *World Values Survey* data, tells us first how well active Roman Catholics, attending Church services each Sunday, accepted Jewish neighbors; second, whether active Roman Catholics more accepted Jewish neighbors than the society surrounding them; and third, whether the acceptancy of Jewish neighbors among practicing Catholics increased or decreased over time. Our data show that among the world's top performing Roman Catholic active communities, we find the *Dominicantes* in the Czech Republic, the United States, the United Kingdom, Portugal, and Argentina, while among world's Catholicism worst *Nostra Aetate* performers, we find the active Catholic communities in Spain, Poland, Malta, Slovenia, Mexico, and Slovakia. In those countries, social realities among the active Catholic faithful could not be more distant from the ideas and perspectives expressed in *Nostra Aetate*.

In our interreligious comparison, we also found that only the Catholic *Dominicantes* in Argentina and the United States were among the world's top 10% performers in overcoming Antisemitism, while the Catholic *Dominicantes* in Venezuela, Bosnia, Nigeria, Slovakia, South Africa, and South Korea were among the world's lamentable bottom two-thirds of communities in overcoming Antisemitism.

We also analyzed *PEW* data on the support or rejection of the Jewish State and *European Social Survey* data on the acceptancy of Jewish immigration to Europe among religiously active Roman Catholics in comparison with the respective total populations. We also highlighted the drivers of Antisemitism by interreligious comparison, using an OLS regression procedure applied to *World Values Survey* data, and analyzed the connections between general religious tolerance and Antisemitism.

Practicing "Good Catholics" and Yet Against Jewish Immigration to Europe?

European Social Survey data for 2014 seem to confirm that only the *Dominicantes* in the Netherlands, the Czech Republic, and France are more positively oriented toward Jewish immigration than the totality of the baptized Roman Catholics in the respective country, while practicing Roman Catholics in Slovenia, Poland, Ireland, Switzerland, Belgium, and Austria by and large rejected Jewish immigration in dismal proportions and also fell behind the more secular Catholics in their support for Jewish immigration in their respective country. One also finds that only in Germany a more significant proportion of persons (all denominations and secular and religious groups among them) was in strong favor of Jewish immigration at all.

Eight decades after the beginning of the Second World War, it is also interesting to note which denominational groups lend greater or lesser support to Jewish immigration in preference or rejection of the immigration of other groups to Europe. The *Dominicantes* in Slovenia, Poland, Switzerland, and Belgium all preferred some other immigrant groups over Jewish immigrants. More and more, the preferred immigrant groups mentioned by the *Dominicantes* in Slovenia, Poland, Switzerland, and Belgium resemble the preferences voiced by European Muslims – all to the detriment of the support for further Jewish immigration.

We also analyze the ranking of the European rejection of Jewish immigration according to religious denomination and religious service attendance. The rejection front is being led by the monthly religious service attenders among Roman Catholics in Slovenia, Poland, and Ireland, followed by Belgium Muslim regular Mosque attenders, etc. Only Protestant and secular populations in the Nordic countries, the Netherlands and in Germany, and active Roman Catholics in Germany really welcomed Jewish immigration to Europe. In the light of *Nostra Aetate*, the rejection of Jewish immigration from the more active Catholic communities in Austria, Belgium, Ireland, Poland, Slovenia, and Switzerland is especially disappointing.

Beyond the Zenith of Ecumenism and Goodwill Toward Judaism?

Our study led us to the firm sociological conclusion that on the Catholic side, the zenith of goodwill and understanding toward Judaism, reached during the pontificates of Popes John Paul II, Benedict XVI, and Francis, has already been reached and that the global Catholic rank and file increasingly threatens to be infected by the rising rates of global Antisemitism and hate of the Jewish State. Going back in history, we found that even the pivotal figure of Cardinal Augustin Bea, who was one of the architects of *Nostra Aetate* on the Catholic side, shunned away from a Catholic identification with the State of Israel and rather tended to view *Nostra Aetate* as a declaration without any Mid-East political consequences.

At the same time, important new shifts in the Roman Catholic Church have to be observed. In a period of growing international migration, even in the rich Western countries, where until now support for *Nostra Aetate* was stronger, new generations of Catholic clergy and faithful, whose home countries did not share the experience of the reckoning and the mea culpa of Christianity after the *Shoah* and the Second World War, slowly enter into positions of leadership and power in the Catholic Church. This could be combined with a more general societal climate of enmity against the Jewish State, brought about by a growing Antisemitism among the global political far right and political far left and the ever more present thought patterns imported by rising Muslim migration to the rich, Western countries.

How Many Practicing Catholics Really Support the Pro-immigration Policies of the Vatican?

According to our results, the "real existing" global Catholicism, which emerges from our data today, can best be described by the following main tendencies:

- 48.05% of all *Dominicantes* in the world are in favor of strict limits in migration policy or even would like to prevent people from coming, as indicated by the population-weighted figures from our figures which cover 91.08% of all global *Dominicantes* in the *WVS* project.
- According to our analyses, in not a single European country, practicing Catholics were more liberal in their attitudes on migration than overall society. Only in Germany was there any relevant active Catholic support for liberal attitudes on migration, as measured by our data, while opposition to them was especially strong in Ireland, Slovenia, and Austria.

In other words, active Catholic publics in Europe could be open to the "populist anti-immigration virus" just as their fellow Roman Catholics in the November 8, 2016, presidential election in the United States.

Global Catholics and Support for the "Open Society" in the West

Our pessimistic European analysis in many ways is reflected also in our global analysis. Our analysis of the *World Values Survey* data was derived from a factor analysis whose design matches what a large social scientific literature has to say on the *Open Society*. Only the active Catholic publics in a handful of countries were more committed to the goals of an overall democratic civil society than the respective overall country population, while in several countries, most dramatically in South Africa, Spain, and Peru, active Catholic publics had to be considered as far less supportive of a democratic civil society than the general publics of their countries.

Measuring Catholic Global Tolerance by International Comparison: Germany Is a Problematic Case

Today, the measurement of religious tolerance across nations has become possible. The *World Values Survey* offers fairly encompassing and comparable data on tolerance items. To calculate the results, we relied on the well-established methodology of the United Nations Human Development Programme and its UNDP Human Development Index (UNDP 2014). For 59 states of the world, there are complete data. While, e.g., in Sweden and the United States 30% or less of the population have no confidence in people with a religious denomination other than their own, these percentages in Algeria, Armenia, Yemen, Kyrgyzstan, Libya, Morocco, Mexico, Palestinian territories, Peru, Romania, Tunisia, and Uzbekistan are over 70% each. Unfortunately, the clear North-South divide of religious tolerance on our globe also corresponds to a clear denominational gap. Among the ten states with the lowest general religious tolerance, based on our five indicators, there are nine predominantly Muslim states. Only one non-Muslim majority country is in this group—public opinion in predominantly Christian Armenia. Our surveys also show the large deficit of religious tolerance in Germany, the worst ranked member of the European Union. Germany occupies only rank 40 of 59 ranked states.

According to our data, the religiously most liberal Catholic community in the world is found in the Caribbean State of Trinidad and Tobago, followed by the practicing Catholics in Australia, Brazil, the Netherlands, and the United States. The worst religious tolerance results for active Catholicism were reported in Peru, Lebanon, Mexico, Germany, and Nigeria. Our data also provide an answer to the question of whether practicing Catholics represent a more tolerant attitude toward members of other religions than the respective total populations. The Catholic communities in the Netherlands, Australia, and Uruguay, in particular, are to be mentioned positively, while the practice of Catholicism in Ukraine, Spain, and Lebanon falls far short of the development of religious tolerance in society as a whole. The disappointing results for Germany both at the national level and at the level of the practicing Roman Catholics and the German Muslim community bode ill for the future capability of Germany as a country to integrate the millions of refugees, which came to Germany since the beginnings of the European refugee crisis in the fall of 2015. A country, incapable of religious tolerance, risks being incapable of societal integration of people from different denominations. But religious tolerance is also a matter for the global South, and not just for the global North and the global migration recipient countries.

Tolerance of Homosexuals

With the publication of Reverend Krzysztof Charamsa's book (Charamsa 2016), written by a Polish former official at the Congregation for the Doctrine of the Faith in the Vatican, accusing the Roman Catholic Church of making the lives of gay and transgender people "a hell," the entire issue of homosexuality and Roman Catholicism has moved again into the focus of international media attention. While Pope Francis went on the record to say "Who am I to condemn the homosexuals," the influential Cardinal Robert Sarah of Guinea, certainly to be considered as a future contender for Saint Peter's throne in Rome, said: "What Nazi-Fascism and Communism were in the 20th Century, Western homosexual and abortion ideologies and Islamic fanaticism are today."

But global value change in favor of accepting homosexuality increasingly also affects the faithful Roman Catholics. According to our figures, less than 50% of the Roman Catholic faithful regular Church attenders in the Netherlands, Andorra, Germany, Canada, Czech Republic, etc. nowadays think that homosexuality is never justifiable.

In Tanzania, Uganda, Lithuania, Indonesia, Hungary, and a host of other countries, the official position of the Catholic Catechism that the homosexual act is a deadly sin is still a majority position among the Catholic faithful. Compared to the opinions of overall societies surrounding the Catholic communities, practicing Roman Catholics in Hungary, Switzerland, France, Slovenia, and Croatia especially heavily discriminated against their homosexual neighbors, while practicing Roman Catholics in the multicultural environment of Singapore, Trinidad and Tobago, Lebanon, and Malaysia and in the Latin American country of Dominican Republic were especially tolerant to homosexual neighbors in comparison with the society surrounding them.

In comparison with overall society, practicing Roman Catholics in Switzerland, Spain, Hungary, Italy, and Uruguay especially strongly rejected homosexuality, while, again, practicing Roman Catholics in the multicultural environments of South Africa, Singapore, Indonesia, and Nigeria and in the Latin American country of Guatemala were the record holders of accepting homosexuality compared to the society around them.

Muslims, Evangelical Christians, and other denominations in these countries often take a still much tougher stance on homosexuality than active adherents of the Roman Catholic Church. Monthly religious service attenders among the adherents of the Jain religion, the Armenian Apostolic Church, Muslims, Pentecostals, Orthodox, Jehovah Witnesses, Hindus, Sikhs, Protestants, Baptists, Buddhists, Taoists, Greek Catholic, Mormons, and others share a higher rejection rate of homosexuality than the monthly religious service attenders among the Roman Catholics.

But seen in the light of our data, decision-makers of the Roman Catholic Church might perhaps start to look for better practice models in this respect among the ecumenical Presbyterian and Anglican fellow Christian Churches as well as among the Confucians—after all, the Ethics of *Love and Responsibility* were written for humankind.

Our analysis cannot claim to tell the decision-makers of the Roman Catholic Church which path to follow here, but it is sufficiently clear from our data that the Church's teaching on this point has less and less followers and that in the name of the relationship with the Open Society, a rethinking of the entire issue would be very necessary. To speak about *Masonic lobbies* in such a context—as Pope Francis recently did—is highly out of place and reminds us, by contrast, that the Roman Church throughout its history from around 300 A.D. to the end of the Second World War had so many problems in adapting to the global trends toward democracy.

The Final, Multivariate Perspective

Summarizing our results and putting them into perspective with new and especially designed statistical analyses developed for the aims of Chap. 7, we first of all emphasized that differences between cultures are far less decisive than differences between countries in determining value development. There is a breathtaking variety of Catholicism around the world.

In terms of the combined performance on the *Nostra Aetate* Index (Chap. 3), the Civil Society Index (Chap. 4), overall religious tolerance (Chap. 5), and the tolerance of homosexuality (Chap. 6), the US active Catholic community leads the international comparison of countries with complete data, followed by the *Dominicantes* in Germany, Chile, Argentina, and Poland, while the *Dominicantes* in Spain, Slovenia, and Mexico are in the lower ranks in our comparison of Catholic tolerance. We emphasize that liberation theology must become a global theology of tolerance. We debate the neoliberal critique of liberation theology and concede that accepting economic competition has an overwhelming positive consequence for other Open Society attitudes.

Our empirical results suggested that there are enough *Dominicantes* communities of the global South, serving as role models for the global Catholic Church to follow.

We also presented in Chap. 7 a brief synoptical promax factor analysis, in which the following dimensions from the *World Values Survey* data base were studied in conjunction with Catholic Antisemitism:

- Acceptancy of homosexuality versus homophobia
- Age
- Attitudes on family and work
- Attitudes on labor and labor rights
- Attitudes on the sociopolitical and economic
- Position in the economic and social hierarchy
- Strength of the adherence to the Church in fundamental religious questions
- Value in education
- Xenophobia versus a culture of welcome

55.55% of variance were explained, and the following factors resulted after the appropriate promax rotation of the factors:

- Secularism
- Xenophobia
- Distance to sociopolitical and economic order
- Poverty
- Acceptancy of homosexuality
- Trade-unionism
- Unimportance of family and work (Nihilism)
- Age
- Obedience (value in education)
- Education: tolerance and respect for other people

We summarized the factor analytical main characteristics of the opinions of Roman Catholics in important countries of global Catholicism. We also highlighted the factor loadings for global Catholic Antisemitism, ranging from the lamentable connection of Catholic to working class trade-unionism with Antisemitism to the Antisemitism reducing effects of the acceptancy of homosexuality, again emphasizing the importance of the findings of Hadler and Inglehart about the close connection between tolerance for homosexuality and overall tolerance in a society (Inglehart 2008; Inglehart and Baker 2000; Inglehart and Welzel 2010).

In our regression analyses, presented in Tables 7.14, 7.15, and 7.16 of this work, it emerges that—apart from Antisemitism rising and then falling with rising per capita incomes—religious tolerance and the acceptancy of homosexuality wield an especially strong negative effect on the country rates of Antisemitism. Our equation explains three-fifth of Antisemitism in the 47 countries with complete data. Two-thirds of religious tolerance are explained by first rising and then falling per capita incomes, by the share of Protestants per total population, and—negatively— by the share of Muslims per total population.

Almost three-fifth of the success or failure of *Nostra Aetate* among active Catholics (*Dominicantes*) in the 20 countries with complete data can be explained by the following processes:

- A function of a rising and then falling implementation of *Nostra Aetate* along per capita income levels.
- *Nostra Aetate* could best be implemented where Roman Catholicism is not the dominant culture.
- The satisfaction of the country's population with the overall safety situation had a considerable effect on the prevalence or absence of Antisemitism of practicing Roman Catholics.

We concluded this chapter by a summary of the best- and worst-practice models of global Catholicism.

Literature

Anti-Defamation League (ADL). (2014). *ADL 100 Index*. Download April 10, 2019, from http://global100.ADL.org/

Bergson, H. L. (1935). *The two sources of religion and morality* (R. Ashley Andrà & C. Brereton with the assistance of W. Horsefall Carter, Trans.). New York: Henry Holt.

Charamsa, K. (2016). *La Prima Pietra. Io, prete gay a la mia ribellione all'ipocrisia della Chiesa*. Milano: Rizzoli.

Fukuyama, F. (1995). *Trust*. New York: Free Press.

Fukuyama, F. (2006). *The end of history and the last man*. New York: Simon and Schuster.

Fukuyama, F. (2016). American political decay or renewal? The meaning of the 2016 election. *Foreign Affairs*, Summer 2016. Available at: https://www.foreignaffairs.com/articles/united-states/2016-06-13/american-political-decay-or-renewal

Inglehart, R. F. (1988). The renaissance of political culture. *American political science review, 82*(04), 1203–1230.

Inglehart, R. F. (1990). *Culture shift in advanced industrial countries*. Princeton, NJ: Princeton University Press.

Inglehart, R. F. (2000). Globalization and postmodern values. *Washington Quarterly, 23*(1), 215–228.

Inglehart, R. F. (2006). Mapping global values. *Comparative Sociology, 5*(2), 115–136.

Inglehart, R. F. (2008). Changing values among western publics from 1970 to 2006. *West European Politics, 31*(1–2), 130–146.

Inglehart, R. F. (2015). *The silent revolution: Changing values and political styles among Western publics*. Princeton, NJ: Princeton University Press.

Inglehart, R. F., & Baker, W. E. (2000). Modernization, cultural change, and the persistence of traditional values. *American Sociological Review, 65*(1), 19–51. Download April 10, 2019, from http://my.fit.edu/~gabrenya/cultural/readings/Inglehart-Baker-2000.pdf

Inglehart, R. F., & Norris, P. (2003). *Rising tide: Gender equality and cultural change around the world*. New York: Cambridge University Press.

Inglehart, R. F., & Norris, P. (2009, November 4). The true clash of civilizations. *Foreign policy*. Download April 10, 2019, from http://foreignpolicy.com/2009/11/04/the-true-clash-of-civilizations/

Inglehart, R. F., & Norris, P. (2012). The four horsemen of the apocalypse: Understanding human security. *Scandinavian Political Studies, 35*(1), 71–95.

Inglehart, R. F., & Norris, P. (2016). *Trump, Brexit, and the rise of populism: Economic have-nots and cultural backlash*. Download April 10, 2019, from SSRN: http://ssrn.com/abstract=2818659 HKS Working Paper No. RWP16-026.

Inglehart, R. F., & Welzel, C. (2003). Political culture and democracy: Analyzing cross-level linkages. *Comparative Politics, 36*(1), 61–79.

Inglehart, R. F., & Welzel C. (2009, March, April). How development leads to democracy. What we know about modernization. *Foreign Affairs*. Download April 10, 2019, from http://www.foreignaffairs.com/articles/64821/ronald-Inglehart-and-christian-welzel/how-development-leads-to-democracy

Inglehart, R. F., & Welzel, C. (2010). Changing mass priorities: The link between modernization and democracy. *Perspectives on Politics, 8*(02), 551–567.

Inglehart, R. F., Ponarin, E., & Inglehart, R. C. (2017). Cultural change, slow and fast: The distinctive trajectory of norms governing gender equality and sexual orientation. *Social Forces, 95*(4), 1313–1340.

Lipset, S. M. (1959). Some social requisites of democracy: Economic development and political legitimacy. *American political science review, 53*(01), 69–105.

Lipset, S. M. (1969, December). The socialism of fools—The left, the Jews and Israel. *Encounter*, 24.

Maritain, J. (1936). *Humanisme integral. Problemes temporels et spirituels d'une nouvelle chretiente*. Paris: Aubier (1936). 334 S. 8°. Aubier.

Maritain, J. (2012). *Christianity and democracy, the rights of man and natural law*. San Francisco, CA: Ignatius Press.

Sacks, J. (1998). Morals and markets: Seventh annual IEA Hayek Memorial Lecture given in London on Tuesday, 2 June 1998. London: Institute of Economic Affairs (1999).

Sacks, J. (2003). *The dignity of difference: How to avoid the clash of civilizations*. New York: Continuum.

Sacks, J. (2005). *To heal a fractured world: the ethics of responsibility*. Ithaca: McGill-Queens University Press.

Sacks, J. (2014). The religious other: Hostility, hospitality, and the hope of human flourishing. Lanham, MD: Lexington Books

UNDP. (2014). *Human development report*. New York: Oxford University Press.

UNDP. (2017a). *Human development data (1990–2015)*. Download April 10, 2019, from http://hdr.UNDP.org/en/data

UNDP. (2017b). *Human development report*. New York: Oxford University Press.

Author Index

© Springer Nature Switzerland AG 2020
A. Tausch, S. Obirek, *Global Catholicism, Tolerance and the Open Society*,
https://doi.org/10.1007/978-3-030-23239-9

Subject Index

© Springer Nature Switzerland AG 2020
A. Tausch, S. Obirek, *Global Catholicism, Tolerance and the Open Society*,
https://doi.org/10.1007/978-3-030-23239-9

Lightning Source UK Ltd.
Milton Keynes UK
UKHW020948100919

349515UK00002B/19/P